Highland Fling

Highland Fling

Bill Anderson's journey
from farm boy to World Champion

Jack Davidson

ARGYLL ✠ PUBLISHING

© Jack Davidson 2009

Argyll Publishing
Glendaruel
Argyll PA22 3AE
www.argyllpublishing.com

British Library Cataloguing-in-Publication Data.
A catalogue record for this book is available from the
British Library.

ISBN 978 1 906134 22 8

Printing: Bell & Bain Ltd, Glasgow

To the memory of
Bob Watson and Ewan Douglas
And to all games heavies, past and present

The Highland Games

They sit on the heather slopes
and stand six deep round the rope ring. . .
. . . in the centre
a waddling 'heavy' tries to throw
the tree of life in one straight line.

Norman MacCaig

Bill Anderson looks over some of his trophies from a lifetime of sporting achievement

Contents

Bill Anderson and Stephen King (Inveraray) at Crieff, mid-1990s

Aboyne Games 1995: Bill Anderson seated on left next to Sandy Gray, Alistair Gunn, Stephen King and Francis Brebner; standing among the Committee members are heavies, Colin Morrison (3rd from left), Bruce Aitken (5th from left), Gordon Martin (7th from left) and Bill's son Craig (3rd from right)

Introduction

BILL Anderson MBE and member of Scottish Sports 'Hall of Fame' is without doubt one of Scotland's greatest ever sportsmen. The 'King of the Heavies', as sports page headlines often dubbed him during an honour-laden thirty year career in Highland Games, was a well merited title. His name became synonymous with caber tossing and hammer throwing as he dominated the world of the heavy events at the Games, amassing eighteen Scottish championship titles as well as British, European, American, Canadian and World titles.

Highland Games are one of the most emblematic of Scottish institutions. There are good reasons for this. The games' origins can be traced back centuries to when chieftains summoned their clansmen to gatherings which took various forms but which usually included contests in archery, running, wrestling, putting the stone and tossing the caber – the forerunners of the modern games. After the unsuccessful Jacobite rebellion of 1745 many facets of Highland culture and way of life were suppressed including clan gatherings and it was not untill 1819 that the first recorded Highland Games of the modern era took place, at St Fillan's in Perthshire. Subsequent patronage by Queen Victoria of Braemar Games made a huge contribution to their development. Nowadays they are a major tourist attraction in Scotland with over one hundred taking place between the end of May and middle of September each year.

The 'heavy events' are the centrepiece of the games, a magnet for spectators. Other activities, such as piping, dancing, running, jumping, tug o'war can all be seen and enjoyed outwith a Highland Games setting. But the only place where the heavy events are held is at the Highland Games. Some years ago a survey of spectators was carried out at the famous Aboyne Games asking them to name their favourite activity. The winner, by a clear margin, was the heavy events.

The Shot/Stone Putt

Drawings of Heavy Events on pages 10–13 Courtesy Doug Fales

As they enter the games arena the heavies, that amazing breed of men who toss cabers as if they were garden posts, cause quite a stir. They simply ooze strength and power as in their kilts and vests they make their way ponderously across the field. To spectators they may look a casual and convivial bunch as they banter and exchange drinks and share tubs of resin which they rub on their hands to improve grip. But such apparent conviviality often masks a fierce rivalry. A lot is at stake – there are significant financial rewards and good performances can lead to invitations to compete abroad.

There are five standard heavy events, putting the shot or stone, throwing the hammer, throwing the weight for distance, throwing the weight for height and tossing the caber. The most spectacular event of course is the caber.

A typical caber measures about eighteen feet long and weighs about one hundred and twenty pounds, with one end thick and the other tapered. The heavy athlete hoists it up by the tapered end to cradle it next to his chest before embarking on a short dynamic sprint which he brings to a sudden halt. He then seeks to maximise the built-up momentum by tossing the caber upwards to make it land on its thick end and turn over with the thin end pointing away from him. The throw is not judged on distance but on the angle at which the thin end of the caber lands, using the clock-face system. Thus a perfect 'toss' is twelve

28lb Weight for Distance

o'clock, the next best would be one o'clock and so on. While strength is required, considerable skill is also needed to manoeuvre the length of the caber, as is evidenced by the occasional almost comic scenes as the drunk-looking 'heavy' battles to keep his balance with the caber wavering high above him.

The shot putt is the same as the mainstream event, the shots at the Games being the 'light' one at 16 pounds and the 'heavy' one at 22 pounds, with some games including both events. The games' shot putter is best characterised by the figure depicted for years on the Scott's Porage Oats packet. However, some games, instead of using standard shots, use a 'light' and/or 'heavy' stone, a more traditional form of the event. The stone is often of irregular shaped granite taken from a river bed and consequently very smooth. Some heavies prefer the stones while others prefer the standard cast iron putts. Some games, such as Braemar and Glenisla, feature a standing putt competition with a 28 pound stone, which calls for considerable power.

The Scots hammer is different from the Olympic hammer in that it is wooden shafted with an iron ball embedded in the end of the shaft, while the Olympic hammer has the iron ball connected by a length of cable to a triangular steel handle. The Scots hammer comprises the 'light' hammer (16lb) and the 'heavy' hammer (22lb). The Olympic hammer is 16lb. Throwing techniques are different, too, as the Scots'

Scots hammer

hammer is thrown from a static position while the Olympic hammer is thrown following several turns in a concrete circle. The Scots hammer thrower takes up his stance behind the wooden trig board with his back to the direction of throw and, using the spikes attached to the soles of his boots, anchors his feet into the ground to provide a stable base for throwing. Having rubbed resin into the shaft, to improve grip, he takes a few preliminary swings round his head, accelerating each time until he has built up sufficient momentum to send the hammer soaring skywards before descending in an arc to thud resoundingly into the turf well over a hundred feet away. This also is a spectacular event capable of provoking much drama, not least when a wildly thrown hammer heads towards a rapidly scattering crowd.

The 28lb weight for distance is perhaps the most graceful of all the heavy events and, well executed, is almost balletic in nature. It consists of a ball or box weight attached by links to a metal handle, which the heavy grips in one hand. Standing at the rear of the circle, the heavy takes a couple of swings about waist level before executing a couple of turns, similar to a discus thrower, accelerating each time while trailing the weight just behind him, to arrive in the optimum position at the front of the circle to enable him to heave it a distance of over seventy feet. It calls for strength, balance and coordination. Some games also feature throwing the 56 pound weight for height event.

The last of the standard heavy events is also a crowd favourite: throwing the 56lb weight over the bar. The weight is usually a box weight (sometimes spherical) again attached by links to a metal handle which the heavy grips with one hand. Positioning himself under the bar, back to the bar, the heavy bends at the knees to take a preliminary swing with the weight backwards between his legs, before thrusting it upwards with a mighty heave to clear the bar at heights often over fourteen feet. Much to the crowd's amusement, the thrower nonchalantly takes a last-minute step aside as the weight crashes down, narrowly missing him. To put this feat in perspective, it has been compared to throwing a seven-year old boy over a double-decker bus.

Cash prizes and points are awarded for each of the events, usually down to fourth place and the athlete with the highest total of points at the end of the afternoon is winner of the heavy championship, which earns him an additional prize. To aspire to be a top heavy it is necessary to be adept at all the different events.

The size, format and settings of the games in Scotland vary greatly; from those in the far north-west at remote Durness, set in stunning surroundings atop cliffs overlooking the North Atlantic, to the more prosaic urban surroundings of Bathgate Highland Games in densely populated central Scotland; from the small traditional Glenisla Games, held on a Friday each mid-August, where the tiny games' field is fitted in between the River Isla on one side and a grassy banking on the other, serving as a natural amphitheatre for spectators, to the regal splendour of the world-famous Braemar Games on Royal Deeside, the best attended of all the games in Scotland. Crowds of more than twenty thousand regularly cram into the Princess Royal and Duke of Fife Memorial Park there with the record standing at thirty-one thousand.

The Lonach Games in Strathdon, Aberdeenshire, first held in 1836, feature the

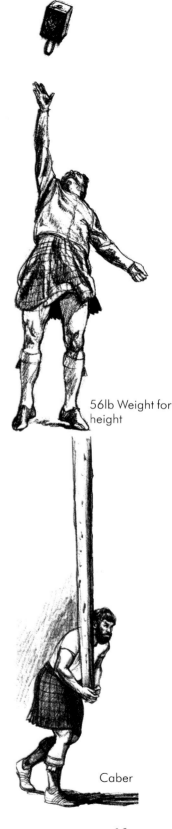

56lb Weight for height

Caber

highly colourful March of the Clansmen – the Men of Lonach – in full Highland dress, armed with pikes and Lochaber battleaxes. About 7.30 in the morning they set out on their march round the houses of the Gathering's patrons, at each of which they sink a dram before reaching, still upright, the games field at Bellabeg Park to signal the opening of the Games.

However, there are many features common to all games. Often held on a gently undulating and recently cut field, tartan and kilts are everywhere and Scottish flags and the banners of local landowners flutter over the arena. Pipe bands march to and fro. Young female Highland dancers, immaculately coiffured and clad, nimbly perform their steps on a platform under the watchful gaze of judges. In a far corner of the arena a sole piper paces slowly back and forward playing pibroch scrutinised intensely by judges, some aided by a glass of whisky tucked discreetly under their chairs. Runners run raggedly round the rudimentary track as others return exhausted from the hill race. Jumpers leap into makeshift sand pits while loud cheering salutes the efforts of the strapping tug o'war teams. Marquees entertain a flow of foreign visitors and clan society members as drams of whisky are dispensed in the refreshments' marquee. Kilted announcers clutch their microphones, crackling out information.

All the while, presiding in patriarchal fashion over this colourful scene is the Chieftain of the Games, a gent of distinguished appearance impeccably attired in Highland dress usually sporting outsize feathers in his headgear and carrying an ornate cromach. But in the middle of the arena, it is the heavies and their incredible feats which are the centre of attention.

A supplementary question in that survey at Aboyne Games asked spectators to name their favourite Games' athlete. The winner, also by a clear margin, was Bill Anderson. This is his story, set in the context of the history of the heavy events and the Games and including profiles of his main rivals and features on many games.

Bill Anderson about to toss the caber at the Scottish Championship, Crieff Highland Games in the late 1960s

Drum Major Ian Morrison, Lonach Pipe Band

Highland Fling

Highland Games overseas
(above)
Sunday 31st August 2008, drummer Tim Donihee and piper Robert Henderson of Calgary warm up for Tim's event at the Canmore Highland Games in Alberta. The day before had been sunny and warm but things can change in the mountains.
Photo by Andrew Joo

(left)
Grandfather Mountain Games, Linville, North Carolina, America's most iconic Games; Bill Anderson competed here and at many other Games overseas (see Chapters 7 and 9)

A young Bill Anderson is congratulated by his father at Aboyne Games in 1961 on breaking AA Cameron's 1904 record for putting the 22lb stone

1. From Alford to Crieff
1956 – 1987

THE black Austin 16 carried a substantial load as it made its way that fine Saturday morning from Bucksburn, on the outskirts of Aberdeen, to Alford in Upper Donside thirty miles west. In the front passenger seat was 18 year old Bill Anderson, 6'1" and 15 stone, while at the wheel was one of his older brothers, John, of similar substantial proportions. It was Saturday 21st July 1956 and it was to the 117th annual Alford Agricultural Show and Sports where the Anderson brothers were headed. The day was gloriously sunny and as the old Austin nudged its way along the A944 west, past Elrick and Dunecht, the countryside became increasingly prettier.

But in the front seat, Bill's mind was not on the countryside. Occasionally, he looked sideways at his brother John, wondering why he had allowed himself to be persuaded the previous night and what he had let himself in for. Bursts of inconsequential conversation did little to calm the feeling of apprehension that was beginning to take root in Bill. There was no turning back now – he would never live it down, far less be allowed to.

The previous night, Friday, at the end of the working week, the Four Mile Bar at Kingswells, near Aberdeen, was doing a roaring trade. Bill and brother John were there along with a friend of John's, Angus Johnstone. This was their regular Friday night get-together, when the rigours of the week were shaken off with the help of pints of McEwan's heavy beer. It was usually a good going session and this Friday night was no exception. The Four Mile Bar was a country pub on the main road just west of Aberdeen, about a mile from the city boundary. Much of its custom was drawn from the surrounding rural population of farmers and farmworkers, many of whom were in attendance.

As the pints eased the stresses of the week, Bill's group became more animated. John mentioned that the Alford Show and Sports was to take place the following day and that it was about time Bill made his debut at the heavy events, instead of just practising with his Scots hammer all the time. Over the previous four years or so Bill had indeed practised a lot with the old Scots hammer that had been lying about his father's farm at Greenferns, Bucksburn. During that time he had improved a lot, thanks to his increasing natural strength and better technique. But all that throwing had been done for fun in non-competitive surroundings, well shielded from the public gaze. Bill well knew there was a world of difference between that and competing in the open heavy events at the games.

He had been toying with the idea of competing for some time – after all, what was the point of just training and improving but not putting your ability to the competitive test? He had been following with increasing interest the press reports of the feats of heavies like George Clark of Grange by Keith, Bob Shaw of Ballater, Jack Hunter of Dunecht, Ewen Cameron of Lochearnhead, Sandy Gray of Leochel-Cushnie and others.

At that time press reports of the top heavies' performances at the games were extensive, especially in the local *Press & Journal*. Their photographs appeared frequently and by now Bill knew them all by sight. As a result, these heavies were on a pedestal in a sense and in Bill's mind were in a different league. His desire to compete was blunted by his perception of the enormity of that step. He needed to be pushed and his fairly reserved nature made it seem an even more difficult decision. Yet, some weeks previously, he had been given a strong vote of confidence by an athlete familiar with the games' scene. Jimmy Simpson, a former schoolmate of Bill's, had quickly established a reputation as a middle-distance runner on the local games circuit. One night, while out on a training run in the country, he chanced upon Bill practising his Scots hammer and stopped to watch. Afterwards, clearly impressed by what he had seen, his advice to Bill was unequivocal, 'Get competing in the Games – you'll hold your own, nae bother.'

Despite such encouragement Bill had not yet taken the plunge nor was he minded to do so that Friday night. How could he possibly compete against these icons when he did not even possess a tape to measure his own training throws? But John and Angus were not for taking 'No' as an answer. John himself had competed in a games on the west coast, near where he went on holiday every summer. They kept on at Bill, reminding him of his great natural strength, his improvement at the hammer and the accolade of Jimmy Simpson. Thanks to their persistence, and fortified by a few pints, Bill's intransigence began to weaken as his competitive instincts began to overcome his inhibitions. Apart from anything else, there was the prospect of a few bob to be won if all went well, as the Sports were professional and cash prizes were awarded. Buoyed by such encouragement, Bill finally agreed. Yes, tomorrow would mark his debut, he declared.

All these thoughts came flooding back into Bill's mind as John eased the Austin into Alford, among what seemed to be hundreds of cars, buses and cycles all making their way there for the same reason.

At this time Alford was a vibrant community, a major agricultural centre with a thriving cattle market and home to the famous Aberdeen Angus beef cattle. It was well served by the Alford Valley railway, connecting it with Aberdeen and beyond, and was the main town in the area for the surrounding agricultural hinterland. The Vale of Alford Agricultural Association's Show and Sports was being held for the 117th time. Primarily, it was an agricultural show featuring competitions for various categories of cattle, horses and sheep but the Sports were an important adjunct. Although called sports they were, in effect, a

Highland Games because apart from the heavy events there was also piping, dancing and running and jumping events. But there were also events not usually seen at a Highland Games – pony jumping, five-a-side football, fancy dress parades and 'blind' boxing. As it was technically a 'Sports' and not a Highland Games there was one important difference – it was not mandatory for the heavies to wear kilts. From Bill's perspective this was significant as he did not own a kilt!

The brothers soon located the Showground and after parking the car made their way there on foot. Bill's attempts at achieving inner tranquillity were not made any easier when he saw the large numbers of people also flocking there. It would be just his luck that this year attracted a record crowd in excess of four thousand spectators, many attracted by the excellent weather. Once they paid their admission money they headed towards the arena where the events were to take place.

This was a rudimentary grass track ringed by spectators. Adjacent to two sides of the arena behind the spectators were a number of agricultural pens holding a variety of sheep and cattle. In the middle of the arena was a marquee for the officials and at either end were two more marquees, one providing basic changing facilities for the athletes and the other the beer tent. After the parade of prize cattle and horses at 1.15pm the Sports were due to start at 1.30pm, the first Heavy event being putting the heavy stone (22lb).

Bill's nerves were hardly calmed by the sight of some of the heavies sauntering easily into the arena to begin warming up. First he spotted Sandy Gray of Leochiel-Cushnie, 6'5" and 19 stones of solid muscle and winner of the Scottish Heavy Events title in 1954. Gray was reckoned to have the strongest grip in the country, which gave him a particular advantage in the weights and hammer events. Then he saw Bob Shaw of Ballater, an excellent shot putter and one of the top heavies for many years, and then Jack Hunter of Dunecht, an imposing figure at 6'6" and 20 stones and holder of the Scottish title from 1950 to 1952. Both were perhaps past their very best but still formidable opponents. Next he caught a glimpse of Hugh Fraser, a well known north-east heavy and Aberdeen prison officer.

John kept encouraging Bill, telling him not to be awed by reputations and to keep as calm as he could in the circumstances. Then he saw Bob Aitken, of Auchenblae, a top all-rounder who excelled at both the 'light' and 'heavy' events.

They were all sporting their kilts and had with them their special spiked boots for use in the hammer throws, to give them more purchase on the ground. Bill, on the other hand, tried not to look self-conscious in his light full length trousers and football boots.

As the parade of cattle and horses made its way out of the arena, that was the signal for the Sports to begin. John helpfully whispered to Bill, 'You'll have to go in now,' and Bill tentatively started what seemed at the time a very long walk into the arena, to speak to the judges about competing. He knew one of them a little, Mr. Henderson of Torphins, which helped but he did not know the other, James Gordon of Strathdon. As Bill was to learn later, his nickname was 'The Duke' because in games circles his word was law! Both were quite friendly and told Bill he could compete. Meantime, the heavies looked rather bemusedly at him, mildly curious as to who this simply attired stripling of a youngster might be. New faces amongst competitors in the heavy events were uncommon. Normally they would be known to someone or known to one of the others. Simply walking in from the crowd to compete as a complete unknown was unheard of.

There were seven heavy events that afternoon: light and heavy stone; light and heavy hammer; 28lb weight for distance; 56lb weight for height and tossing the caber. The only event Bill had ever previously tried, and that not in competition, was the hammer. The heavy stone, (22lb, as opposed to the 16lb weight of the Olympic shot) got under way with Bill, being the new boy, designated last to throw. Although nervous, he was relishing the prospect of competing. Never having tried the shot putt previously he eagerly studied the technique of the others as they heaved the stone, apparently effortlessly, to send it thudding into the turf. Shaw appeared to be in the lead as 'The Duke' barked, 'Anderson, ye're next!'

Bill grasped the stone and took his place in the square behind the trig board. Mentally rehearsing first what he had to do and concentrating intensely, he glided towards the board before releasing the stone with all the power he could muster. However, it was a cautious effort and while to the rear of the field he was at least not last. And he had made a start! By the second round Shaw had established a lead but Bill's effort, more confident this time, was not far behind. Rumblings began among the other heavies on seeing Bill's second putt – who was this guy? When it came to the final round, Shaw was still in the lead despite not having improved his distance. Realising he was in with a chance of a shock victory Bill gave it all he had with his last throw, timing his final push perfectly to send the stone out just beyond Shaw's mark. This was a truly unbelievable start for Bill, beating the great Bob Shaw at his best event and this Bill's first time. He was delighted but could not show it for fear of alienating the others, whose party he had just gatecrashed.

Suitably encouraged, he set about the other events with gusto. Next was the light stone, 16lb weight as in the Olympic shot. Here the natural order of things was restored, with Shaw winning, Bob Aitken second, and Bill third with a throw of about 39feet. Such success far outweighed his expectations or those of anyone in the Four Mile Bar the previous evening.

The 28lb weight for distance was a highly technical event which Bill was unable to make much of, despite help from Hugh Fraser as to how to do it. With the light hammer, 16lb, he only succeeded in throwing his three attempts out of bounds as he was hooking the throw at the end, probably because of trying too hard. Sandy Gray won with a distance of 118 feet. But in the heavy hammer, 22lb, he came an excellent second to Gray with a throw of about 89 feet, to Gray's record throw of 94 feet. Gray also won the next event, the 56lb weight over the bar, with a height of 14 feet, while Bill did very well to claim a share of third place, with 12 feet.

Finally came the caber, which Bill failed to lift successfully because of problems with balance. It was a very demanding task for a novice such as Bill to be able to lift the caber even though Sandy Gray was giving him tips on how to do it.

By the end of the afternoon Bill eagerly counted his winnings – the princely sum of £9.10/-, £9.50 nowadays. At that time Bill's weekly wage was £4.50 – in the course of an afternoon he had earned more than two weeks' wages. He was pinching himself to believe it. And while the other heavies initially had kept at arms' length from him, as the afternoon's events unfolded and they saw Bill's prowess and potential emerge, they became reasonably encouraging. They all knew, however, they had just witnessed the start of a new era in heavy events.

Needless to say, it was a very happy return car journey for the brothers Anderson, with Bill thanking John for his encouragement. Where else could such a day end but back in the Four Mile Bar, where Bill willingly stood his hand several times as he and John went over the events of the day. By now Bill was well and truly hooked on the Games, 'bitten by the bug' as he said. Now there was no need for him to be pushed – he had all the motivation he needed.

Bill Anderson with rival, Australian Scot, Colin Mathieson

Move forward to 1987 and the Scottish Heavy Events Championship at Crieff Highland Games. Between his Alford debut in 1956 and 1987 Bill Anderson had gone on to enjoy a stunningly successful career as a heavy athlete and in the opinion of many well-qualified observers, had demonstrated during those years that he was the greatest ever in the history of the games. During that time he had amassed Scottish championships, British and European championships, American and Canadian championships, World championships, World Caber Tossing championships and more cups, medals and prizes than he could possibly ever hope to accommodate in his house.

Of all these worthy championships, the one which undoubtedly carried the most kudos was the Scottish one, held annually at Crieff. For the heavies this was the Blue Riband, the annual cup final, and Crieff was their Hampden, their Murrayfield. In the public's mind Braemar was the annual showpiece of the games season, understandably so, but for the competitors Crieff was the place. Bill was now approaching fifty and if Old Man Time was not yet knocking on his door, he was certainly walking up the path. Over the last years, he had become aware of his physical capabilities diminishing. He was not so strong at the weights in the gym and his hammer throwing, once his outstanding event, was no longer so good although he still maintained a good all-round level of performance. Despite nature's inroads, his competitive spirit still burned brightly and the lure of the Scottish championship at Crieff remained a powerful one.

As he and seventeen year old son Craig, an aspiring heavy himself, drove off from Aberdeen to start the hundred-mile trip to Crieff that Saturday morning, 15th of August 1987, Bill reflected on his unparalleled success there during his career to date. Champion fifteen times in his own right and two titles shared with the great Arthur Rowe. Never once out of the top three in all his twenty-nine appearances in the championship since his debut in 1958, although his last win had been in 1980.

In the intervening years other younger heavies had begun to impose themselves – men like the celebrated strongman and former international shot putter Geoff Capes and Scots' heavies like Grant Anderson, Alistair Gunn, Hamish Davidson and others. While Bill still competed well he no longer dominated as he once did. Another title to add to the seventeen already in his locker would be a great achievement before retirement beckoned, he continued thinking as he and Craig neared Crieff. The thought of retirement had of course occurred to him. But walking away from the games after more than thirty years' involvement was not easy and something he preferred not to dwell on. That would be a decison for another time.

As he and Craig made their way into the Games in Crieff's Market Park, it was overcast with hardly any wind. The park is quite close to the centre of Crieff and was once graced by an ornate grandstand which sadly burned down in 1971. It has no immediate outlook although in the distance the pleasant wooded slopes of the Strathearn valley can be seen. Although its setting is not particularly special, the Games themselves are special because of the calibre of competition and high standards of organisation and officiating.

As he entered the arena Bill again saw the sights so familiar to him. Partly encircling the park were a large number of shows blaring out music, stalls of various types and fast food outlets, the unmistakable smell of whose products hovered over the arena. A number of marquees were dotted about over the ground and the wooden boards of the Highland dancing platforms resonated to the dancers' footsteps as they sought to keep time to the piper's notes. As the crowd slowly grew, pipe bands could be heard warming up.

The local events, confined to athletes from the area, were winding up. A three hundred and thirty yard grass track had been marked out in the middle of the arena which runners could be seen lapping, as cyclists waited their opportunity to warm up. The local heavies, among them the Simpson brothers and that fine all-round athlete John Robertson from Logierait, Perthshire, departed the arena to make way for the Championship contestants.

As anticipated, Bill's main rivals had all turned up, among them Alistair Gunn, from Halkirk in Caithness; Grant Anderson from Dundee; Brian Robin from Oban; Stephen King from Inveraray; Neil Fyvie from Aboyne; Alan Sim from Fettercairn and Chris Black from Edinburgh.

Black, then aged thirty seven had an outstanding pedigree in the amateur ranks particularly as a wire hammer thrower. Scottish and British champion numerous times, the high point of his career came at the Montreal Olympics of 1976 when he finished seventh in the hammer final. He had also been Scottish shot putt champion and a very good discus thrower. Although immensely strong, through years of heavy weight training, he did not have a lot of experience at the traditional heavy events which would count against him.

Robin was an excellent heavy who had won the world caber tossing championship two years previously while King was a promising young heavy who would go on in the future to claim Bill's light hammer world best mark. Fyvie and Sim were also creditable well known heavies on the circuit and more will be said of Gunn and Grant Anderson shortly. In brief, this was a formidable field ranged against Bill. The stakes were high – not only for prestige but also for the prize money. The winner could walk away with between £200 and £300 in cash plus a gallon of whisky. Being champion could also earn one invites to lucrative events overseas and elsewhere in the UK. Some of Bill's rivals definitely fancied their chances, privately reckoning the great man was 'past it'.

The heavy events in sequence were the heavy shot (22lb), the light shot (16lb), the 28lb weight for distance, the heavy hammer (22lb), the light hammer (16lb), the 56lb weight over the bar and tossing the caber. By about 2pm the ground was virtually full with about eight thousand spectators ringing the arena. The pipe bands were in full swing, the dancers were nimbly creating their patterns, the runners were straining sinew and muscle for the tape, while the cyclists appeared to defy gravity by staying in the saddle as they hurtled round the tight bends of the grass track.

Meantime, in the centre of the arena, the focus of most attention, the heavies started to slog it out. Over the course of the afternoon the competition was very close, with the lead changing – between Grant Anderson, Alistair Gunn and Bill.

Grant could justifiably claim to be the outstanding heavy of the time. In the 1980s he had won three Scottish titles outright and shared two more with Capes. He had also won the US title four years in a row between 1981 and 1984, been world champion and world caber tossing champion and on his day was the best in the world.

Gunn was progressively making his mark on the games scene, having first figured, winning prizes at national level about four years previously. In 1986 he had won the Glenfiddich Qualifying Heavy Events Championship – a season long competition restricted to under 25s and involving a number of games, with points being awarded at each and the winner decided by aggregate. He had also acquitted himself very well in the equivalent senior competition and was a tenacious competitor. Nor was he above trying to gain an edge over opponents by psyching them out verbally, taunting them about 'poor performance'. That fell on stony ground as far as Bill was concerned. He was extremely good at shutting everything else out and concentrating on his performance.

The Scottish championship was decided on the aggregate of points scored for the seven heavy events, six being awarded for first, down to one for sixth place. Success therefore depended on the heavies' all-round ability. The success of Bill's career owed much to the fact that he was excellent at all events. Gunn had won both putts, Grant Anderson both hammers and the 56lb weight for height, while the only event Bill won was the 28lb weight for distance with a fine throw of 73 feet.

As the final event, the caber, loomed, Bill held a marginal overall lead because of high placings in all events. Despite his best efforts he could only finish third in the caber, behind his namesake and Gunn, but held on to secure the championship by half a point from Gunn, with Anderson third, a few points behind. Incredibly, Bill had won his eighteenth Scottish title when two months shy of his fiftieth birthday, the oldest winner ever. He had also maintained his astonishing record of being in the top three in the championship over thirty consecutive seasons.

His rivals and the crowd were generous in their applause as Bill stepped forward to receive the grand old trophy once again from the Chieftain of the Games, together with his gallon bottle of whisky. Never an over-demonstrative character, Bill again succeeded in hiding his elation while giving the impression of being modestly content at the way things had turned out. Seven years had passed since his last title, making this win particularly sweet, especially given his recognition of his diminishing powers. Had he known then that this was to be his last participation in a Scottish Championship, the victory would doubtless have tasted even sweeter. In the circumstances a more fitting finale to Bill's association with the Scottish Championships could not have been scripted.

Needless to say, Bill and Craig enjoyed the trip home to Aberdeen with the Scottish trophy in the boot. Craig enjoyed opening the individual events' prize money envelopes and the Championship prize envelope, which he totalled to the grand sum of £250. Bill never disguised the fact that he enjoyed winning money at the games. There had not been an abundance of it around in his youth and he and his family appreciated the contribution it made to their standard of living.

However, this time Bill and Craig went straight home with the winnings – unlike after Alford Show in 1956 when Bill blew most of them on his brother and himself in the Four Mile Bar at Kingswells.

The Anderson family home at Greenferns Farm, Bucksburn, Aberdeen

An Anderson family wedding 1950; Bill third from left, back row

Highland Fling

2. Early Days

WILLIAM Smith Anderson, first saw the light of day at Greenferns Farm, Bucksburn, on the northern outskirts of Aberdeen on 6th October 1937. Although his weight was not recorded, due to his birth being at home as was then common, he certainly was a large baby. The Anderson family was a large one, Bill being the sixth of nine sons, with an elder and a younger sister. In chronological sequence they were Andy, twins John and Frances, James, Douglas, Alexander, Bill, Edward, Jean, George and Donald. About twenty years spanned eldest to youngest. Alexander died at age thirty-five, due to rheumatic fever, since when Andy, John and James have also died. Bill's parents were John and Jeanie who also were from large families, John being one of eleven and Jeanie being of seven.

The Andersons had been farming at Greenferns since the final years of Victoria's reign, when Bill's paternal grandfather, Andrew Anderson, took over the farm. Going further back, to the early 1800s, the Andersons originally came from Monymusk in west Aberdeenshire before gravitating into Aberdeen where they worked as gardeners and shopkeepers prior to Bill's grandfather farming Greenferns.

There was a farming connection also on Bill's mother's side of the family as her father, James Parley, was a farmer at Northfield, also on the northern outskirts of Aberdeen only a few miles from Greenferns. Several centuries earlier her forebears had come to Scotland from France, possibly as Huguenot refugees, to work as servants at Slains Castle. The now ruined castle sits perched on the cliffs above the North Sea to the north of Cruden Bay, Aberdeenshire, where it forms an imposing landmark on the rugged coastline. It is considered one of the inspirations for Bram Stoker, the creator of Dracula, who used to holiday in nearby Cruden Bay.

Bill's wife Frances, whom he married in 1960, was also from farming stock, having been brought up at Blacksmith's Croft, Sheddocksley, Aberdeen, a small farm near Greenferns. Given that Bill himself worked in farming till he was aged twenty-seven it is clear that this farming background was an important formative factor in his upbringing and development. It also contributed significantly to laying the foundations of his career as Scotland's greatest ever heavy athlete.

Greenferns was a dairy farm extending to about one hundred acres, which belonged to Aberdeen Town Council, from whom John Anderson leased it. In those days this was quite a common arrangement. There were usually about a maximum of sixty head of cattle, of which at any given time about forty would be milking cows. Apart from the cattle, crops such as turnips, oats, barley and corn were grown, some of which was used as feed and bedding for the cattle. There was also a wide variety of vegetables grown for consumption by the family.

Bill's recollections of childhood are good. 'We all got on well. Inevitably, there were some disagreements and arguments but they were short lived. I used to think my dad was strict but now I realise he had to be with so many of us, particularly nine boys, to handle. This was wartime and, in common with many families, there wasn't much money about although we were fortunate in being on the farm that we never wanted for food or other essentials.'

His earliest memory on the farm was of a near tragedy involving his younger brother, Edward, in about 1942 when he was five and Edward four. The two had started following the binder during the harvest and then they got a lift on it. Edward's child's curiosity got the better of him as he leant down for a better look and fell through the covers of the binder, resulting in his head becoming stuck between the rollers. Bill, although virtually frozen in fear, had the presence of mind to shout loudly at the horseman, Charlie Bain, who immediately brought the horse to a standstill before beginning the delicate task of extricating Edward, with Bill's help, by his legs from his life-threatening position. They succeeded but Bill has never forgotten the anxiety he felt for Edward.

Horses were still very much in use then on farms as it was not really till after World War II that tractors began to be introduced. They did many tasks, including ploughing and pulling carts to carry feedstuffs for the cattle. They were used to 'muck out the midden' and had many uses at harvest time. There were three horses at Greenferns, 'one pair' and a 'spare' horse, the 'pair' working together all the time. The horseman, who was in charge of them, was a very important worker on the farm. Lunch lasted an hour and a half, to ensure the horses were properly rested. As well as horsemen, in those pre-mechanisation days, farms usually employed a cattleman or dairy cattleman, sometimes an 'orraman' – a worker so called as he was left to do everything, and sometimes a 'halflin', so called as he was a youth under the age of eighteen and was reckoned only half a man!

Bill and his brothers had good cause to remember the first tractor at Greenferns. About two years or so after the end of hostilities his father purchased a gleaming new tractor, which naturally was his pride and joy. One Friday night not long after, he and his wife went out to visit relatives, leaving the boys at home. Temptation was too much and minutes after their parents' car had disappeared from view five Andersons junior set about acquainting themselves with this new wondrous piece of machinery. After some anxious tinkering, the tractor sputtered into life whereupon the five, at the same time clinging on to different parts of the driver's seat, the wheel arches and the bonnet, sought to control the vehicle's forward motion, initially with some success. But disaster was just round the corner, literally, as an attempt to negotiate the left hand turn between the stable and the bothy proved to be disastrous as an assortment of ten hands reaching simultaneously for control of the steering wheel ended with the tractor crashing into the stable wall, causing serious damage to the tractor, with its formerly pristine bodywork now markedly less so. Mr. Anderson was displeased.

Bill and his siblings all got on together notwithstanding the occasional difficulties and as adults that harmony endured. He acknowledges that much of the credit for that is due to the excellent values instilled in them by his parents who were good, honest, hard working people, well respected members of the local farming community. Being such a large family also meant that it was in all their interests to co-operate with each other. In addition, all helped out from an early age doing jobs on the farm. Those two elements combined to foster a spirit of togetherness.

Having an array of elder brothers as well as a big sister was an advantage for Bill when he started school for the first time, as he had their reassuring presence. He clearly remembers his first day at Bucksburn Primary School. It entailed leaving home at 8.15am, trailing a number of brothers, to set off on the two-mile walk down the Howes Road to Bucksburn, escorted by his big sister Frances.

'I can remember being left outside the school gates and making my own way into the school. I didn't feel particularly apprehensive about it. I just took it in my stride really. Maybe having older brothers at the same school helped.'

Even at that early age Bill was demonstrating the equable temperament that was to serve him so well in the competitive arena of the Games circuit. Miss Bruce, 'a fine lady' he recalls, was his first teacher in a class of about thirty-five pupils. While school was not his favourite place he did alright, without excelling at any particular subject although he was good at arithmetic. He encountered no major difficulties, thought well of his teachers and particularly enjoyed the football in the playground. At the end of the school day there was the long walk back to Greenferns, this time uphill. Over the course of his primary schooling there was always a number of his brothers and sisters walking together to and from school, with some innocent mischief usually going on. Other kids from neighbouring farms also walked the same route and added to the fun of the daily trek.

There were times, though, when it was less fun than others, particularly in winter when sometimes biting cold, wind, rain and snow had to be contended with – winters then in Aberdeenshire tended to be very hard.

Although Bill claims never to have been in any real trouble at school he does remember his brother Edward one day stealing a teacher's belt, before cutting it up into small pieces and hiding them under various boulders on the return walk home. He also remembers a time when some of his brothers thought a day spent roaming the surrounding countryside was preferable to sitting doing boring lessons in a stuffy classroom. Despite their taking care to leave home properly equipped for school at the correct time and returning home at the expected hour, their ruse was short-lived and there was no more truancy.

Much of his primary schooling, of course, took place during World War II. Although it did not impinge greatly on his upbringing he remembers the gas masks in the farmhouse and the frequent blackouts. Although Aberdeen was far from the theatres of war its harbour had been subject to bombing raids and one night, in about 1942, Bill recalls a raid when bombs fell on the farm. The siren at nearby Dyce Airport sounded, which was the signal for Bill's dad to cram all the youngsters into a small room beneath the stairs till the 'all clear' signal was given. The silence of the night was first pierced by the drone of the bombers' engines before being shattered by the sound of bombs exploding nearby. The Luftwaffe had been trying to hit water supply lines to Dyce Airport and the next morning Bill saw the bomb holes in the farm fields. He and his brothers were about to pick up pieces of metal debris left lying around till their father's admonition dissuaded them. All were relieved to be unscathed although an aunt's theory that 'maybe a nice pilot didn't want to bomb anyone' seemed a little implausible.

At this point Bill's life outwith school revolved round the family and the farm. For all the boys the farm was a fantastic playground. With so much company at hand, so much open space and so many outbuildings available, the boys had no difficulty in finding diversions. However, from relatively young they were all expected to make a contribution to the working of the farm and did so, at first on an occasional informal basis which became a more formalised arrangement as the boys grew older.

'It was just something that you grew up with. I never thought much about it. We all did our bit, it was part of our way of life. It was certainly something I never resented. When we were a bit older and did weekend rotas to help with the dairy operation, it meant my brothers and I couldn't go to watch Aberdeen play football at Pittodrie as often as we might have liked, but you just accepted that and got on with it,' recalled Bill.

When younger, Bill did a variety of tasks round the farm – gathering potatoes, weeding carrots, skimming neeps and weeding the drills. Either his father or his elder brothers would instruct him in these tasks.

Mealtimes at Greenferns were quite an occasion as the whole family sat down to eat together. Because of the number of mouths to feed and the numerous other household tasks that had to be undertaken, domestic help had to be employed – ladies known rather unflatteringly as 'skivvies' helped Bill's mother but also took their turn at milking the cows, which then was all done by hand. These ladies used to 'live in' at Greenferns and were treated as another member of the family.

Much of their food was produced on the farm, with meal and porridge forming a large part of their diet and vegetables being plentiful. Twice per week the baker delivered a dozen loaves. Being a farming family they were fortunate in having such food resources available to them, given the restrictions and rationing imposed on the rest of the population during and following the war. Although mealtimes could occasionally be chaotic, they did serve to foster that spirit of togetherness in the family, a spirit that was not diminished by the three elder brothers having to sleep in one of the bothies because of lack of room in the farmhouse.

As Bill grew up he and his brothers began to take an interest in sport, particularly football initially. More significantly perhaps, Bill remembers the first sports meeting he ever attended which made a big impression on him. This was the Stoneywood Mill Sports Day in 1947, held at the Polo Park, Stoneywood, which adjoined Bucksburn on the north side of Aberdeen.

The following year his big sister, Frances, took him by train on an excursion to Turriff, the market town some forty miles north-west of Aberdeen, to see the then famous Turriff Show, an agricultural event which also featured sports, including the traditional Scottish heavy events.

'I can remember,' says Bill, 'taking up my position in the crowd opposite where the heavies were throwing, in order to get a good view of them. Subconsciously my interest was being stimulated even then and I can remember Jimmy Reid of Skene competing that day as well.'

Also stoking that interest was the fact that during the war Bill's father had been the Home Guard champion for Aberdeen area at throwing the Scots hammer and putting the shot. Like all the Andersons, Bill's dad was a big man whose strength derived from years of heavy farming work but he only ever competed in Home Guard competitions.

A year or so after the end of the war Bill remembers one Sunday two ex-employees of his father coming back to visit at Greenferns. Once they had been entertained in the house the three men then went to the nearby field, collecting the Scots hammer from the barn en route, and held an informal hammer throwing competition. There was always a Scots hammer or two lying around the farm and at many other farms in Aberdeenshire then. Prior to World War I in Aberdeenshire informal inter-farm Scots hammer competitions were a regular event and also carried on, albeit to a lesser extent, between the wars. After 1945 the practice virtually came to an end with the exception of the time when 'neighbouring' was taking place. 'Neighbouring' occurred during harvest times when threshing was being undertaken. Farms in the same area lent men to each other on a reciprocal basis, principally to work the threshing mill which required between twelve and fourteen men to operate it. It was essentially a co-operative exercise between neighbouring farms for their mutual benefit. In their free time the men thrown together in this way often took part in informal Scots hammer competitions. But the days of 'neighbouring' were numbered, with the advent of the combine harvester towards the end of the fifties when the practice became redundant.

As a result of all these factors Bill's interest in hammer throwing began to form. It was shared by some of his brothers and when still very young Bill and Edward played with a 'pretend' hammer, of a ball with a hole through it attached to a rope, before graduating on to play with a ball attached to a makeshift wooden shaft. Within a few years, by the time Bill was in his early teens, he had started throwing the real thing, albeit only for fun.

By the time Bill was of age to attend secondary school at Bankhead Academy, also at Bucksburn, his duties at the farm had come to occupy more of his time. One of his regular tasks was to carry milk in three gallon pails from the byre to the milkhouse, where they had to be lifted and emptied into the cooler. This involved carrying about thirty pails, each weighing thirty pounds, twenty five yards or so before lifting them to empty them. Another task was to assist in loading the Scottish Milk Marketing Board lorry, which called every day, with ten large cans each containing ten gallons. This involved swinging the cans up to about chest height and then manoeuvring them into position on the top deck of the lorry, with one hand.

'I always had strong legs,' commented Bill, 'but this heavy work with the milk made them even stronger and also strengthened my back. In fact, I remember the lorry driver saying to me several times, "You're a right strong loon (boy)." By age fourteen Bill was a strapping specimen, a shade under six feet tall and weighing in at fourteen stones.

Meanwhile, he carried on at school enjoying the sport but not so much the academic side although he was awarded a prize for technical subjects and did well at geography. He was a regular for the football team where he played at either centre half or right back. School games were played on Saturday mornings, at Harlaw playing fields in Aberdeen, with Bill cycling there and back. Bankhead played other Aberdeen schools such as Torry, Hilton, Powis, Frederick, Oakbank etc. For his size he was surprisingly quick and agile, which he demonstrated a few times by winning the one hundred yards sprint and high jump at the school sports in the summer.

In the summer of 1951 an outdoors sports meeting against Inverurie Academy had to be transferred indoors to Bankhead's gym because of poor weather. One of the events was to be 'shying the football' but as the gym ceiling was reckoned to be too low, putting the medicine ball was substituted instead by Bill Harrower, Bill's games teacher. Bill demolished the opposition despite never having tried the activity before and counts this as his first competitive throwing success. By now he was very aware of his growing strength and his interest in the heavy events of the Games was increasing. He began to scour newspapers for the then extensive reports of the various Highland Games and took note of the names of the better known heavies and their performances – men such as George Clark, Sandy Gray, Jack Hunter, Bob Shaw, Jock McLellan of Alness, Ewen Cameron of Lochearnhead and Sandy Sutherland of Ardross.

Mainstream, or amateur, athletics as it was then, held no great interest. In that part of Scotland the Games were the thing and the activity to which young men from a rural background aspired. The stars were the heavies who could earn useful money if successful. These Games were professional only in the sense that prizes consisted of cash, not items such as clocks or cutlery sets which were awarded at amateur Games. The north-east was the hotbed of the professional Games and the area from where many of the best exponents came.

He was now practising the hammer regularly at Greenferns and becoming quietly optimistic about his potential as he soon outdistanced his brothers who threw with him. His father gave him some elementary pointers but at this stage it was all informal, a fun activity that he enjoyed for its own sake without any serious thought of competing. After all, there was not even a measuring tape at the farm and distances achieved could only be estimated. At the same time Bill's football interest continued, with him and some of his brothers playing for the local amateur team, Kingswells, in the summer league. Often there were three or four Anderson brothers in the same team and on one occasion there were actually six of them!

On his fifteenth birthday Bill left school to start working full-time at Greenferns, as he had always known would be the case. He was not unhappy to leave school and the prospect of working held no fears for him as he had already been doing it part-time for some years. However, despite his obvious diligence at work it was becoming apparent that with all the brothers on the farm there were too many of them to support at Greenferns. Accordingly, in early 1953 Bill's father told him and elder brother Sandy they would have to find work elsewhere. Bill took a job as cattleman on Quarry Farm at Persley, a few miles east of Bucksburn, while Sandy obtained work on a farm at Dyce. This entailed Bill living at Quarry Farm where he was housed in a 'fairly basic' bothy which he shared with another worker of the same age. Again, Bill's equable temperament came to the fore. 'I never thought that much about it, probably because I was from a farming background. I was never really homesick. I'd go home once a week on my bike.'

One such trip home Bill remembers particularly well. Having cycled back and stood his cycle outside the house he was surprised there was no sign of anyone. This seemed very strange as usually there was always someone engaged in some activity going about the farmyard or at one of the outbuildings. On entering the house which at first seemed eerily quiet, all then became clear – the whole family was squeezed into the living room sitting in total silence watching the family's first ever television set!

Bill adapted well to life at Quarry Farm although the work routine was quite demanding. Most days he had to be up by half past five which was the start of a long working day, usually into the early evening. The farmer, Stanley Fyfe, was a decent man to work for and meals were taken with him and his family in the farmhouse. So keen was Bill becoming on his hammer that he took one with him to Quarry Farm to enable him to practise there, especially once the lighter spring evenings started. Although he had no formal coaching, he began to think about technique and improvements to maximise distance. Till then, most of the heavies tended to throw in a rather stiff legged fashion without much movement and essentially using only the top half of the body. Bill reasoned that involving the big muscles of the legs and lower back more would help to accelerate hammer head speed and he experimented with technique by rotating the hips and upper thighs, to extend the arc of the swing. However, this was still a purely recreational activity while football with Kingswells in the summer league remained his competitive sport and one in which his performances were beginning to become noticed.

Indeed, it is possible that a career as a footballer could have beckoned had Bill accepted an offer made to him. That same summer, 1953, he was back for a few days at Greenferns helping out. He and a couple of his brothers were working on clearing out a ditch when two men in their twenties appeared out of the blue on foot there. After a few pleasantries they asked him to confirm he was Bill Anderson before explaining they were officials of Hall and Company, then a well known junior football team in the Aberdeen and District Junior League. As Bill and his brothers' bemusement grew, they went on to say they had watched him play several times for Kingswells and wanted to sign him.

Junior football, despite its name, was particularly then seen as a stepping stone to the senior game and was properly considered the level below senior. Their offer came as a big surprise to Bill who, for some reason that even today he is unsure of, failed to express any great enthusiasm for the project, keen as he was on football. Despite that, the officials were not to be easily put off and spent about an hour trying to cajole him to sign, to no avail. Thinking about it in retrospect, the prospect of having to travel into Aberdeen by cycle, to train two or three times a week, did not appeal to him. Flattered though he was, it just did not seem right to him at the time. But it begs the question whether, had he taken that option, he would have graced Pittodrie and Hampden instead of Braemar and Aboyne?

Another significant event took place in Bill's life that summer – he met Frances, who was to become his wife and to whom he is still happily married. The hub of social activity for the youth of the area was the Kingswells Village Hall which, among other activities, used to host traditional dancing on Friday nights. Bill remembers that some of his older brothers used to attend there and spoke of the fun they had. One Friday evening while out on his trusty bicycle he pedalled past the hall and heard the dance music blaring out. Being a typically curious youth he decided to take a look and gingerly edged his way in. The place was alive with dancers doing a medley of reels, fox trots and Gay Gordons to the jaunty tunes of a local two-piece band. It immediately appealed and he started attending regularly, even going to dancing classes. Frances was also a regular there and that was the start of their lifelong romance.

Although Frances lived only half a mile or so from Greenferns and Bill knew her by sight, it was only at the Kingswells dancing that they got to know each other and started courting. Dancing has in fact played a large part in their lives as even today much of their free time is spent doing Old Time dancing.

After about two years at Quarry Farm, Bill moved to Upper Mill Farm at Tarves, about twelve miles north of Aberdeen. There he was employed as a dairyman in one of the three byres there and shared a cottage with another six workers. The work schedule there was even more demanding than at Quarry Farm. The day started at twenty past four, with the option of a couple of hours back in bed in mid morning before having to clean up the byre preparatory to starting again at about two-thirty in the afternoon, till about six o'clock. For three weeks it was seven days a week, with a weekend off on the fourth week. All this hard work was contributing to Bill's physical development as he was now a solid fifteen stones plus but was restricting his opportunities to practise the hammer which, again, he had taken with him. Often he simply did not have the energy to do justice to his practice although his enthusiasm for and interest in the Games did not weaken. Such a punishing work schedule was affecting his social life adversely too. He enjoyed a night out, particularly now as he was courting Frances, but a night out followed by a 4.20 start was not a happy combination.

Like all young men of that age throughout the country, Bill was served his call-up papers for National Service in the army on his eighteenth birthday in 1955. Conscription, abolished in the mid sixties, lasted two years and at least in the short term could be a life-changing event which was not popular with all the youth of the time. Bill realised the likelihood was that he would be posted overseas as Britain then still had an Empire. While the prospect of being away from his familiar surroundings and particularly Frances did not delight him, on the other hand he had become a little dispirited with the relentless life of a dairyman at Upper Mill. Mr Durno, the farmer there, was rather an autocratic individual who ran a tight ship but who appreciated Bill's working qualities. He suggested to him that he could obtain him an exemption from National Service because working in dairy farming was considered a 'reserved' category. Although Mr Durno's offer was appreciated Bill felt there had to be something more in the world than what Upper Mill had to offer and politely declined.

With his call-up anticipated in the summer of 1956 Bill stopped work at Upper Mill and returned to Greenferns where he helped out as well as on neighbouring farms. Again, once the lighter nights arrived, he resumed training with his hammer which led to his successful debut at Alford. Buoyed by that success – 'I was a wee bit elated,' Bill understated his reaction – he headed to Dufftown Highland Games the following Saturday, again driven by big brother John. Despite the atrocious conditions and the increased pressure on his shoulders following that debut at Alford he again excelled, winning the light hammer and the stone putt which earned him about £8. The competitors were the same as the week before, with the exception of Bob Shaw who was absent. Once Dufftown finished, Bill began looking forward to the next week's Games at Aberlour, Morayshire, particularly as these would be the last before his call-up to the Army. At Aberlour there lay in wait, among others, two of the most accomplished heavies on the circuit, each at different stages of their careers.

Sandy Sutherland of Ardross, in Ross-shire, was then in his prime, aged twenty-five, and had a legitimate claim to be considered the country's best heavy at that time. An excellent all-rounder he was an outstanding shot putter and hammer thrower with throws over 45 feet and 125 feet to his credit. Blessed by good looks and an excellent physique he was an impressive figure. Jock McLellan of Alness, on the other hand, was reaching the end of his career. Aged forty four, his better days were behind him but he was still a gritty competitor who enjoyed the games too much to retire. An outstanding hammer thrower he had held the Scottish record for the 16lb hammer at 129 feet 1 inch since 1949, which he achieved at Pitlochry Games.

Given this level of competition Bill was pleased to win three seconds and £6 in the putt and both hammers, all behind Sutherland who swept the boards by winning all events. McLellan, not best pleased at this young pup relegating him to third in the hammers, commented pointedly on Bill's light hammer throw, 'I've thrown heavy hammers further.' Despite this acerbic start to their relationship, Bill and he were to go on to become firm friends.

Having tasted such success in his first three Games, Bill was desperately keen to build on that to make a real name for himself on the circuit. But first there was the small matter of the Army to deal with.

On 8th August 1956, the Monday after the Aberlour Games, Bill reported to the Cameron Barracks at Inverness to join the 1st Battalion of the Cameron Highlanders and become Private WS Anderson. Once initial formalities had been dealt with he was taken to meet the Commanding Officer who asked him about any sporting prowess he may have, there being healthy inter-battalion rivalry on the sports field. Having mentioned his football interest Bill proceeded in a low key way to explain that he could putt the shot forty feet and throw the hammer about one hundred and twenty feet. From the officer's lingering, sideways look at him Bill could tell he thought Bill was a fantasist. Undaunted, he sought permission to attend Strathpeffer Games the following Saturday which was granted. There he won prizes in both hammers and weight over the bar, netting some £5 in prize money. As 18/- (90p) was the weekly army 'pay', £5 was very welcome. A strong field had turned out there including Sandy Sutherland, John Jack of Alness, Louis Stewart of Corpach and that outstanding all-rounder Jay Scott of Inchmurrin. Someone in the Army hierarchy must have been impressed because when Bill asked for permission a few weeks later to compete at Braemar Highland Games, it was granted as he was to be representing the Cameron Highlanders.

The Battalion pipe band was to be performing there and as Bill knew the Pipe Major, Johnny O'Rourke, he travelled down by bus with the band from Inverness. Braemar represented a significant progression for

Bill. It was the biggest Games of the circuit, famous for its royal family connection which boosted the crowd to over 20,000, far greater than any of the crowds Bill had performed before. Being Braemar, it also attracted a strong quality field of athletes and 1956 was no exception. Since joining the Army Bill had been unable to practise the hammer due to the emphasis on good old-fashioned army 'square-bashing' which, while excellent for general fitness, did not amount to ideal preparation for heavy event competition. In the circumstances Bill was pleased to notch two fourth prizes, each in the hammer competitions, behind Sutherland, Gray and McLellan. Exposure to that size of crowd and that level of competition in that lovely arena whetted his appetite for more.

And there it was for the first time he met perhaps the best known heavy – who was a legend on the circuit and about whose exploits he had read copiously – George Clark, formerly of Grange and now of Torphins. By now aged forty nine he was in the twilight of an amazing career which had begun in the 1920s and was to creep into the 1960s. During the 1930s and the post war period he was undoubtedly Scotland's number one heavy while at the same time a champion wrestler, who had competed all over North America and in Western Europe. Clark has sometimes, with good reason, been referred to as the *enfant terrible* of the Games, as will become apparent.

But that was the end of the Games at this stage for Bill as he resumed his training at Inverness for a further six weeks. An overseas posting was expected, particularly with the Suez crisis then well under way, but it was to Aden that Bill's battalion was sent. Aden was a British protectorate in Yemen, strategically positioned at the southern end of the Red Sea and Suez Canal, where it was an important refuelling port for shipping en route to India and the Far East. Its stability was under threat from the nearby Suez crisis and from feuding tribes in the north, some of whom wanted independence from Britain. His first experience of flying was shared with a number of his colleagues on a military plane which took them initially to Entebbe in Uganda, as flying over Suez was prohibited. After a break for refuelling the flight continued north to Aden where this group of raw and exhausted soldiers disembarked, to be hit by searing heat of temperatures in excess of 37° Celsius. Bill recalls how the first lad off the plane fainted due to the heat and fell flat on his face. Welcome to Aden.

After initial acclimatisation Bill's Company was sent to Dhela in Yemen, where a variety of containment duties were undertaken. The inherent danger in their assignment was tragically underlined one day when (while out on a route march) a colleague from Buckie was shot dead by a Yemeni sniper and the Company Commander was seriously injured. Most of Bill's time was spent on guard duty and practising riot control. However it was soon time for the Company Sports at which Bill won the shot, discus and hammer quite easily. That was the first time he had thrown the discus and the wire hammer.

Next came the Battalion Sports, where he repeated his success, and that was followed by the 'big one' – the Aden Command Sports – which included athletes from the RAF and Police. Underlining the keenness of the inter-force rivalry, the RAF had brought over from Cyprus an apparently accomplished hammer thrower in a bid to secure that title. But despite Bill's being a complete novice at the wire hammer he saw off all rivals, throwing the prodigious distance of one hundred and thirty three feet from a standing throw! He also won the shot and discus for a clean sweep of the throws. That success was repeated the following year despite a protest having been received about Bill being a professional and thus ineligible to compete in these sports.

Another sport where Bill achieved success in the Army was boxing. A good friend, John Reid from Alness, was a keen boxer and persuaded him to start training for the Company heavyweight championship, which he won comfortably. The next contest was for the Battalion title which again he won. Reid won the light heavyweight title and another friend, Jocky Ellington, from Oldmeldrum, won the middleweight title. Bill had no particular illusions about his boxing – he recognised he was not an outstanding stylist but at sixteen stones and six feet one inch tall he had considerable physical advantages. Lieutenant Colonel Maitland McGill-Crichton, Second in Command of the battalion, enthused, 'At last we've got someone now to stand up to these big Guardsmen.' Another bonus to being in the boxing team was it entitled you to time off soldiering duties to train and also to double rations in the cookhouse.

The Aden Command Championships were next, when Bill was scheduled to box an RAF corporal who exclaimed at the weigh-in on seeing his opponent's sizeable frame, 'Ah'm no' fighting him!' From that moment on, his fate was sealed, Bill recording a comfortable win. As there were no more contests to be had that was the end of Bill's boxing career. Like Rocky Marciano he retired unbeaten. After being in the Duty Company for about a year he was transferred to the HQ Company in Aden where he joined the Regimental Police.

Although he had not experienced danger at first hand while in Aden, there was a constant undercurrent of tension as the enemy was mostly unseen, waging guerrilla type campaigns. It therefore did not come as a huge disappointment when after eighteen months he and his colleagues were posted back to Dover, where he continued as a Regimental Policeman. That was a fairly torrid spell in his military career as there were frequent outbreaks of fighting among the soldiers based there, fuelled in part by the availability of cheap cider which when mixed with fortified wine provided a lethal and disinhibiting cocktail. The presence of rival regiments, including the Gordons, added to the tension already existing with the locals. There were many weekend scrapes that Bill and his colleagues had to try to defuse. Indeed, only a few years ago one former Gordon's national serviceman stopped Bill in the street in Aberdeen to thank him for stopping someone giving him a beating one night in Dover about forty years previously.

Meantime, in Scotland, the Games season was getting under way and after a spot of home leave in May, when he managed some hammer practice, Bill was granted permission to compete at Oldmeldrum Games, near Aberdeen, in June, his first since Braemar two years previously. On a bright sunny day Bill's debut at Oldmeldrum went better than expected as he won the shot putt, both hammers and placed in the 56lb weight for height. His heavy hammer was particularly good, reaching about one hundred and eight feet. Considering the calibre of opposition – Sandy Gray, Sandy Sutherland, Ewen Cameron, George Clark, among others – and his two-year absence in the military with no opportunity to practise the heavy events, his performance was very pleasing. It amounted to a declaration of intent to the other heavies, one of whom – Charlie Allan – had been overheard saying, 'Why are we lettin' this sodger beat us?' The impact Bill made was acknowledged particularly by George Clark who commented afterwards to the assembled throng, 'All your records are goin' to get broken now, boys, by yon Anderson.'

For Bill it was back to Dover, with some extra cash in his pocket, to complete National Service and on 7th August 1958 he was demobilised. Although he did not consider himself a particularly accomplished soldier he had acquitted himself well as a Lance Corporal in the Regimental Police. The authoritarianism of army life did not appeal to him but he was able to handle it and kept himself out of trouble. There were two particularly positive aspects. One was that it matured him greatly as a person and the other was the camaraderie he enjoyed with his fellow servicemen, the great majority of whom were first class individuals and mutually supportive. An important source of support was Frances whose regular weekly letters not only were eagerly anticipated and replied to but enabled their relationship to develop despite the distance between them.

On completing National Service each soldier was issued with a Discharge Book containing details of service and comments by his Commanding Officer. Bill's Commanding Officer wrote, 'A good and reliable man. His size belies his disposition and he has a most pleasant character.'

Upon demob. Bill had no fixed plans other than anticipating a return to farm work and more Games competition. The Scottish Heavy Events Championship was due to take place on 20th August at Crieff but Bill was not going to participate as he had no means of transport. The night before Crieff Games he received a surprise phone call from George Clark suggesting he should go to Crieff. When Bill replied that he had no transport the bold George said he would take him there but not back as he himself was going to compete at Cortachy Games in Angus instead.

At this stage of his career Bill was not really attuned to the wily George's machinations and accepted what he took to be a kindly offer. However, the next day, after three hours as passenger in George's Packard car Bill emerged at Crieff a nervous wreck. George was not an ardent disciple of the Highway Code, preferring to drive on whichever side of the road suited him at any given time. It seemed a miracle they had reached Crieff unscathed.

Once competition begun, George's motivation for his 'good deed' became clearer. The front runners for the title were Jay Scott and Sandy Gray and it was the latter whom George wished to win. Apart from not being a huge fan of Scott's, George had a beneficial harvesting arrangement in place with Sandy Gray and felt that Bill's presence would take points off Scott, enabling Gray to triumph. However, the best laid plans 'gang aft agley', with Bill's efforts actually taking points off Gray, enabling Scott to scoop the title by a point with Bill third. But it was a hugely significant day for Bill who set his first major Games record at the light hammer which he threw one hundred and nineteen feet. This was an excellent throw, surpassing his best in competition by five feet. However, it came at a cost as he tore his stomach muscles while throwing which meant his season was over. That was hugely frustrating but only made him more determined to make up for lost time the following season.

So far he had received scant encouragement from other heavies, a number of whom reacted to his arrival on the scene less than graciously and gave him the 'cold shoulder' treatment. There were exceptions, notably Sandy Gray who gave him advice on how to pick up the caber. Often he had to resort to travelling to Games on his own while others shared car travel to keep costs down. Instead of discouraging him it had the opposite effect. He was discovering that he was a very competitive young athlete with a strong will to win. That had also been evident in his football but in the individual contest of heavy versus heavy it figured even more strongly, particularly as significant prize money was involved.

Whether the established order liked it or not Bill was here to stay. Throughout much of the 1950s the heavy events at the Games had been going through a rather stagnant phase without much progress in terms of performance levels and by the end of the decade a number of the heavy athletes, many with illustrious pasts, were continuing beyond their best days. Into the latter category fell men such as George Clark, Jack Hunter, Jock McLellan, Bob Shaw and Louis Stewart while Ewen Cameron was approaching veteran status.

George Clark had certainly had a most illustrious career but, at aged fifty-one in 1958, was no longer the force he had once been. Clark dominated the heavy scene from the 1930s through to the early fifties, although rivalled in his earlier years in particular by Ed Anderson of Dundee. Again he was of farming stock, from Grange near Keith, and possessed great natural strength and power. Weight training was alien to him although he had apparently done a form of resistance training when younger by strapping an agricultural roller to his back with a harness and repeatedly pulling it across a field. He had what might be described as a forceful personality and was fond of getting his own way. He intimidated rivals at times by verbally abusing them and intimidated officials because of his status and domineering manner. He was 'sledging' years before it had occurred to the Australian cricketers. In 1951 he became the first man to toss the special Braemar caber, 19'3" long and 120lb. Despite being the outstanding heavy athlete of his generation, he was not above a spot of chicanery. He would strategically place a towel just beyond the trig board behind which athletes had to throw and when he fouled by overstepping the trig, he would bend to pick up the towel in one continuous movement pretending he was only retrieving his towel. In 1936 he had been banned from Aboyne Games for complaining about poor prize money, as had the well-known hammer thrower, AJ Stuart of Glenlivet. After Stuart apologised to the Committee, his ban was lifted but due to George not being the apologising type, he did not return there to compete till the 1950s. He was also a famous 'all-in' wrestler who competed all over Britain and Western Europe and in

1937 toured North America where he defeated former world champion, Danny O'Mahoney.

In the early 1960s Bill and other athletes from the Aberdeen area, such as Sandy Gray and light athletes such as Jimmy Gibson and Ian Gilbert, would stop at the Panmure Hotel in Edzell, near Brechin, for a couple of drinks on their way back from Games. Clark, who was very well connected with the police and who seemed to know each Aberdeenshire Chief Constable personally, warned them the police knew of this and intended to stop them to check if they were driving under the influence of alcohol. Indeed, a few weeks later, Bill was stopped by police but there was no question of his being under the influence.

Jack Hunter was another who by this stage was past his peak. A very big and handsome man – about 6'6" and 20 stones – Bill thought he flattered to deceive somewhat in the sense that his power was not commensurate with his bulk. However, he had been an accomplished heavy, having won the Scottish title between 1950 and 1952. Despite being an Aberdeenshire farmer his accent was not local to the area and he did not appear to mix in readily with others. Bill found him rather aloof and had the impression that because he and Clark were married to sisters, Hunter's presence on the Games field had a lot to do with Clark. It was said, no doubt scurrilously, that he was often to be seen wearing his kilt in the vicinity of the nearby Crathes Castle, always ready to be photographed by tourists.

Another heavy in this category was Jock McLellan of Alness. An excellent hammer thrower – it was his Scottish record of 129'1" at Pitlochry in 1949 that Bill was destined to break – he was an athletically built 6'2" who weighed in about fifteen stones. Originally a farmworker in the Black Isle he became a roadman for the local Council. Although he won the Scottish heavy events title in 1955, like Hunter his career came to an end not long after Bill started.

The 1953 Scottish heavy events champion Ewen Cameron had a different background from the other heavies being a former public schoolboy and successful hotelier. However, his grandparents had farmed near Fort William before acquiring the Lochearnhead Hotel in the 1920s which Ewen went on to develop into one of the country's best known hotels. He demonstrated his youthful sporting potential by sharing the Victor Ludorum (Games Champion) prize at Glenalmond public school in Perthshire before he and some schoolmates falsified their age to enable them to volunteer for war service. Ewen spent the final part of the war in the Royal Navy based in Sri Lanka where he represented the Combined Services at rugby. After the war he began running the family hotel while continuing to play rugby firstly for West of Scotland and Glasgow and then Perthshire Accies . By now about 6'4" and weighing in at about 20 stones, he decided to enter Killin Games to try the heavy events which he did with some success. His father was a Games' enthusiast and he and Ewen helped re-establish the Lochearnhead Games in 1948.

Ewen began taking the games more seriously and soon he was competing on the circuit with a lot of success, his major one being the Scottish title in 1953. His particular strengths were the hammer, with which he reached about 125' with the light one, and the caber. So keen did he become that his widow Anne recalls their taking their car on honeymoon to Jersey and customs officials being rather bemused on checking the boot to find an assortment of shot putts, weights and hammers. She recalls a lot of fun trips in the company of other heavies, Clark, Gray, Hunter, McLellan, the Scott brothers and later Bill, to a number of Games to which each would bring their own picnics. She recalled one occasion, 'I was driving the car with Ewen in front and George Clark and Sandy Gray sitting in the back and the two of them chatting away constantly with me unable to understand a single word because of their broad Aberdeenshire accents.'

Ewen continued competing with some success till the early 60s and was a very well known figure on the Games' scene. He appeared in the film 'Geordie', about the fictional Highland hammer thrower who went to the Olympics and won the gold medal. Ewen did the Scots hammer sequences but as he was not an Equity member he was not allowed to speak! He also took part once in an exhibition of heavy events in Copenhagen sponsored by Carlsberg, which involved him shipping his own caber across there – its arrival caused a certain amount of consternation.

On retiral from competing he judged at a number of Games, including Crieff where he was Chieftain in 1975. He became a very successful businessman developing water ski-ing on Loch Earn and becoming involved in politics and was awarded the OBE in the late seventies.

Another renowned heavy still on the circuit then was Bob Shaw of Ballater who had been born at Inverenzie, Deeside, in about 1911. Of farming stock he was an extremely pleasant character who was universally popular. When in his prime, in the late 30s and throughout the 40s, he was a serious rival to Clark and Ed Anderson and was credited with being the 'unofficial' Scottish heavy events champion in 1937.

Standing 6'1" and weighing in at about sixteen stones, his best event was the shot putt. Once he retired from competing he became a familiar figure judging at Games in the north-east.

Louis Stewart from Corpach, Fort William, was an excellent left-handed hammer thrower whose career was winding down when Bill started. It was Louis' record which Bill broke at Crieff in 1958. At about 6' and 15 stone he was also a very good caber tosser but weaker at the weights' events.

Louis McInnes from Taynuilt, near Oban, was another heavy who had been on the circuit for some years. A good all-rounder he excelled at the caber and was to join Bill and the others on the 1964 trip to North America.

Another two heavies who had been competing since the early 1950s but who would carry on to the 70s were Jock McColl of Oban and Eck Wallace of Strathmiglo, Fife. McColl, originally from Luss and a descendant of Rob Roy, was an immensely strong man but not the most athletic. He tended to compete mostly in the west coast Games where he carved a decent reputation as an all-round heavy. During a six-week trip to the USA and Canada in 1964 Bill recalls that he remained unbeaten at arm wrestling contests – much to the locals' frustration. His working life was spent with the Council at Oban and he now acts as a judge at Games such as Inveraray, Tobermory and Lochearnhead.

Wallace was the local police officer in Strathmiglo, Fife. He too was very strong and, despite not being the most agile, was particularly adept at the weight for distance, where he exceeded seventy feet, and caber toss. He was also a noted wrestler.

These were the principal established heavies who had been on the circuit for years by the time Bill Anderson started making his breakthrough. His arrival accelerated the demise of the more senior among them as it was becoming apparent that this young heavy was about to rack up standards to previously unimagined levels. But in addition to them Bill was also facing good competition from other men then in their prime, including Jay Scott, Sandy Sutherland, Charlie Simpson of Wick and Bob Aitken. Sandy Gray, although a little older than these, was also a doughty opponent and we shall hear more of them in chapters that follow.

Bill (standing left hand side) at harvest early 1950s with family

Bill in 1957 in Aden during National Service

Bill at Banchory-Devenick, c. 1961

3. Bill Makes His Mark

A FTER army life and his all-too-brief success at the Games that summer of 1958, Bill settled down again to life at Greenferns determined to be fit for the following season. He embarked on a punishing work schedule at the farm, rising at 5.30 am to feed the cattle in the byre. Thereafter, throughout the day a variety of tasks had to be undertaken such as cleaning out the byre, milking the dairy cattle, feeding them, loading milk on to milk lorries and other jobs, with the working day usually finishing about 8 pm.

After several months of this schedule Bill's general fitness improved considerably and by spring 1959 he was a solid 16 stones plus and looking forward eagerly to the season starting. By now he was out training every day at the farm, sometimes in the evening, sometimes at midday. Mostly he was practising his favourite event, the hammer, of which he now had three. One was a 12lb hammer which he used to develop his speed and the other two were the conventional light (16lb) and heavy (22lb) hammers.

He had already thought deeply about hammer technique and began to do so again. He realised that speed of turn was the key to success and that depended on strength, particularly of the lower half of the body and on balance. Hitherto throwers had not rotated much on their turns but Bill began to do so, using his knees and pelvis to increase the arc of rotation while doing so at optimum speed and retaining his balance. In this he had an advantage because of his low centre of gravity. He endeavoured to swing the hammer as fast as he could, beginning with his first turn to build up momentum immediately rather than start with a slow first turn which had been the usual practice.

His quest for speed was also aided by two factors. Firstly, he applied resin to his hands, to effect a better grip on the hammer shaft. Secondly, during the 1959 season for the first time he began to use boots with metal spikes attached to the sole which extended beyond the toe and which he then embedded in the ground. This enabled him to 'anchor' himself better and to lean more into the throw to impart more speed without losing balance.

His hammer practice gave him cause for optimism for the season ahead but he also realised that to fulfil his ambition to be the best of the heavies it was not enough to be the best hammer thrower. He had to be adept at the other events too, particularly as national championships and individual Games' titles were decided on an aggregate of best points total for all events. Accordingly, with this in mind, he also trained for the shot putt and the 28lb weight for distance as well as the hammer. A blacksmith friend of his had made up a shot putt and 28lb weight for him – no question of going to a sports store and buying them! Bill was quietly pleased with his training and was keen for the season to start.

The opening Games of the season were, as usual, to be at Blackford in Perthshire at the end of May. These Games were run by local blacksmith and well known heavy events' judge and enthusiast, George Hally, who over the years was to prove a good friend and support to Bill.

Bill set off from Aberdeen on the three hour car trip to Blackford in good spirits but had he known what lay in store for him there it would have caused deep depression. Back then some Games insisted that athletes wishing to compete completed an entry form a week or so in advance and Blackford, unknown to Bill, was one such Games. As he made his way into the arena, looking forward to the tussle, he could see George Hally and a clutch of heavies assembled, among them Sandy Sutherland, Bob Aitken, Sandy Gray, Eck Wallace, Jay Scott and in the middle of them, holding court as usual, George Clark.

Although Bill did not expect his arrival to prompt an outbreak of communal glee among his rivals he certainly did not expect the ripostes delivered on his bidding them, 'Good day lads'. 'Ye cannae compete – you've to enter first,' barked Clark, followed by: 'Aye, ye better awa hame laddie, ye're no getting to compete.' Bill was crestfallen but dared not show it, to avoid giving Clark more satisfaction.

The rules were the rules, clearly stated on the programme and although George Hally was obviously embarrassed and apologetic he could not make an exception for Bill, particularly given Clark's stance. Bill knew there was no option but to take it on the chin while also realising this was but round one of a long fight with plenty opportunity to make amends in the weeks and months to come. Clark's objectionable behaviour merely hardened Bill's resolve to succeed whatever obstacles were put in his way and Clark's intimidatory tactics were to backfire.

One positive consequence of this debacle was that Bill ensured nothing would be left to chance in future – he would find out well in advance which Games required prior entry.

In the weeks to come he certainly made amends by doing well, firstly at Alloa where he won the shot putt and hammers. As illustration of the remarkable Clark's longevity at the top it is interesting to note that at Alloa he won the 28lb weight for distance with a throw of 73'2". His then national record for the event stood at 80'8", established in 1938 at Pitlochry Games. That was followed by more success at Crook of Devon, in Kinrosshire and at Comrie Games, both now defunct.

The Crook of Devon Games were run by the late Willie Shand who at this time was unaware of Bill's existence. Had he been, it is doubtful if he would have offered the same amount of prize money. In an admirable effort to encourage improved performances, an additional prize was awarded for breaking a record plus £2 per foot for the distance by which the old record was surpassed. This was Bill Anderson's first Crook of Devon Games and he literally had a field day smashing not only the ground record for the light hammer but also Jock McLellan's Scottish record of 129'1" set at Pitlochry in 1949, with an outstanding throw of 131'11" to claim his first Scottish record. Not only did that cause a significant dent in the prize fund but Bill went on to eat further into it by breaking the ground records for the heavy hammer and heavy stone, with throws of 103'5" and 38'9" respectively, and for good measure also winning the 28lb weight for distance with 67'5".

The following week, at Comrie, he claimed his second Scottish record in a week by improving McLellan's national heavy hammer mark from 103'9" to 105'4" and also broke the ground record for the light hammer with a throw of 121'2". His long hours of practice at the hammer were now paying off as he established himself as the country's number one exponent of the art.

In the weeks following these high points, he noted a slight decline in his level of performance which he attributed to playing summer football for Kingswells in the Echt District League twice a week. He therefore, with regret, brought the curtain down on his football career as the two sports were not compatible. Doubtless this provoked huge sighs of relief from opponents confronted with Bill's daunting presence.

This had the desired effect as his performances began to improve again at a series of Games, including Echt, Alford, Dufftown, Fort William, Tomintoul and a number of Games during the Glasgow Fair fortnight in July, including Luss, Inveraray and Tobermory.

That summer Bill also competed for the first time at Dornoch Highland Games where, each year, the coveted prize of a Gold Medal was at stake for the best all-round heavy athlete. The first event was putting the shot which Bill had a tendency to hook. However, he won the event only for George Clark to complain to the judges that as Anderson was not throwing straight his efforts could not count. Although this was nonsense it was illustrative of Clark's influence that the judges agreed and the event was re-run. Much to Clark's chagrin, however, not only did Bill throw straight but three feet further second time around! And thereafter Bill went on to win the first of seventeen Gold Medals at Dornoch.*

While, as noted, Bill was ahead of the field with the hammer this was not so with the other events and these Games gave him the opportunity to hone his technique in the weights and caber events under competitive conditions, with a view to being at his best for the Scottish Championship in Crieff.

This was to be Bill's second visit to Crieff and he was keen to claim his first Scottish title and follow in the footsteps of heavies such as Ed Anderson, Jim Maitland, Bob Starkey, George Clark, Jock McLellan and others. The preceding weeks had gone well and Bill's optimism was justified when on 20th August 1959 he claimed his first Scottish Championship and in some style. He won the light putt with a throw of 45'5", the heavy putt with 38'8", broke his existing light hammer record by eight feet with an excellent throw of 127'2" and smashed Sandy Gray's record in the heavy hammer by improving it from 100'4" to 111'8". Sandy Gray won the 28lb weight for distance with 69'2", the 56lb weight over

---

* As an interesting footnote to that anecdote, Douglas Edmunds, a top heavy in later years, recalls competing at Tomintoul Games in 1977 against Bill and others, with George Clark there as judge. Edmunds sometimes could beat Bill at the putt but on this occasion finished about two inches behind him. Clark then intervened saying to Edmunds, 'Aye, hae another yin, I could see ye werena quite ready there.' Flabbergasted, Edmunds did so but still could not beat Bill. Clark was not afraid to bend rules if it meant Bill might be beaten. Edmunds also remembers how unflappable Bill remained in the face of such provocation by Clark, simply not rising to the bait.

the bar with 13'6" and the caber, with a perfect 12 o' clock toss, to finish runner-up to Bill. Bill was absolutely delighted with his success, which earned him about £40 in total prize money. That may not sound much now but it was pretty good at a time when in England a footballer's maximum weekly wage was still £20 and Rangers' and Celtic players were earning about £15 per week. This success for the first time brought Bill publicity in the national press, as well as extensive local press coverage.

For the rest of the season he enjoyed further success. By now he had invested in a Ford Thames van which he was using to travel to Games and later that month drove to Invergordon Games, in the company of his now fiancée Frances. On their arrival the local events (confined to competitors from the locality) were still going on, in which Sandy Sutherland was doing well. As they sat alongside the van having a cup of tea and taking in the action, a group of spectators approached to announce to Bill, 'Ye'll no win the day, Anderson. Sandy's unbeatable the day.' Bill replied laconically, 'We'll see' and cast his eye around the arena where he noticed George Clark in conversation with Sandy Gray. He just knew Clark was behind this attempt to psyche him out.

As so often, this had the opposite effect as Bill proceeded to defeat Sutherland in every event, breaking the records for the light and heavy hammer and light and heavy putts in the process for a thoroughly successful day. In fact, the more Clark tried to intimidate Bill the more it spurred him on to better performances. Clark should have realised Bill was not the type to be intimidated. His desire to win was unquenchable and Clark's tactics would not deflect him. There is no doubt that the crown that Bill was now slipping into place on his head had last been worn by the great Clark, who was decidedly unwilling to smooth the path for the coronation. Not seeking his assistance with coaching was bad enough but to start beating his records, as Bill had done at a number of Games, was adding insult to injury.

Still to come after Invergordon were what many considered the two biggest Games of the year, Aboyne and Braemar. Then, Aboyne took place on the first Wednesday of September followed the very next day by Braemar. It was not until 1979 that Aboyne Games changed its dates to the first Saturday of August, Braemar having done so in 1968 to the first Saturday of September. At Bill's first appearance at Aboyne he broke both the ground records for the light and heavy hammers, recording 128'5" with the former, breaking AJ Stuart of Glenlivet's 1934 record of 125'3". His heavy hammer distance of 102'5" beat Sandy Gray's record of 96'8", set in 1954. And there the heavy hammer weighs 24lb, not the standard 22lb He also won the heavy stone with a heave of 38'8".

It is worth noting that the 56lb weight for distance event was won by the evergreen Clark with a throw of 35'3" at age 52. That compared well with his own national record of 39'6" set at Pitlochry in 1933. For the first time at Aboyne, Bill won the trophies awarded to the best heavy, the Dyce Nicol medal, the Dinnie Challenge Trophy and the Dinnie Stone Trophy. In his opinion Aboyne was the best Games for the athletes as everything was extremely well organised, thanks to its extensive committee. Warm-up throws were allowed, the officiating was impeccable and measurements and record-keeping were meticulous. All these factors plus good prize money attracted all the best athletes to compete in a very picturesque setting on the Green, in the middle of Aboyne, nestling among the Deeside hills.

Bill thought of the next day at Braemar as his real début there, as he was only a very raw novice when he appeared in 1956 just as he started national service. The big crowd, usually about 20,000, had little effect on Bill as he was always capable of great concentration. The Royal Family used to arrive about 3 pm, as they still do, which coincided deliberately with the staging of the caber and hammer events. In those days when security meant no more than locking your door at night the Royals sometimes walked on to the arena and mingled with the athletes. In particular that year Bill recalls the Duke of Edinburgh asking him details about the hammer and the spiked footwear being used. Their presence, he felt, added much to the occasion but in itself did not spur him on to greater throws. A competitive environment was enough to stimulate his competitive juices. That day brought him three new ground records – he broke the light stone record with a putt of 45'6", the light hammer record with a throw of 126'9" and the heavy hammer record with a throw of 102'7$^1/_2$".

With the final Games of the season at Pitlochry bringing him more success Bill had good reason to look back on his first full summer circuit as a very successful one. A first Scottish title together with numerous records and very welcome prize money all combined to make Bill a very happy heavy.

Another reason for the feelgood factor was that he and Frances had become engaged that summer and had agreed to marry early the following year. By now Bill had moved from Greenferns to work at his eldest brother, Andy's farm, Cowford, at Banchory-Devenick a few miles to the south of Aberdeen. There Bill worked mostly with the dairy cattle while an older brother, Sandy, mostly did the tractor work. Although Bill and Frances had bought a flat in Aberdeen to live in once married, using some of Bill's summer prize money, there was a cottage available with the job at the farm and the flat was sold without being occupied.

The wedding took place on 23rd January 1960 at Kingswells Church, near the Hall where they had first met. A huge snowfall the previous week had blocked many roads but a thaw set in two days beforehand and all went ahead as planned. The reception took place at the Queen's Hotel in Aberdeen, after which Bill and Frances spent a week's honeymoon in Edinburgh. They used to joke that was the only time of the year they could marry due to Bill's summer commitment to the Games but in part it was true. Bill is in no doubt that marrying Frances, who worked as an accounting machine operator with Aberdeen Journals, was the best thing he ever did. Not only have they had an extremely happy marriage but he credits her with giving him every support in his Games' career and ensuring that his feet stayed firmly on the ground.

But soon the 1960 season was beckoning. Once Spring arrived, Bill was out training hard in a sheltered area in the wood next to his brother's farm. Subject to weather conditions he trained every evening. There was still no question of his doing weight training or being coached by anyone – he simply organised his own training sessions as he saw fit. Conscious, for example, that his throwing the 56lb weight over the bar for height was not as good as his hammer throwing, he began practising it more intensely, utilising tree branches as makeshift bars. Equally aware that his throwing the 28lb weight for distance was, comparatively, average, he stepped up his practice of that event. The lack of a caber prevented his training for that speciality.

The opening Games of the season near the end of May were, of course, at Blackford. Bill avoided his error of the previous year, ensuring he had entered well in advance and gained some consolation for the previous year's fiasco by winning both putts and hammer throws. In the light putt he achieved his best throw to date in competition, with a mark of 48'11", while his light hammer sailed out to an excellent 129'. Blackford was the first successful step in a season which was to be full of success.

For the second year in succession he won the Scottish Championship at Crieff, creating new ground records in the light hammer with a throw of 129'7" and the heavy hammer with a throw of 112'1", the latter being a new national record. At Greenlaw Games in the Borders he set a new national record in the light hammer with a throw of 135'2". Again in the light hammer he set new ground records at Aboyne with a throw of 128'10", beating his own record by five inches, and Braemar with a throw of 130'7", again beating his own record. Meanwhile, at Comrie Highland Games for the second year in a row he set a new national record for the heavy hammer, with a throw of 110' (later beaten by him at Crieff) and in the same event later created new ground records at Braemar and Oban with throws of 109'3" and 105'9$^1/_2$" respectively. With the heavy hammer at Aboyne (24lb) he increased his own record to 104'10", in the process defeating Sandy Sutherland by 12' and Bob Aitken by 15'. In putting the light stone he set a new ground record at Braemar with a throw of 46'10" and in so doing equalled the national record which had stood since 1907 to Charles McLean of Fort William who set it at Aboyne Games. His best putt of the season with a 16lb ball, as opposed to a stone, was at Auchterarder where he reached an excellent 49'4". With the heavy ball he reached 38'8$^1/_2$" at Crieff, a mere 8$^1/_2$" behind the national record set by the legendary AA Cameron at Aboyne in 1904.

Over the 1960 season his wins in each of the light and heavy putts and light and heavy hammers reached double figures, in the course of which numerous records in addition to the ones detailed here were set. But in the other events his successes were fewer. In the weights and caber events for the most part athletes such as Sandy Gray, Sandy Sutherland and Jay Scott monopolised the top prizes. In the caber Sandy Gray was recognised as the top man, recording numerous successes, while Sandy Sutherland and Jay Scott each chalked up a few victories. Gray again dominated in the 28lb weight for distance, with Scott and Sutherland notching a few wins each. The remarkable George Clark, at fifty-three years of age, had an outstanding win at Alloa Games with a throw of 72'7$^1/_2$". To put that in perspective, the best recorded throw of the year was Sandy Gray's ground record at Crieff of 75'4". In the 56lb for distance and for height, again it was Gray who dominated with a best heave in the former of 38'4" at Aboyne. Again, Jay Scott and Sandy Sutherland were closest to Gray, with several wins in each of the disciplines, Scott achieving a notable toss of 13'7$^1/_2$" at Oban Games with the 56lb weight for height. Bill's lack of mastery of these disciplines apart, the season had been nonetheless a resounding success for him.

And Bill was by now doing the entire Games' circuit, travelling each weekend up and down the country throughout the summer. In addition, some Games took place midweek and, indeed, for the first week of the Glasgow Fair holiday fortnight, which began in mid July, a Games took place virtually every day of that week. Because Bill worked for his brother, he was able to agree flexible working hours to enable him to attend as many Games as possible. During the season, which opened with the Blackford Games at the end of May and closed with the Pitlochry Games in the middle of September, Bill would participate in about thirty Games at various venues as far apart as Halkirk in Caithness, Portree in Skye and Thornton in Fife. Life on the circuit in summer was enjoyable and rewarding, although at times demanding and tiring.

For Bill in the meantime though it was back to farm work at Banchory-Devenick for the winter. The physical rigours of that work kept him in good shape but it was not till about March of 1961 that he again began training for the summer season. Again, that training followed the same pattern as the previous year, with Bill practising the different events in the clearing in the wood next to his brother's farm. Again he did so on his own, without any coaching or outside assistance, while weight training remained some way off in the future.

Given the strength of Bill's motivation to succeed further and the sheer enjoyment he derived from throwing, the solitude of his training regime proved no hardship. And it was to be the foundation of another hugely successful season. Again on 19th August he clinched the Scottish title, for the third year in succession, at Crieff Games. In doing so, he secured five 1st places: in the 16lb shot with 46'1$^1/_2$"; the 22lb shot with a ground record of 39'; the 16lb hammer with a throw of 126'10"; the 22lb hammer with a throw of 104'6" and the 28lb weight for distance with a throw of 75'2". However, he eclipsed that outstanding achievement at Aboyne Games just over two weeks later, on 6th September, where in also securing five 1st places in cold and wet conditions he broke four records, two of which had been set as far back as 1904 and 1907.

Despite the miserable conditions, an estimated crowd of 12,000 had crammed into the Green to witness Bill's record-breaking feats. The first one to fall, in the late morning session, was the oldest, set in 1904 – the legendary AA Cameron's record for putting the 22lb stone, of 39'5". Initially, Bill edged 3" past it but in an additional throw permitted him he extended this to a magnificent 40'8$^1/_2$" thereby comfortably bettering Cameron's hitherto mythical mark. As the applause deservedly rang out for this outstanding feat, according to one press report of the time, the emotion of the occasion got the better of Bill's father who left his seat in the stand to run across the field to hug his son. Some seven feet behind, in second place, was the 54-year old George Clark. Half an hour later he broke his second record of the day when he extended his own heavy

(24lb) hammer record by 4" with a throw of 104'10", leaving Sandy Gray trailing in 2nd place almost seventeen feet behind.

The first event of the afternoon session, putting the 16lb stone, saw Bill's record breaking spree continue when he beat Charles McLean's 1907 record of 46'10" with an excellent throw of 47'8", eight feet clear of Bob Aitken in second place. To complete his quartet of records he next broke his own light hammer record by $1^1/_2$" with an extra throw of $130'4^1/_2$", having won the contest itself with a heave of just over 125 feet. Second again was Bob Aitken, with a throw of 113'7", almost seventeen feet behind. To round off an outstanding day's work Bill also clinched first place in the 28lb weight for distance with a throw of 69'10", came 2nd in the caber to Sandy Gray and 4th in the 56lb weight for distance which, astonishingly, was won by Clark. Not content to rest on his laurels, at Braemar Games the next day Bill collected four first prizes, winning the light stone (44'1"), the 28lb stone ($31'1^1/_2$"), the light hammer ($129'7^1/_2$") and the heavy hammer (103'2").

Those three weeks spanning the Crieff Games to the Braemar Games represented a purple patch of form for Bill. But, apart from that, he dominated the entire season. In the light shot putt he was first on at least a dozen occasions, including a ground record at Oban and a season's best at Lochearnhead of 48'4". In the heavy shot he won numerous times including that ground record at Crieff. In the light hammer he was utterly dominant, also setting ground records at Auchterarder and Oban. In the heavy hammer it was the same and his high points included ground records again at Auchterarder and Oban. He showed marked improvement in the caber and 28lb weight for distance, winning both these events at a number of Games. His performance at the 56lb weight for height was better than the previous season and at Comrie Games he set a ground record of 12'11". However, in these latter events, Sandy Gray, Sandy Sutherland and Eck Wallace claimed most of the first prizes and Bill acknowledged that in these events he still lagged somewhat behind. But in the other events not only was he beating all opposition but beating them out of sight, as was demonstrated by his winning margins at Aboyne.

He was now unassailably the number one heavy events athlete in the country and at a mere twenty-four years old he looked set to take a stranglehold grip on the Games for years to come. There was no sign of any young heavy emerging to challenge Bill's supremacy. On the contrary, he was distancing himself from his existing rivals by ever increasing margins and in his weaker events – weight for distance and height and caber toss – he was rapidly closing the gap between him and the likes of Gray, Sutherland Wallace and sometimes even beating them.

For the 1962 season Bill adopted the same formula as in previous years, emerging from winter farmwork in about March to start preparing. And once the circuit was under way he again immediately asserted his position, mopping up success after success. The highlight of the season was his fourth successive Scottish title at Crieff Games on 18th August which beat the record (at least in recent times) of three successive titles held by Jack Hunter, between 1950 and 1952. In doing so he won five events, setting ground records in three of them. He won the 16lb shot in a ground record throw of 49'6", the 22lb shot in another ground record (and national best) throw of 40'7". He won the light and heavy hammers with throws of 126' and 106'2" respectively and he won the 28lb weight for distance in a ground record throw of 79'3$^1/_2$" which smashed Sandy Gray's 1960 record of 75'4". At Luss Games he set new national bests for the 16lb ball at 49'10" and the light hammer, with a throw of 137'4". At Aberdeen Games on 1st September, with an exhibition putt with the 16lb stone he broke the fifty feet barrier for the first time, with a magnificent heave of 51'3$^1/_2$". Again with the 16lb ball he set ground records at Crook of Devon and Comrie in addition to numerous first places elsewhere. With the 16lb hammer and 22lb hammer he was again unbeatable, setting ground records with the light hammer at Crook of Devon, Comrie and Oban and winning the event at every Games he participated in.

1962 was the first season when he had a number of wins with the 28lb weight for distance, the highlight being his ground record at Crieff of 79'3$^1/_2$" which was only 1'5" short of George Clark's national record of 1938. It was also the first season when he recorded a number of wins with the caber, including Braemar, where he tied with Sandy Gray, and with the 56lb weight for height and for distance, including a toss of 40'7" in the latter at Mallaig which beat George Clark's national best set in 1933.

1960s Heavy Events Rivals

Sandy Gray, sometimes known as Henry, was the sixth generation of Grays to have farmed the hundred acre farm of East Eninteer on Craigievar Estate in the parish of Leochel Cushnie, near Alford. As there was an old Scots hammer lying about the farm he began throwing it just for fun. The Estate had an annual picnic for tenants, staff and their families at which sports would also take place. In 1947 at aged eighteen Sandy made a winning début there with the hammer and went on to compete locally at games at Kennethmont, Wartle and Keig, all now defunct. While competing at Tarland Show in 1949 Lady MacRobert of Douneside, who was a Patron of Aboyne Games, suggested he enter there and sent him to the Tarland kiltmaker, Mr Blackhall, to have a kilt made for him at her expense, to enable him to compete at Aboyne. He made his début there later that summer but was overwhelmed by the size of the crowd, especially when he heard one spectator shout, 'He'll never mak' a thrower!'

But he did not give up and was given some coaching by George Clark who had seen his potential. As a result, the next year he won his first prize at Aboyne in the heavy hammer throw and a very successful career as a heavy was truly under way. At 6'5" and 19 stones he was well equipped for the job. He also had very big hands with reputedly the strongest grip in the country. He excelled at the caber and 56lb weight for height, with which he reached 15'6". His best in the light

hammer was about 120', about 100' in the heavy hammer, about 75' in the 28lb weight and about 40' in the light putt, which was his weakest event.

Highlights of his career included winning the Scottish title at Crieff in 1954 and tossing the Special Braemar Caber five years in succession and winning the extra £10 prize each time. That prompted a Braemar official to comment, 'Ye'll soon hae the Society ruined.' A genial giant, Sandy was well liked by all at the Games, a plaudit not easily gained in that deceptively competitive environment. He seldom trained nor did he ever lift weights and one can only speculate what he might have achieved had he done so.

In 1953 he took on the challenge in Aberdeen's Music Hall of lifting the smaller of the two Dinnie Stones (340lb) and walking twenty yards with it, single handed. Having manfully reached eighteen yards, he could do no more and had to drop the Stone. When the announcer said he had not won the money the crowd went wild, shouting, 'Give him the money!' and the organiser had to relent and pay up!

Sandy competed till about 1974 after which he became a judge at many of the Grampian Games, including Braemar. In 2006 to mark his long association with Braemar Games he was presented to the Queen and Duke of Edinburgh, the latter of whom stated, 'You've been coming here nearly as long as I have.'

Sandy Sutherland, who won the Scottish heavy events' title in both 1956 and 1957 was another from a farming background, in Ardross, north of Inverness. Born in 1931 he became involved in the heavy events almost by chance. One night in the late 1940s he and some friends attended the Ardross Games' night dance in the hall next to the Games field. The shot putt and hammer were still on the field and he began throwing them out of curiosity. It soon became apparent he was throwing as far as some of the heavies had done that afternoon in competition and this encouraged him to try the heavy events. He acquired an old hammer head which he tied string round to give him a primitive type of hammer for training. He then graduated on to a proper hammer by locating a handle which he secured into the hole of the hammer head with lead. He can remember summer evenings at Ardross Mains when eight or nine men would be throwing the hammer. After such rudimentary beginnings he soon achieved success on the circuit, travelling all over the country and competing till the end of the 1960s, latterly mostly in the 'north' Games.

He was a very good all-round heavy with a best of 141' at the light hammer, 118' with the heavy hammer, about 47' in the light putt, 73' in the 28lb weight for distance and 38' in the 56lb weight for distance. His best at the 56lb weight over the bar he laughingly recalls was '13'6" plus two fish boxes at Lochinver', reference to the use of fish boxes once the equipment had reached its maximum height.

Like most of his contemporaries, he did very little weight training and was essentially self coached. A near neighbour of his was Jock McLellan of Kildary, the Scottish heavy events champion of 1955 and national record holder in the light hammer, with a throw of 129'1½" in 1949. Sandy and another heavy from the area, John Jack, used to train with McLellan in the hope of picking up some tips but McLellan was not keen to impart his knowledge, saying of Jack, 'That yin is like a hen, goin aboot pickin things up.'

Like others, once he stopped competing he began judging at Games in the north and still does so at Lochinver and elsewhere.

Jay Scott was another top athlete who was still very active when Bill Anderson started. He and his brother Tom, a noted light events Scottish champion, owned the island of Inchmurrin in Loch Lomond where they operated a farm and had business interests connected with local tourism. Jay and his brother had attended the prestigious boarding school, Keil Academy, at Dumbarton. Jay was 6'1" handsome and well built at 15 stones, whose background was more privileged than the average Games athlete. He was married to well known actress and entertainer Fay Lenore and was Scotland's Sports Personality of the year in 1957.

So far as Bill Anderson was concerned he was less than welcoming initially and rather disparaging about his potential. When David Webster, well known Games enthusiast and writer, was preparing a book on the Games in the late 1950s Scott told him, 'Anderson would not make the grade' and, as a result, David omitted mention of Bill from his book. However, industrial action delayed the book's publication and, by the time it emerged a year or so later Bill had won the Scottish title which made his omission seem very curious.

While that anecdote may not reflect well on Scott's appreciation of rival talent, his own range of talent was breathtaking. He excelled in all disciplines of athletics and, had he been an amateur, would have been a world class decathlete. He was a first class sprinter and had come close to winning the famous Powderhall Sprint several times. He was an outstanding jumper and pole vaulter who in 1964 at Tobermory leapt an incredible 6'3^1/$_2$" using the scissors style, a Scottish games high jump record which stood for many years. On one occasion after the Tobermory Games it is said that he arrived at the harbour late, to see 'his' ferry beginning to edge its way out from the quayside. Undaunted, he took a run, planted his pole firmly on the quayside and vaulted aboard, much to the passengers' amusement but much to the dismay of the captain.

He was also a top all-round heavy events exponent who won the Scottish title in 1958 and for a number of years was among the very best on the circuit. Scott was an extrovert, livewire character with a well-developed sense of fun and mischief. In Bill's opinion, he took on too many commitments which contributed to his career being shorter thanit may otherwise have been.

(Previous page, l to r) Aboyne Games 1971 (l to r): Charlie Allan, Arthur Rowe, Bill Anderson, Sandy Gray, Charlie Simpson, Geordie Charles, John Freebairn and Jim McBeath

Bob Aitken was another heavy from a farming background who became involved because an old Scots hammer was lying about at the farm and he began throwing it for fun. Born in 1935 he was brought up at Inchbreck Farm near Auchenblae, Kincardineshire. His recollection was that all the farms in the area had Scots hammers and men would spend some of their spare time throwing them. He first competed in light events at sports held in conunction with the Glenbervie Flower Show near his home. Having tasted success there, in 1951 he moved up a league to compete at the Banchory Show, winning the junior high jump and placing second in the senior event. Bob cycled there, a twenty mile trip each way, having to cross the 2000 feet plus Cairn O'Mount on the way, hardly a recommended preparation for the sports.

This reminds one of William Grewar of Glenisla who in 1886 walked from there the twenty three miles over the Cairnwell Pass (2200 feet) to Braemar to compete in the Games, before walking back home that evening to Glenisla!

After Banchory Bob Aitken began competing in the heavy events as well as the light events and soon developed into a very successful all-round athlete. At Aboyne he won the Chieftain's Challenge Cup for the best combined heavy and light event athlete nine years in a row, from 1960 onwards. He was another heavy who benefited from coaching assistance from George Clark whom he said, 'ruled the games'.

Many are the stories he remembers of Clark, one being the time he was a passenger in the Packard then being driven by Clark in Perth when a policeman stopped him to say, 'Do you realise you are on a one-way street?' To which the bold Clark replied, 'Aye, but ah'm only goin' the one way.' Bob remembers Clark coaching Arthur Rowe and helping Rowe occasionally himself in exchange for Rowe helping him with his shot putt.

Bob also used to travel to Banchory-Devenick to train sometimes with Bill at his brother's farm but thought Bill was less forthcoming with advice. Despite that he, Bill and Sandy Gray often used to travel together to games. In common with most others at the time Bob hardly ever lifted weights, gaining his strength from his farmwork. By the time he retired in the early seventies he had reached 45' with the light putt, over 130' with the light hammer and 100' with the heavy hammer and about 75' with the 28lb weight. In the light events he lays claim to a 6' plus high jump, using the scissors technique, at Fort William and elsewhere regularly threatened the six feet mark while his best pole vault was 12'. In 1977 he along with some others, as part of the Queen's Jubilee Appeal Fund, was responsible for starting the Drumtochty Games, near Auchenblae, held in the lovely setting of Drumtochty Castle grounds. Once retired, he judged at a number of Grampian Games including Braemar before giving his sons, Bruce and Stephen, some coaching. Both have since won the Scottish heavy events championship, Bruce three times and Stephen once, with the former considered by many to be Scotland's consistently best heavy following Bill's retirement.

Charlie Simpson had a long and successful career as a heavy beginning in the mid 1950s through to the late eighties, finally retiring when aged fifty eight. His background was farming and fishing, having been brought up on the Isle of Stroma in the Pentland Firth. He recalls going out in the 'yawl' boats whose engines were unreliable and as a result having to row seemingly interminable distances. He also recalls he and his brothers throwing their father's forehammer at the farm for fun and helping out with farmwork. That combination of farmwork and rowing built up his strength and while in the RAF from about 1951 to 1955 he competed with distinction in the shot putt, discus and hammer and was an excellent heavyweight boxer. Mike Ellis, then British wire hammer champion, told him that despite his basic technique he had great potential at the hammer.

Once he left the RAF he competed at Highland Games in Wick and others in the area. As he put it, there was nowhere else to go as there was no amateur athletics in the area. From those beginnings he carved out an excellent career on the circuit as one of the top heavies throughout the sixties and into the seventies. Although Charlie Allan used to claim being known as 'Charles III', through finishing third so often behind Bill Anderson and Arthur Rowe, Charlie Simpson claims that title as rightly his as he often finished third behind them in Scottish and British championships. He was an excellent all-round heavy with best marks of about 49' in the light putt, 129' in the light hammer, about 72' in the 28lb weight for distance (once doing 75' with a weight known as 'Hally's Flyer', reference to the maker George Hally of Blackford and the fact it was slightly underweight) and 14'6" in the 56lb weight over the bar. He was also a very useful caber tosser but if anyone criticised his caber he would reply with a twinkle in his eye, 'Aye, but there's no trees in Caithness.'

He was full of admiration for Bill Anderson who he describes as a 'brilliant heavy' who was also a real sportsman and a true friend. He enjoyed his trips abroad with Bill particularly to Tokyo where he was grateful to Bill for sharing a room with him, despite his snoring!

Although Charlie only did a very little weight training later in his career he always did general fitness training, including running. Like others, once he retired from competition he began judging at Games in the north which he still enjoys.

4. Arthur Rowe's Arrival
amateurism and professionalism

TOWARDS the end of the 1962 season, as sports' page headlines referred to Bill Anderson as 'The King of the Heavies' and just as it began to seem that he wielded absolute power in the realm of the heavies, brooking no opposition, there occurred a development that was to have a huge impact on the heavy events' scene. As has been observed, prior to Bill's taking part, the Games had been somewhat in decline with a number of established heavies reaching retirement age and public interest was low. Bill's arrival had provided a welcome boost but by now his domination was such that from the public's perspective results were predictable and that again led to loss of interest.

All that, however, was set to change dramatically with the arrival of Arthur Rowe from Barnsley. This would initiate the most intense head-to-head rivalry in the heavy events over the next dozen years ever seen in the history of Highland Games.

On 5th September 1962 Yorkshireman Rowe appeared at Aboyne Games to compete. His reputation preceded him – five times British shot putt champion and record holder, European champion and record holder and Commonwealth Games champion and record holder, ranked third best shot putter of all time in the world in the previous season and an Olympic competitor. Aboyne was basking in sunshine with a crowd approaching the 10,000 mark as a supremely fit-looking and well-muscled Arthur Rowe, clad in shorts and t-shirt, made his way from the crowd into the centre of the arena at the Green to enter the heavy events.

Rumours had been circulating that he was coming north to compete and the arrival of this superb athlete, all 6'1" and 18 stones of him, raised the crowd's sense of expectation. Bill and the other heavies, including Sandy Sutherland, Sandy Gray, Charlie Simpson, Charlie Allan, Bob

Aitken and Eck Wallace, suddenly realised the cake was now going to be shared differently. There was only one problem – the official in charge, Mr Gordon from Strathdon ('The Duke') refused to let Arthur compete as he was not wearing the kilt. There then ensued much animated discussion resulting in Charlie Simpson, the genial policeman from Wick, offering Arthur the use of his, which Arthur gladly accepted. Needless to say, Charlie's name was mud for the rest of the afternoon among his colleagues! But the ribbing was all good-natured.

As far as Bill was concerned, he viewed Rowe's arrival fairly philosophically – the simple fact was he was entitled to compete and Bill knew that Rowe would beat him in both the light and heavy stone events but not the others. Rowe proceeded to smash Bill's light stone record set the previous year with a magnificent heave of 57'6", although Bill countered with an excellent effort of 49'7", itself two feet better than his previous year's mark. Rowe also broke Bill's heavy stone record albeit by a lesser margin, recording a throw of 42'9". Bill also broke his own record with an excellent toss of 41'10".

It was no surprise that Rowe failed to place in any of the other events, this being the first time he had competed. Bill broke his own records in the heavy and light hammers with throws of 106'7$^1/_2$" and 131'4$^1/_2$" respectively, came third behind Sandy Gray and Eck Wallace in the caber, won the 56lb weight for distance and was second to Sandy Gray in the 28lb weight for distance to clinch his fourth successive Aboyne heavy weight title and the usual trophies. In an effort to win the Chief's Challenge Cup, awarded to the best all-round athlete in light and heavy events at the Games, Rowe entered the long jump where he leapt 18'11", a valiant effort for a non-jumper but not enough to secure him the Cup which, again, went to Bob Aitken of Auchenblae.

While initially his appearance had taken the heavies aback, Rowe went on that afternoon to prove himself a congenial competitor refreshingly free from any baggage that might have attached to an athlete of his celebrity. As a result, although there may have been some private gnashing of teeth, there was no animosity expressed towards him. Bill recalls nothing being said about Rowe's long term plans as regards the Games, the only thing for sure being that he would also be competing the next day at Braemar.

At that time at Braemar, to preserve the finely manicured turf of the arena, warm-up throws were not permitted. The rule was zealously enforced by former champion heavy, now judge, Ed Anderson who kept the implements under lock and key till the competition began. Consequently, in the light stone it took Rowe till his third and final putt to master it, creating a new record of 52'10$^1/_2$".

He found similar difficulties with putting the heavy stone Braemar style. The heavy stone weighs 28lb, 6lb heavier than the standard heavy stone, while Braemar style entails its having to be thrown from a standing position without the benefit of a preliminary glide, nor must either foot leave the ground prior to release of the stone. A challenging test indeed but one which Rowe eventually mastered, with a new record of 33'6$^1/_2$". However, as at Aboyne, Bill went on to win the championship, notching wins in the hammers, 28lb weight for distance and sharing the honours in the caber with Sandy Gray. And the following Saturday at Pitlochry, the final Games of the season, Rowe again competed, again winning both putts with Bill winning most of the other events and the heavy weight title.

A significant marker had been put down by Rowe. Bill had reached the point where his superiority was effectively unchallenged but it was clear that once Rowe became adept at the other traditional Scots heavy events he would pose a serious challenge.

Though in effect contemporaries (Rowe was a year older than Anderson, being born on 17th August 1936), age was the only common factor in their backgrounds. Rowe was born into a mining family in the village of Smithies on the outskirts of Barnsley, in the middle of the then booming and densely populated South Yorkshire coalfield. While Bill was brought up in the wide open spaces of the farm, with its own inbuilt adventure playground, Arthur's parameters were defined by the tell-tale signposts of heavy industry – pit bings, cooling towers and a scarred landscape. After attending Raley Secondary Modern School, where he shone as a gifted all-round sportsman, Arthur started work aged fifteen as apprentice blacksmith at the nearby North Gawber pit, where his father also worked. As well as being an outstanding swimmer at school (he used to joke that as an 11-year old he had won a cash prize at a swimming gala and so was a professional from an early age) Arthur also excelled as a footballer, signing as an amateur for both Barnsley FC and Rotherham United. He was also a useful cricketer and it was that sport which was to lead him indirectly into athletics.

Shortly before his seventeenth birthday, while waiting his turn to bat in a local cricket match, he observed some young athletes nearby practising the shot putt. To pass the time before wielding the willow he sauntered over, with his pads on, and asked if he could have a try. After a few efforts it became clear that he had a very special natural talent as he gradually outdistanced the others, his best throw with the junior ball reaching forty-three feet. For a complete beginner this was exceptional.

Rowe began intensive practice at the shot putt. He was constantly training, even in the street, under the streetlights during the winter. Soon cricket's loss became athletics' gain as he began winning local and county titles. This brought him to the attention of Geoff Dyson, the Amateur Athletics Association National Coach. Dyson was an outstanding technical and far-sighted coach who was largely responsible for dragging British athletics single handedly out of the postwar doldrums and into the modern era. He gave Rowe some expert tuition and advice and set him targets, telling him to contact him again if he reached those targets. Rowe duly did and Dyson began to feel he had a truly special talent on his hands. To help determine if this really were so he arranged for Rowe to participate in a series of physiological tests and experiments at Leeds University, to assess his physical capabilities. His heavy manual work as a blacksmith in the pit had obviously built up his physique but he also had a lot of natural athleticism and good co-ordination. These tests determined that he had 'outstanding explosive power' and that he was in the category of 'a phenomenon' in respect of his general physical condition.

In short, Arthur Rowe had outstanding natural physical gifts but these were augmented and developed by his dedication to training. In those aspects – natural physical talent and capacity for hard training – it can be said that Bill and Arthur had much in common. But whereas Bill's development was entirely dependent on his own unschooled input garnered from his own observations and reliant on instinct and enthusiasm, Arthur had the advantage of being able to draw on the support of the best technical coaching available in amateur athletics. That in itself would not have taken Arthur far without his own determined application.

It is ironic that, as a professional athlete, Bill was self taught, essentially unaided by anyone other than himself, whereas as an amateur, Arthur was the recipient of the very best of technical advice. Weight training, for instance, now so universal, was then in its infancy as a training aid for athletics. Dyson soon advocated it for Arthur Rowe and devised a series of training programmes. These were undoubtedly of huge benefit to him and he soon had his own set of weights, made at the forge, with which he trained avidly, even setting a British record for the press behind the neck of 280lb and winning the only 'Mr Adonis' competition he ever entered. On the other hand, as will be seen, Bill never even lifted a barbell till 1964 and that was only done in response to Arthur's success.

At about the same time Anderson was being demobbed from National Service in 1958, Rowe was building on his success of the previous year by winning his second AAA shot putt title, this time with a new British record of 56'9", but more prestigious titles awaited Arthur that summer. First in Cardiff, at the Empire and Commonwealth Games, he won the shot putt with another British record of 57'8". Second, at Stockholm, in the European Championships with his very last throw he edged past Lipsius of USSR to clinch the title with yet another British record of 58'4". A party of Barnsley schoolchildren accompanied by a former teacher of Rowe's, a Mr Goodman, cheered him on with cries of 'C'mon Barnsley!' He thus became the first and, so far, only British athlete ever to win the European shot title.

Despite his rising star Rowe stayed true to his roots, remaining in Barnsley and continuing to work as a blacksmith at the pit. He did most of his training in a makeshift circle at the rear of the Tollgate public house in the town and continued competing at local events. On 14th August 1959 at the White City in London he finally broke the mythical sixty feet barrier with a putt of sixty one feet in an international against Poland, and that summer won his third successive AAA title. Such excellent form created high expectations for his prospects in the Olympics in Rome the following year.

These expectations were scarcely dimmed in Olympic year by his winning his fourth AAA title with a new best performance of 59'2". But about a month before the Olympics, he caused controversy by electing to compete at Mansfield Miners' Gala instead of representing Britain in an international against France at the White City. To an extent he silenced his critics by setting a new European and British record there of 62'1". That summer he was also credited with an exhibition putt of 64'6". All seemed to augur well for Rome.

However, Rome was an unmitigated disaster for Rowe as well as a number of other British athletes. His best putt was 54'8", not even good enough to reach the final which was won by Bill Neider of USA with 64'6". Rowe was on the receiving end of much criticism from the British press and a photo of him fraternising with female athletes did not help. The press effectively accused him of having crumbled on the sport's biggest stage. But this was very unfair. The British team had only three days' acclimatisation amid temperatures that rose to 100°F. Rowe suffered dysentery, causing him to lose about ten pounds in weight. In those circumstances his drop in form could be understood. By way of redemption, a month after Rome in miserable conditions in East Berlin he extended his European record to 62'8$^1/_2$", having previously registered a putt of 64'11" in training.

The following season, during which he remained undefeated, was perhaps his best ever. He won the AAA title for a record fifth successive time and within the space of three days in early August twice extended his European record. On 5th August, in an international against Hungary, he added over a foot to his existing record by reaching 63'9" and two days later at Mansfield, again at a Miners' Gala meet, established another record with a putt of 64'2". That effort ranked him third on the world all-time list behind two Americans, Olympic champion Bill Neider and Dallas Long. He was also credited with a training putt of 66'1$^1/_2$" which, had it been done in competition, would have fired him to top of the world all-time list.

Although inside the arena itself his star was firmly in the ascendancy, there were rumblings that he was dissatisfied with his lot as a leading international amateur athlete. In those times, representing Britain entailed heavy demands and called for big sacrifices from athletes like Rowe. While celebrity and a measure of glory followed there were no material rewards available, at least officially. Rowe was a 'high maintenance' athlete with a prodigious appetite for the plentiful quality food needed to sustain his powerful seventeen stone plus frame through taxing training regimes. International vests or blazers did not put food on his table and absences from work because of international duty usually left him with a deficit in wages as a result. Tension between him and the AAA had arisen in the past when he had sometimes opted to compete in local miners' galas rather than represent his country internationally.

But he began the 1962 season in the excellent form of the preceding season, winning an indoor international in April, at Wembley, against West Germany with a putt of 63', following that in June with excellent efforts of 63'6" and 63'11" at White City, London, and Sheffield respectively. On 24th July at Doncaster, he nudged past his own European record by one inch but the shot was found to be marginally underweight and the 'record' was not ratified.

The very next day Rowe stunned the athletics world by signing professional rugby league forms for Oldham, thereby bringing an abrupt end to his amateur athletics' career. He had been dissatisfied with his lot for some time and had begun to feel resentful about the lack of recompense representing his country, given the sacrifices he had had to make to do so in terms of finance, time and effort. Following his marriage the previous December and with a baby on the way Arthur felt the financial pressures more keenly and was anxious to secure his family's future as much as he could. He was also becoming aware of the beginnings of steroid abuse in his event which caused him considerable dismay.

So when Oldham offered him a generous signing-on fee – variously reported as between £1,500 and £6,000 – Arthur had little hesitation in accepting it. Whatever the exact amount it was extremely welcome to Rowe who later wrote in his autobiography that it bought him a house, a car and left him some money in the bank. The fact that he had never played rugby in his life seemed of little moment to either him or Oldham Rugby League Club. With his powerful physique and all-round athleticism Rowe certainly seemed to possess the necessary physical attributes. But it was not to work out, his career lasting less than a season during which he only played four reserve games. He was a very high profile signing who added 4,000 to the gate on his début as well as attracting the television cameras. Rowe soon felt opponents were targeting him and there were disagreements with the club, who insisted on playing him as a forward while he preferred to play in the backs. At his age, with no previous rugby experience, it was a difficult transition to make and it was not a success.

At this time, the world of amateur and professional athletics were poles apart. A chasm separated them. Under no circumstances could an amateur athlete earn money from his athletics, either directly as a participant or through coaching. Lottery funding for amateurs was a long way off. Nor were amateurs allowed to compete alongside professionals even when no monetary prize had been won. It was akin to a form of apartheid. These rules were strictly enforced and transgression inevitably resulted in banning from the amateur ranks.

Tom McNab, former national athletics coach and four times Scottish amateur triple jump champion, dabbled in the Games once, to his cost. In 1957 he won a few pounds at Nethybridge Games, but this reached the notice of the amateur authorities who suspended him from amateur competition for a year. He reckons his punishment would have been much more severe had he not had influential contacts in the hierarchy. Even at that, this was particularly hard to bear as he had previously been selected for a Great Britain 'B' team, a place which he had to renounce and he suspects that the fall-out from all this cost him a place in Scotland's Commonwealth Games team of 1958. He recalls, 'The divide between the two – amateur and professional – was particularly pronounced then. In amateur eyes the 'pros' were tainted, considered a lesser species and to be kept at arm's length. On one occasion a number of guys from my club (Shettleston Harriers) went on a training run with an old 'pro' athlete and thereafter were written to by the authorities warning them not to let this happen again! Playing professional football barred players from participating in amateur athletics. Perhaps the best known, relatively recent, example was George McNeil of Tranent.

In his youth McNeil played part-time professional football for Hibs. and Stirling Albion. Although he never established himself in that career and gave it up in his early twenties, he was thereafter barred from amateur athletics. McNeil went on to become the world's best professional sprinter, achieving the unique double of winning the Powderhall Sprint in Scotland and the Stawell Gift in Australia, the Blue Riband of professional sprinting. In the mid-seventies he ran an officially authenticated 110 metres at Meadowbank Stadium, Edinburgh, in 11.06 seconds, a time which equates to faster than Allan Wells' gold medal winning time over 100 metres at the Moscow Olympics. Yet his talents were denied access to such championship tracks as all the major domestic and international championships, such as the AAA Championships, Commonwealth Games, European Championships and the Olympics, all came under amateur jurisdiction.

This dichotomy derived from Victorian times when 'pedestrianism', or professional footracing, was in its heyday. Fuelled by betting, huge crowds at the time were attracted, especially in its hotbeds such as Sheffield and Edinburgh. But 'where there's brass there's muck', and as much of the racing was done on handicap that gave rise to various forms of chicanery and instances of serious public disorder were not uncommon at stadia, where punters perceived they had been duped on the part of their 'ped' or his coach. Partly in reaction to such distastefulness the Corinthian ideals of amateur athletics, with emphasis on fair play and a total absence of 'filthy lucre' were embraced initially by the public schools and universities, with their ethos of muscular Christianity. This led to strict regulation of the sport by the imposition of standardised rules for track and field events imposed by newly created national governing bodies. Such regulation soon extended into the international arena, establishing a uniform set of rules for the sport.

On the other hand professional athletics never succeeded in imposing such uniform regulation. In professional athletics, the dimensions or state of the running track or the weight of throwing implements could vary from one part of the country to another, as could the level of qualifications, if any, of the officials. Its continued association with betting and money was seen by many as tainting it and tarnishing its image. Such attitudes to professionalism were, of course, not confined to athletics. In golf, for example, a professional was not usually permitted into the clubhouse till after World War II. The legendary Walter Hagen used to delight in ostentatiously parking his luxurious Rolls Royce in front of the clubhouse to change in it. In cricket, professionals were ostracised by having to change in a separate part of the pavilion from their amateur colleagues.

The continued co-existence of professional and amateur athletics inevitably led to some celebrated cases of 'shamateurism'. In 1895 Scotland's outstanding champion sprinter Alf Downer and several top English athletes were found guilty of accepting appearance money to run at Burnley Cricket Club Sports and promptly banned from amateur athletics. Shamefully, after the 1912 Olympics in Stockholm Jim Thorpe, the winning American decathlete, who was part North American Indian, was stripped of his gold medal when it was discovered he had as a youngster played junior league baseball, which was nominally professional. And by the mid 1950s nationally condoned 'shamateurism' was taking root.

In the communist countries of the eastern bloc talented athletes were often allocated 'posts' in the country's military, with all the requisite support enabling them to be effectively full-time athletes, while in the USA, 'sports scholarships' were often generously awarded to top athletes, enabling them to train full-time under the guise of being a student. Indeed, once Arthur Rowe had established himself as an international athlete, he was offered such a scholarship at an American university. Conscious of only having a basic education, when he asked what he could study he was told, 'Oh, that's not a problem, you can do basket weaving or something!'

While at international level such methods of beating the system were an open secret and tolerated through the turning of a blind eye, at domestic level amateur regulations were strictly enforced. Thus, for example Bill, having competed as a professional at Alford and earned prize money, had no prospect whatsoever from then on, had he wished to do so, of competing as an amateur. Accordingly, any prospect of his representing Scotland at Commonwealth Games or Great Britain at Olympic Games or European Championships was denied him. Participation at domestic level in championships or even at club level was also denied him. Looked at from today's perspective, when the sport is completely open, that does seem an unduly harsh penalty not only for the individual athlete but also in terms of the sport's having been deprived of the services of a number of excellent performers. This seems particularly so given that in this context the term 'professional' was a misnomer. It properly describes a person who earns his livelihood through exercising his profession whereas, in the case of Bill Anderson and others, there was no question of their earning a livelihood through competing as a heavy on the Games' circuit – the amount of prize money simply did not allow for that. They, in participating in Highland Games, were simply continuing a long tradition of over a century's standing.

The Games had begun, as shall be seen, as local celebrations, often in then relatively remote areas, at which small cash prizes were awarded. Once amateurism took hold in late Victorian times, these Games carried on as before which thereafter meant they were categorised as professional athletics. This was so even though at the traditional Games there was never any betting or consequent crowd disturbances, as no organised pedestrianism took place. It was something of an anachronism to classify them still as professional by the time Bill Anderson and Arthur Rowe were competing.

Ironically, while engaged in army National Service, and despite a petty objection about his being a professional, as has been seen Bill competed in amateur athletics in the shot, discus and hammer. At about the same time, in August 1957, at the White City Stadium, London, Arthur was notching his first national shot putt title at the AAA championships with a throw of 53'7". No doubt at that time the furthest thought from each of their minds was that five years later they would be pitted against each other as professional heavies at Aboyne Highland Games.

Becoming a professional was never a conscious decision by Bill Anderson. In part it was geographical and in part cultural. The north-east could fairly lay claim to being the stronghold of the Games and was where the majority of the top heavies belonged. Men such as Donald Dinnie, Jim Maitland, George Clark, Ed Anderson and Sandy Gray were all north-east men. When Bill began, as well as the two biggest on the calendar, Braemar and Aboyne, there were countless small professional Games throughout the district. Then, unlike now, these Games were given extensive press coverage and heavies like Clark, Gray, Anderson and others, such as Bob Shaw and Jack Hunter, were household names. Most of these men were from agricultural backgrounds and the natural arena for aspiring young heavies of agricultural or manual working background to head to was the professional Games circuit. Many came from relatively isolated rural locations. At a time when by no means everyone owned a car and public transport was limited, there was little possibility of gaining access to an amateur athletics club in a city such as Aberdeen or Dundee. In any event, there was no real tradition of people from such backgrounds taking part in amateur athletics.

Generally speaking, amateur athletics was still the preserve of the middle classes, a hangover from Victorian times. This was admittedly less true of the runners' side of the sport where many harriers' clubs, with a working class membership, had evolved from cross country running. But in the technical field events, especially the throwing events where specialist equipment and facilities were necessary, such as throwing implements and throwing circles conforming to regulations, most of the participants were of middle class background. In the mid 1950s Scotland's shot putt champion was Tom Logan, a Glasgow policeman; the discus champion was Jim Drummond of Heriot's FP Athletic Club, Edinburgh; the hammer champion was Doctor Ewan Douglas, an old Fettesian who was succeeded by a fellow Fettesian, Ian Bain; and the javelin champion was Donald MacKenzie, a Watsonian representing Edinburgh University Athletic Club. While the popular comic-book character of the 1960s, Alf Tupper, 'The Tough of the Track', reflected working class involvement on the running track there was no equivalent character for the field events. Accordingly, in the same way as it could be said Arthur Rowe's initial involvement in amateur athletics arose from his environment, Bill Anderson's did also in professional Highland Games. But someone from Arthur's background was really an exception at the top level of amateur throwing events and this factor was to be a major influence on the form of his future career.

After turning professional, Rowe admitted in a number of newspaper interviews that while still an amateur he had often accepted 'backhanders', ie cash payments of about £25 or £30 a time to appear at local athletics' meetings such as miners' galas instead of participating in higher profile meetings in London. As he was quoted, 'Maybe if you have gone to Eton or Oxford, you can afford to turn down these offers but if, like me, you haven't got the brass, you take backhanders.' For lack of a measure of financial support there is little doubt that Britain lost the services of its most outstanding shot putter ever. Had that been available Arthur would not have turned professional. But up to this time, as has been noted, world class throwers in Britain from a working class background were unknown till Rowe appeared. His loss to Britain and the sport was amply demonstrated later that year in November when the Commonwealth Games were taking place in Perth, Australia. As Englishman Dr Martyn Lucking was winning gold in the shot putt with a throw of 59'4", the *Daily Mail* organised a shot putt event in Barnsley for Arthur Rowe under competitive conditions. Despite this being out of season and Rowe having no proper preparation he threw an excellent 63'2".

No doubt encouraged by such form and becoming conscious that his rugby league career was failing to fulfil its potential Rowe wrote to Jack Crump, then the Senior AAA official and 'Mr Athletics' in Britain, to seek reinstatement, claiming the newspaper articles about his accepting cash had been exaggerated. But to no avail. In the climate of the time this was no surprise. There was to be no going back and after their initial skirmishes at Aboyne, Braemar and Pitlochry in September 1962 the scene was set for the most compelling and sustained head-to-head confrontation between Bill Anderson and Arthur Rowe, which was to breathe new life into the heavy events and the Games generally.

It was only a short time prior to his début at Aboyne that Arthur Rowe learned for the first time of the existence of professional athletics north of the Border. Although in the wake of turning professional he had run in a few handicap sprints at some Lakeland Games, which were professional, it was not until he received a visit in Barnsley from George Clark that he became aware of a circuit of professional Highland Games in Scotland, where cash prizes were available in a number of throwing events.

Clark was still competing at the time he went to visit Rowe in Barnsley although, at aged 55, he was declining. But he could claim success at Aboyne in throwing the 56lb weight for distance as far back as 1930 and as recently as 1961. George had his own particular brand of humour. His driving was notoriously bad and often attracted gestures from other drivers. When that happened George would comment to his passenger, 'Look, that mannie must ken me, he's waving at me!'

Some years previously, at Lochearnhead Games, before entering the arena he saw JJ Miller, the famous Games' commentator, with whom he had an edgy relationship, holding court, microphone in hand. He persuaded a friend to approach Miller to tell him, 'George Clark died

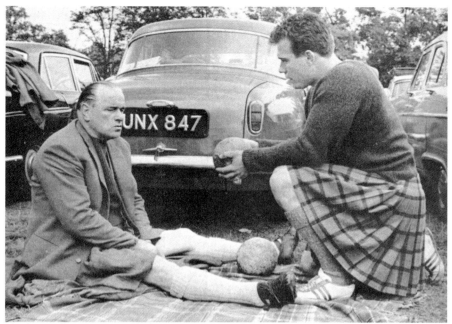

The legendary George Clark giving tips to Arthur Rowe on the art of stone putting – Clark persuaded Rowe to compete in the Games to increase competition

yesterday,' while he remained out of sight. Miller rushed into the heavies' tent, where some were changing, to announce the news which allegedly elicited the response from one, 'Oh Christ, I bet the funeral will be next Friday and that's Durness Games, my favourite.' Returning to the arena he asked for the crowd's attention when he solemnly announced the passing of the great man and requested they stand in silence for two minutes, which they did.

The Games then resumed and after a short while Clark discreetly approached Miller unseen from the rear, tapped him on the shoulder and muttered, 'Cauld day the day, eh?' Miller allegedly exploded with a series of expletives but unfortunately forgot his microphone was still on, leaving the crowd in a very bemused state. Clark tended to dominate officials and organise which heavies would go to which Games when several took place on the same day. However, he also had a deep attachment to the Games and was worried that Bill's complete domination of the heavy events was unhealthy, predicting correctly it would lead to loss of interest among the public. With all that in mind he went off to seek out Rowe in Barnsley to persuade him to come north.

Rowe realised after his initial foray that to challenge Bill Anderson seriously would require him to master the traditional Scottish events as well as the putts. During the winter of 1962/63 Clark travelled to Barnsley several times to give Rowe coaching in the traditional events. Rowe had always been a ferocious trainer and sustained an intensive training regime of weights and throwing even, at one stage, purchasing a telegraph pole from the GPO to hone his caber technique. Meantime, up north, Bill maintained his usual routine doing no winter training, only emerging to do some throwing practice about the end of March.

In readiness for the Games season Rowe and his wife Betty came north and installed themselves temporarily in a farm cottage on the outskirts of Stonehaven, which had been arranged through Clark who continued, sometimes with Bob Aitken of Auchenblae, to tutor Arthur in the art of the Scots heavy events.

Blackford Games in Perthshire, held on the last Saturday of May, had traditionally been the opening Games of the season for a number of years. As such, they were always eagerly anticipated as rivals emerged from winter hibernation to test their form, set down markers and seek to claim the first prize money of the summer. The 1963 Games were not only going to herald the season but were to feature the first of a season-long series of head-to-head challenges between Bill and Arthur.

With the benefit of winter's training and expert coaching, many were intrigued to see how Arthur had improved in the traditional Scots' events. And many were intrigued to see how Bill would react. Nobody was left disappointed, with a contest that went down to the wire. Arthur won the putts with an excellent throw of 59' in the light putt while Bill won the hammers. The 28lb weight for distance went to Bill and 56lb weight for height to Arthur, with a new ground record of 14'6". That left the caber as the deciding event, with Bill securing first equal with Eck Wallace from Strathmiglo to eclipse Arthur by the narrowest of margins.

Arthur had demonstrated great improvement in the traditional heavy events compared with his initial efforts at the end of the previous season. As the season unfolded it became clear that his performance at Blackford had been no one-off. At Thornton Games, in Fife, in June, not only did he win both putts but also the weight for distance and weight for height. At Comrie Games, also in June, he went one better, succeeding in beating Bill at his speciality – the hammer throws – with heaves of 128'2" and 104'4" in the light and heavy hammers respectively, Bill redeeming himself by winning the caber. At Mallaig Arthur had a monster putt of 62'10" and won the 56lb weight for height while Bill won the caber, hammers and 56lb weight for distance.

At the Aberdeen Games, in front of a crowd of over six thousand,

Arthur set a new 56lb weight for height record with a magnificent toss of 15'. This gave him a two point lead over Bill going into the final event, the caber. Stung by Arthur looking likely to defeat him on his home patch Bill, ever the competitor under pressure, dug out a winning performance with a perfect toss to share the honours with Arthur.

At Halkirk Games, near Thurso in Caithness, a cup was awarded to the winner of the heavy events' championship to keep for a year but, in the event of anyone winning it three years in a row, he was allowed to retain it in perpetuity. Bill, having won it in 1961 and 1962, was therefore poised to keep the cup should he win in 1963. The progressive Halkirk Games' Committee was always looking at ways to promote its Games and boost attendances and was alert to the increased level of interest created by the rivalry between Bill and Arthur. But they were also canny and, according to Bill, reluctant to lose their heavy championship cup to him. He suspects that in an effort to achieve the best of both worlds, by increasing their gate and retaining their cup, they paid Arthur appearance money to compete. However, on this occasion the ploy backfired as Bill defeated Arthur to win the cup, which he still has!

By now a pattern was beginning to develop that Bill had the upper hand in the hammers, Arthur in the putts, with Bill edging it in the weights for distance and Arthur the weight for height, with the caber often being the deciding event which each on his day was capable of winning. In terms of matchmaking it was a promoter's dream, with the two of them often level going into the drama of the final event – the caber. Games' secretaries up and down the land were reporting increased attendances, thanks in part to the Scottish-English aspect of their rivalry increasing interest in the Games not only in Scotland but throughout the UK. The two were becoming utterly dominant, comfortably ahead of their rivals and it was becoming a rare occasion when someone other than either of them won any of the events.

Reflecting that state of affairs in late July that summer Bill received an interesting if rather plaintive letter from fellow heavy Charlie Allan, then a lecturer in Glasgow. In it he stated that Eck Wallace, had told him that Arthur was going to Auchterarder Games next Saturday but was saying he was going elsewhere in the hope that Bill would go to Auchterarder too! Charlie continued, tongue in cheek, that as he was going there he did not want to see either, let alone both, Bill and Arthur there. Further on he writes, 'I know there is a good day for me somewhere but I don't know where they are all going. Could you tell me where they are going or where you think they are going?'

That letter encapsulated one of the heavies' principal concerns. During the height of the summer it was quite common for there to be four or more Games on the same day. Which heavies went where depended on a number of factors. There was the geographical, as a heavy from the central belt would not immediately opt to go to the north of Caithness. Then there was the question of which events were held at which Games as some Games held eight heavy events while others only five and potentially there was more money to be won out of eight events. Then there was the question of prize money as some Games' prize lists were more generous than others. And finally, perhaps most critically, there was the question of which Games which of one's rival heavies were going to as this clearly impacted on potential winnings.

Not surprisingly, at this remove, Bill Anderson is unable to recall who went where that particular Saturday but is certain that he never at any time avoided Arthur Rowe. Indeed, competing against Arthur brought the best out in Bill and *vice versa*. The record books suggest Bill, however, did not go to Auchterarder that day as Arthur is credited with a clean sweep of all the heavy events, most unlikely had Bill been there.

The closeness of their rivalry through the season added extra spice to the Scottish Heavy Events' Championship at Crieff Games on 17th August, in front of a crowd of about ten thousand. Would Bill retain his crown which he had won convincingly for the previous four years or would Arthur wrest it from him? One of the best ever heavy events' contests resulted in a maiden Scottish title for Arthur Rowe, on the occasion of his twenty-seventh birthday, pipping Bill by the margin of one point – twenty three and a half to twenty two and a half. Bill had lost for the first time in five years but there was no shame in that as he had broken three records that afternoon, as did Arthur. Bill's records came in both hammers with throws of 134'3" and 114'8" in light and heavy respectively and in the 28lb for weight for distance with 84'3", with Arthur second in that event exactly one foot behind.

Arthur's records came in the two putts, with 57' and 47'7" in the light and heavy putts respectively, and 15' in the 56lb weight for height. In the light putt Bill achieved a very creditable 50'9", in second place behind Arthur, a distance which would have won him that year's Scottish amateur title by almost three feet and would have placed him second on the Scottish amateur all-time list behind the outstanding Mike Lindsay, fifth in the Rome Olympics of 1960. This is all the more impressive considering the putt was reckoned to be Bill's weakest of the heavy events. The destiny of the title was in doubt till the last event, the caber, which was won by Sandy Gray, but Arthur pipped Bill for second place to clinch the title. This was the first time a non-Scot, far less an Englishman, had claimed the title leading to predictable headlines such as 'Sassenach Hammer of the Scots' and the like.

Early September, at the Aboyne Games, another tremendous tussle took place, Bill just edging ahead of Arthur to claim the heavyweight championship for the fifth year in a row. In the process the crowd was treated to four new records, three to Arthur and one to Bill. Arthur's were in the light and heavy stones, with 57'7" and 43'11" respectively, and the 28lb weight for distance with 79'8$^1/_2$", in the process breaking his mentor George Clark's record of 76'4" which he had set in 1934.

Bill's record was in the heavy hammer with a heave of 107'$^1/_2$". The following day at Braemar Games, Rowe went one better by setting four new records on his way to pipping Bill to the championship. His records came in the stones, 53'11$^1/_2$" in the light stone and 36'8" in the heavy stone, the latter of course being the Braemar stone, 28lb, and putt from the standing position. His other records were in the 28lb weight for distance and 56lb weight for height with 77'7" and 14'2". Meanwhile, Bill extended his own heavy hammer record with a throw of 111'5$^1/_2$".

That was the end to a season which had also seen some other outstanding performances by Bill and Arthur – the 16lb shot putt of 62'10" by Arthur at Mallaig; the 22lb putt of 48'1" by Arthur at Pitlochry and a 138'1" light hammer throw by Bill at Luss.*

Arthur had clearly announced himself as a serious rival to Bill and in a relatively short space of time had demonstrated an impressive mastery of the Scots' traditional events. Given his innate athleticism, power and co-ordination this was perhaps no real surprise but much of it was also down to hard work on his part. During a weight training session at the

---

* It should be pointed out that an element of caution has to be applied in accepting some Games' performances at face value. In the professional Games conditions varied considerably from Games to Games. Some arenas had measured tracks that were level but others were not; some Games' fields had flat throwing areas whereas others were on a slope; each Games had its own implements which meant some could be heavier or lighter than the regulation weight; and the standard of officiating (even at times the impartiality!) varied widely, most of the officials being untrained volunteers from the local community and the consequent reliability of performance recording could vary. Generally speaking, of the big Games, Aboyne were always considered scrupulously run, with performances being accurately recorded, while Crieff and Braemar were on a similar level. But among the lower profile Games significant variations in standards of facilities, officiating and recording of results existed.

Spartan Weight Lifting Club in Aberdeen, the intensity of his training, which caused a puddle of sweat to form at his feet, created a big impression among the gym's regulars. With his rugby league career over, he was free to concentrate on the Games during the summer when he was effectively a full-time athlete. He had also signalled his serious intentions with regard to the Games by installing himself and his wife in Scotland during the Games' season. Another indicator of the seriousness of his intentions was that he had purchased his own kilt, Royal Stewart tartan. In fact, so attached did he become to this kilt that long after he had retired from the Games he used to don it for family Christmas celebrations at home in Barnsley – surely the only Englishman in Yorkshire wearing the kilt that day!

There were not huge amounts of money to be won but a successful Arthur or Bill could make a living out of it over the summer months, although Bill at this time was still fitting the Games in around work on his brother's farm. The highest prize money in the early 60s was awarded by Braemar where in most of the heavy events first prize was £6, reducing to £2 for fourth place, as well as a special £10 prize for the Braemar caber. Accordingly, a successful Braemar could net Bill and Arthur a sum of between £40 and £50 each depending on results. This was at a time when the average working man's wage was about £12 per week and top footballers in England had just rid themselves of the maximum weekly wage cap of £20 and Johnny Haynes was on his way to becoming the first £100 per week player. Allowing for inflation, these approximate Braemar winnings equate to about between £600 and £750 today.

At that time Aboyne Games were held the day before Braemar and although prize money there was a little less than at Braemar there was potential for good earnings over the two days. At other times of the season there were weeks when several Games took place, when sums in excess of £100 per week could be earned, depending on success and subject to deduction of travel and subsistence expenses. It was accordingly of some importance for heavies other than Bill and Arthur to choose their venues carefully as going to the same Games as them effectively meant competing for third place.

Arthur was interviewed by a national broadsheet and asked if he could survive on his winnings from the Games. With characteristic humour he replied, 'Oh, yes, provided you sleep under hedges and eat grass.'

After a period of initial circumspection, Arthur had been well received into the ranks of the heavies despite depriving some of prize money. Despite his pedigree as an amateur athlete he never sought to impress anyone with it and soon became popular with his fellow heavies, officials and Games' enthusiasts. Despite their intense rivalry on the field Bill and he were on decent terms. Both were steely competitors who earned the other's respect but it never spilled over into rancour. From different backgrounds, they were different types with Bill tending to be more reserved but together they were certainly compatible and did enjoy each other's company. Which was just as well as they spent a lot of time together over the course of the season. It is difficult to think of another sport which involved so much regular exposure between two such close rivals. Most weeks they were competing against each other, in addition to which on occasion they travelled together and shared overnight accommodation on the circuit.

Scenes from the Games circuit

(above) March of the Clansmen
– the Men of Lonach – at Lonach
Games, Strathdon

(right) children's races are
popular at many Games

(below left) Atholl Gathering at
Blair Castle

(below right) Doug Edmunds
throwing the caber for distance
at Ceres Games watched by
Grant Anderson

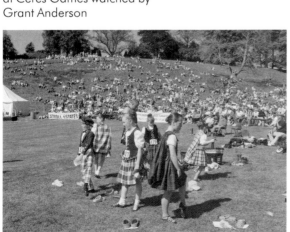

5. The Circuit

THE Circuit is the name given by competitors to the one hundred plus Games that take place up and down the country each year between May and September. 'Doing the Circuit' refers to competitors taking part regularly in a good number of these games. Although many are held on a Saturday or Sunday, by no means all are, some adhering to their traditional weekday dates, eg Inveraray on a Tuesday, Ballater a Thursday, Dornoch a Friday etc. The dates of some games are arrived at by means of a complicated formula, eg the first Tuesday after the second Saturday of the month and it is always wise to check locally the date of the games before setting off to spectate. The 'peak period' of Games is July and August when the weekends feature many games being held on the same day. The first week of the Glasgow Fair holiday from mid July onwards was traditionally known as 'Games week', as games took place every day of the week and for the most part still do.

During the years of Bill Anderson's career as an athlete, a number of games had ceased to exist while new ones had started up and others that had been in abeyance restarted. And the same has happened since he retired. Some games after being held on the same date for many years have changed dates and others have changed venues. In that sense, the face of Scottish games reflects a number of recurring changes.

Broadly speaking, the circuit could be said to consist loosely of four main areas. There are the 'north' games, which cover the area round Inverness and to the north; the 'north east' games, which cover the Grampian area and north Perthshire; the 'Fife' games covering Fife and south Perthshire, and the 'west coast' games, covering Argyllshire and parts of Invernesshire. Some athletes tended to participate mostly in the circuit of the area where they lived while others travelled the country.

By the time Arthur Rowe appeared, Bill Anderson had been travelling the circuit for about four years, averaging about thirty games per year. The circuit began on the last Saturday of May at Blackford Games and finished on the second Saturday of September at Pitlochry Games. Blackford still usually opens the season, a date now shared with Bathgate Games, although some years the Atholl Gathering at Blair Castle is held on the Sunday prior to Blackford. Altholl takes place 'the weekend before the last Monday in May', an example of the complicated date formula referred to above. The Atholl Gathering first took place in 1846 to commemorate the Queen's presentation of Colours to the Atholl Highlanders a year before. They fell into abeyance but were revived in 1984. The season now ends with the Invercharron Games on the third Saturday of September.

First held in 1870, **Blackford Games** were initially held in 'the Coo Park' in this delightful Perthshire village but latterly have been held, thanks to Mr Stirling of Keir, in the Games Park, next to Tullibardine whisky distillery. For years they were run by the inimitable George Hally, already mentioned, who first became Games Secretary there in 1939 and continued to be so till his death in 1984. Blackford and George Hally were inseparable. He was a highly respected heavy events judge who went on to become President of the Scottish Games Association. Active mostly in the Fife and Perthshire Games he was instrumental in the postwar years in persuading some heavies who competed in Games there wearing shorts to switch to wearing the kilt, which soon became the norm.

An individual of some candour he did not suffer fools gladly. Over the years he had acquired detailed technical knowledge of the heavy events and occasionally coached aspiring heavies, including Douglas Edmunds and John Freebairn among others. He used to go round the Games in a small truck carrying hammers and weights and the like. These implements and others were cast at a foundry in Forfar and George, being a blacksmith, would attach links, handles and shafts to them in his forge before having them stamped by Customs and Excise to authenticate their weight. He would export some to the USA, Canada, Australia, New Zealand and other places for use in their games. In the course of his judging career at home he met the then Australian Prime Minister, Sir Robert Menzies, who attended Comrie Games, and the British Prime Minister, Sir Alec Douglas-Home, who was Chieftain of Crieff Games in 1965. His many contacts enabled him to promote a number of heavies' careers through liaising with Games' organisers to arrange appearances and by setting up exhibitions of heavy events here and abroad.

Several times George arranged for Bill Anderson to do exhibitions at agricultural shows throughout the UK and to do demonstrations as part of summer evening entertainment programmes for visitors, in places such as Oban. In a sense he was a form of prototype of today's sports agent except his principal motivation was the promotion of the heavy events and Games.

Despite the low prize money and the bitterly cold conditions that usually prevailed, being the opening Games, Blackford usually attracted a decent crowd with a good field of athletes. As illustrative of the low prize money then on offer it is interesting to note that in the early 1970s first prize in most of the heavy events was £3 whereas at Birnam Games, by Dunkeld in Perthshire, back in 1867 the corresponding figure was £2!

The Blackford Games have included special attractions on occasion, such as the Golden Lions freefall parachute team, and novelty events like sports cars racing sprinters over a short distance. And for over fifty years, part of the games' profits are allocated to an annual old age pensioners' village outing.

When competing Bill would some-times travel there with Sandy Gray and Bob Aitken, after meeting at Brechin and thereafter sharing a car. On the return trip they often stopped at the Panmure Hotel at Edzell for refreshments where they would sometimes meet other athletes returning from other Games and discuss the day's events. At any rate they did so till George Clark tipped them off about police interest in this activity as already mentioned.

Bill competed at Blackford for over twenty-five years. The Games celebrate their one hundred and fortieth staging in 2009.

The next Games on the circuit usually attended by Bill were at **Strathmiglo**, in Fife, where they took place on the King George VI Playing Fields in the middle of the village. Although they could trace their roots back to the Victorian era they had not been held for many years till local policeman and well known heavy athlete, Eck Wallace (known locally as 'Big Sandy') revived them in 1965. Unlike Blackford they were not affiliated to the Scottish Games Association, there apparently being a personality clash between George Hally and Eck Wallace which prevented this. Wallace could apparently be a feisty character at times and on ocasion sparks would fly between him and his brother on Games day. Often benefitting from good weather, there was a full programme of heavy events, running (including a hill race up Lomond Hill), dancing, cycling and latterly an important pipe band competition. Crowds usually were about two thousand but unfortunately the Games were discontinued in 2002 due to a lack of organisational support.

Next on the circuit was **Markinch**, in Fife, held in Dixon Park in the middle of town. The first Games here were held in the 1920s and, as with a number of Fife Games, the emphasis was on professional sprinting with plenty bookmakers always in attendance and crowds of over 3,000 being common. However, there was also a full programme of heavy events, including the British 28lb weight for distance championship, and over the years Bill achieved much success there.

But the confines of the Park were not really appropriate for throwing the light hammer – there were a number of near misses with the implement landing perilously close to the crowd several times, while Bill himself remembers one year launching it in among a bunch of cyclists, thankfully with no mishap – and as a result the light hammer was withdrawn in the interests of safety. Bill recalled, 'When you're young the dangers involved don't really inhibit you but as you grow older you're much more aware of them.'

Markinch being then dominated by the Haig distillery it was no surprise that whisky featured prominently on the prize list. Although he was often offered a dram at the Games Bill seldom accepted, preferring to return home in good condition!

The next Games was on the third Saturday in June at Oldmeldum, near Aberdeen, always known as '**The Oldmeldrum Sports**'. For years this was Aberdeen's local Games as the Aberdeen Games did not re-start till 1961. They were always a colourful and high profile event which were well publicised by the Committee, who always secured a celebrity to open the Games and act as Chieftain, eg the actress Pat Phoenix (Elsie Tanner from Coronation Street), the entertainers the Alexander Brothers, Bobby Charlton, Jimmy Saville, Frankie Vaughan and Linda Lusardi, among others.

The Games originated in the early 1900s but, due to financial difficulties, ceased in 1923. They were resuscitated in 1930 thanks to the singleminded efforts of Fred Green and five others. Fred Green was the local miller who persuaded five other working men in the area to donate a week's wages to re-start the Games, to provide a Cocoa Fund for the children of Oldmeldrum. In those

times donating a week's wages was a significant sacrifice.

From such beginnings – the first Games raised £36 for the Fund – Oldmeldrum Sports have gone on to become one of the biggest annual attractions in the north east and have sometimes drawn crowds in excess of ten thousand. Their original charitable aims are maintained, with all profits being distributed to local charity and community organisations. Bill always enjoyed these Games and their fun atmosphere. But one of his first memories of them recalls an era when attitudes in certain respects were definitely different. On his first appearance in 1958 there was a 'novelty event', which involved George Clark and Sandy Gray wrestling a donkey. While George had the poor beast in a necklock Sandy had a hold of its tail, with the crowd apparently revelling in the spectacle. But before the donkey could be grounded he struck an undoubtedly painful pre-emptive blow by landing a kick on a certain area of Sandy's anatomy, bringing an immediate halt to proceedings.

Aberdeen Games took place at Hazlehead Park the next day and most of the athletes who had competed at Oldmeldrum would also compete at Aberdeen. Although Aberdeen had held different Games over the years, these began in 1961. They were run by Aberdeen Council and received great publicity due to their hosting the World Caber Tossing Championships. They were reasonably well supported, on occasion having crowds of about six thousand, but despite them being 'home' Games for Bill he never particularly excelled there. He was successful but Arthur Rowe tended to have the upper hand over him there whereas at Aboyne, some twenty five miles to the west, Bill was virtually unbeatable. A large number of international heavies attended, attracted by the World Caber Tossing Championship, the pioneers being the Swedes from Gottland, Erik Heedin and colleagues, and then the American Methodist minister, the Reverend Arnold Pope from North Carolina.

Newburgh Games, in Fife, were usually also on that weekend, which meant competitors were split between Fife and the north east.

The last weekend in June saw Games at **Ceres,** in Fife, **Crook of Devon**, near Kinross, and **Comrie**, in Perthshire, the latter two ceasing in the mid 60s due to economic problems.

Ceres Games, near Cupar, lay claim to being the oldest in Scotland as it is said they were first held in 1314 by celebrating Fife archers returning from the Battle of Bannockburn. However, there is no hard evidence supporting this claim although the archery connection is maintained through the Games continuing to be held in the pretty Bow Butts Park in the middle of the village. Till the end of the 1800s the Games extended over two days, the first being Market Day when animals were sold on the Green, where there were also toy stalls and gypsy caravans. The second day was known as Plack and Penny Day, when races and athletic contests were held and which evolved into today's Games day. Horse racing also featured, with the chain race consisting of six laps of the arena, but that has had to be stopped now because of health and safety concerns.

At Ceres the caber is tossed for distance and is the only Games in Scotland where this still happens. Historically, a number of the Fife Games featured this form of the event as opposed to the standard form, where the winner is judged on the clock face system. A special heavy event here involves the 'Ceres Stone', a heavy stone with a ring attached. Throughout the year it is kept at the Ceres Inn but on Games day it is brought to the Park and used in a throwing for distance contest. Cumberland wrestling is also held here with much sought-after Wemyss Ware plates on offer as prizes. Bill competed here on a number of occasions but regretted there was no light hammer event due to the restricted size of the Park.

A more recently founded games held on the last Saturday of June are the **Drumtochty Games** at Auchenblae, Kincardineshire which were first held in 1977 to celebrate the Queen's Jubilee Year. The following year a new committee headed up by former SGA president Jim Brown MBE in the chair, ably aided and abetted by former heavy Bob Aitken and others, took over the running of the games and fashioned them into one of Scotland's most appealing.

A traditional games encompassing all events, they take place in the lushly wooded setting of the grounds of Drumtochty Castle. A small pavilion accommodates the games' patrons while the atmospheric games field is ringed by bales of straw for seating while brightly coloured flags flutter overhead round the arena. Bill won the inaugural heavy events championship here and competed several times with success over the years. In 1983 Geoff Capes set a new world best here for the 28lb weight for distance with a throw of 91'5". A few years ago Drumtochty formed a twinning arrangement with Regina Games in Saskatchewan, Canada, since when members of the respective committees have made exchange visits. Drumtochty is well served by its committee and is fortunate in having a number of present and former heavies involved – Bob Aitken, son Bruce, Alan Sim and his son Stephen as well as Jim Brown himself. If the weather is favourable, the games usually attract a crowd of about three thousand and rank as one of the best traditional games in the country.

Thornton Games in Fife were held in early July. Believed to have been in existence since 1853, they were once one of the biggest Games in the country, held over two days, attracting crowds in excess of 40,000 during the 1930s. Then they were held on a Friday and Saturday during the Glasgow Fair to attract the Glasgow and west coast holidaymakers from nearby Leven, who would arrive by special trains. At that time Thornton was situated in the busy Fife coalfield and the professional running at the Games with its betting and attendant bookmakers was a big attraction. But there was always a full programme of heavy events too, as well as wrestling. It was here Bill brought to an end his wrestling career after accidentally injuring an opponent. Since the 1920s the Games have been held in the town's Memorial Park, created by local subscription after World War I. Nowadays the Games still thrive but on much lower crowds.

The following weekend, from mid July onwards, saw the beginning of a period of intense Games activity coinciding with the Glasgow Fair fortnight. **Balloch Games** were first held in 1967 after a number of local businessmen came together to set them up. They have always been held on the first Saturday of the Glasgow Fair Fortnight in July which has ensured excellent attendances of between eight and ten thousand spectators. Initially they were held at the Moss of Balloch, which they outgrew, then moved to Christie Park in nearby Alexandria and for the past seven years have been held at Balloch Castle Country Park. Latterly the SGA version of the World Heavy Events championship has been held here.

Balloch always seemed to enjoy sunny weather according to Bill's recollection which, combined with spectators' natural high spirits at the start of their holidays, made for an excellent day out. Other spirits were also in evidence as Bill recalls prizes of bottles of whisky being awarded in addition to the cash prizes. This meant he often had a difficult time leaving the arena, laden with bottles and having to decline many offers of assistance received!

Alva Games were usually held on the same day in Johnstone Park, a very pretty setting overlooked by the Ochil Hills. These Games began life as the Alva Gymnastic Games in 1845 and, since 1856, have been held in Johnstone Park which was donated to the town for the Games by local man James Johnstone. They are the last surviving Games of the 'Wee County', those of Alloa and Sauchie having ceased some years ago and host a famous hill race. Big crowds were common, with a lot of betting on the sprinting, cycling and pony trotting. It is believed these were the first games to stage cycling but pony trotting has been brought to an end because of health and safety concerns. In the early 1970s a well known weightlifter and amateur heavy, Jim Ferguson of Monklands, was spectacularly exposed while competing for cash, despite wearing a wig, when identified by an amateur official who was there as a spectator.

There being Games each day of this week meant Bill took a week's holiday off work to become effectively a full-time athlete. On Monday **Burntisland Games** in Fife took place. These purported to be able to trace their beginnings to the mid seventeenth century when Cromwell's soldiers raced horses along the sands to nearby Pettycur. The Games were held on the Links, the site previously of Burntisland Golf Club, reckoned to be the eleventh oldest in the world. They evolved from the holding of an annual market there and for that reason were known for many years as the 'Market Games'. As the Monday was a local Fife holiday and part of the Glasgow Fair large crowds used to turn up to enjoy the Games and the neighbouring fair ground shows. Despite that, Bill recalls prize money being very low.

On the Tuesday it was on to **Inveraray Games**, in Argyll, held in the lovely tree lined Winterton Park in the grounds of Inveraray Castle below Dun a' Chuaich, the hill on which stands the famous 'bell tower' with its vantage point high over Loch Fyne, to guard against unwelcome visitors. Inveraray also lays claim to ancient roots dating back to 1563 when

Games were allegedly held to celebrate the visit of Mary Queen of Scots to her half sister, the Countess of Argyll, but hard evidence is in short supply. Games were also apparently held in 1844 to celebrate the marriage of the Duke of Argyll's son but that was a single event and it was not until 1890 that the Games were officially set up. Thereafter they ran till World War II, in Stable Park, but did not restart till 1958 when the Duke of Argyll offered the use of Winterton Park, where they have flourished ever since. Their beautiful location always attracted large numbers of foreign tourists.

In 1971, while wrestling here, Bill stepped in a hole in the ground created by a hammer and fell awkwardly, injuring his ankle, wrist and back, as a result of which he was unable to participate further. He had no alternative but to return home to Aberdeen to recuperate, causing him to miss the whole week's Games. He was in such discomfort he had to drive back home all the way in first gear as it was too painful to change gear. Fellow heavy Gordon Forbes and he had travelled to Inveraray in Gordon's car which he lent Bill for his return home. On being asked how Gordon felt about all this Bill replied, twinkle in eye, 'Oh, he was quite happy to see me go – in fact they all were', referring to the heavies who, in Bill's absence for the rest of the week, saw their prospects of prize money immeasurably improved!

Next day, Wednesday, it was **Luss**, on Loch Lomond, a lovely conservation village once referred to as 'the prettiest village in Scotland' and made famous latterly as the location of the television series 'Take the High Road'. Luss Games were traditionally

Luss Games 1935. Courtesy Anne Paterson, Luss Games

a big event which on occasion attracted five figure crowds. They were first held in 1875 having been founded by the Luss Company of Dunbartonshire Volunteers and they benefited from the patronage of the Colquhoun family, whose residence Rossdhu House is in the parish. The Colquhouns made available the field for the Games, at the entrance to which stands a memorial cairn to Sir Ivar Colquhoun erected in gratitude for his and his family's contribution to the Games throughout the years.

When Bill began competing there, gold medals were still awarded to the winners of heavy events and he was fortunate to collect a number of them. At the start of his career there Bill can remember one of the judges was Tom Nicolson, one of the famous Nicolson brothers from the Kyles of

Bute. As a young man he had won the British wire hammer title several times and represented Britain in the Olympics. Despite his then advanced years he enjoyed mildly taunting Bill as he produced his medals, saying, 'You'll never win one of them.' Recently the Games, which have been attracting crowds of about three thousand were moved to Sunday of the same week in a bid to attract more competitors and spectators.

Thursday that week took Bill to one of his favourite Games, at **Tobermory** on the Isle of Mull. Started in 1923 they were first held at Balisgate but now have a superb setting on the Golf Course high above the town, with wonderful views down the Sound of Mull to the Morvern Hills on the mainland. It is an intimate arena,

An early Games in Tomintoul Square

with many spectators seated on the natural amphitheatre provided by the high banking on one side, with all the events unfolding on the fairway below. The springy turf of the Golf Course has yielded some excellent performances in the jumping events over the years, with former well known local Kenny McIntyre credited with an outstanding triple jump in 1965 of 48'7", as well as being the scene of Jay Scott's famous 1964 high jump.

Bill always found the atmosphere here very relaxing, the tone being set on the morning ferry trip across from Oban where spectators and athletes, pipers and dancers would all mingle. The return ferry trip back in the evening was more lively altogether with impromptu ceilidhs breaking out as dancers danced, pipers piped and singers sang to the

accompaniment of numerous drams being sunk. But Bill and his fellow heavies had to exercise restraint as their next port of call the following day was **Dunbeath Games** in Caithness, in the far north of Scotland about two hundred and fifty miles from Oban.

Bill would often drive north in the same car as Arthur, Sandy Gray and Bob Aitken, staying overnight in a guest house in the Inverness area. They would have to leave early the next morning to complete the long drive to Dunbeath (this being in the days before bridges spanned the Cromarty and Dornoch Firths) to arrive at midday, in good time for the start of the Games. Dunbeath, famous as the birthplace of the celebrated Scottish writer Neil Gunn, had held Games since 1851 in the small John Gerrie Sports Field. Being on a slight slope it gave the heavies the benefit of throwing downhill. Spectators' cars usually ringed the arena, a source of occasional concern due to errant hammers. Among the trophies competed for by the heavies were the Townsend Cup, for best caber tosser and the Achnaharish Cup, for best all-round heavy.

This was a planned fishing village created by the Duke of Sutherland during the Highland Clearances, when the occupants of Kildonan and Strathnaver were evicted and relocated here. These were particularly friendly Games where Bill was always made to feel welcome. Dunbeath was also home to the McBeath twins, Tom and Jim, top Games athletes from the late 60s till throughout the 80s. Tom was a light events' specialist while Jim was the best all-round 'heavy' and 'light' athlete of his era and one of the best ever. During his career he won the Chieftain's Challenge Cup at Aboyne (for the best all-round heavy and light events' athlete) a record seventeen consecutive times from 1970 to 1986. Sadly these Games are now defunct.

The next day, Saturday, were **Lochearnhead Games** in Perthshire, home of the British Heavy Events Championship and therefore an important Games. From Dunbeath it was a drive of about two hundred and twenty miles, at the end of a long, tiring, week. The Lochearnhead Games – to give them their full title, the Strathyre, Balquhidder and Lochearnhead Games – will always be associated with the former champion heavy Ewen Cameron, for many years the proprietor of the famous Lochearnhead Hotel. Although the Games had existed since 1872 he and others were instrumental in their

resuscitation in the post World War II era and the amalgamation of the three Games into the one, to be staged at Lochearnhead. The Games were given a big boost when awarded the hosting of the British Heavy Events Championship for the first time in 1967, sponsored by Black and White Whisky.

Despite the basic nature of the Games field there – Bill recalls the cattle having been moved out of it a few days before, leaving tell tale evidence of their recent occupation – performances and crowds were always very good. And although logic would suggest that, after such a punishing week, fatigue would detract from Bill's performances he always found it had the opposite effect and that by the end of the week he was throwing better than he had at the start. This was demonstrated spectacularly in July 1969, when Bill smashed the world record in the light hammer with his magnificent throw of 151'2".

The **Tomintoul Games** near Glenlivet, in the heart of Speyside whisky country, were held on the same day. They began life in about 1840 as a village picnic and sports and were first held nearby at The Haugh at Torbane. Then they were held on the square in the village till an errant hammer throw variously credited to Jim Maitland or AJ Stuart almost wrought serious havoc in the 1930s. Thereafter they were moved to a public park on the edge of the village, in a wooded setting overlooking the Banffshire hills. For a long time they were always held on the Friday after the 12th of August, the start of the grouse shooting season, to attract spectators from the numerous large shooting parties then held in the vicinity. But the number of parties declined and about fifty years ago the Games' date was changed to coincide with the Glasgow Fair holiday. Its record crowd was five thousand in 1976 and now the average attendance is between two and three thousand.

At a later stage **Taynuilt Games**, near Oban, were also held on the same Saturday while, on the Sunday, **Arbroath Games** were held in the town's Victoria Park. On the following Wednesday, the **Fettercairn Agricultural Show and Games**, in Kincardineshire, were held and they were the scene of many a joust between Bill Anderson and Arthur Rowe but have been defunct for some years now.

On the same day, on the other side of the country, **Arisaig Games** took place. Originally held as far back as 1880, they became defunct about the turn of the nineteenth century until 1936 when they were revived and have since been held continuously. For years they were staged in the lovely Morrach Park in the village but because of inadequate car parking facilities a new venue had to be found. Now these traditionial games take place outside the village at Traigh Farm beside beautiful white sands with stunning views over to the Small Isles, a magnificent location. The Chieftain is Ranald McDonald, 24th Captain of Clanranald and Chief of Clanranald who hosts the Clanranald marquee at the Games, a local hospitality point for clan members and others to meet. Recently a twinning arrangement with Loch Norman Highland Games in North Carolina has been formed.

Two days later, usually the last Friday of July, Bill would head up to the extreme north west of Scotland to the **Durness Games**. Situated a few miles east of Scotland's most north westerly point at Cape Wrath these Games were revived in 1970, after a ten year gap. They are held in Shore Park which sits on top of cliffs overlooking the North Atlantic, with spectacular views out to sea, eastwards along the rugged Sutherland coastline and its pretty beaches and south to the magnificent Sutherland peaks of Ben Loyal and Ben Hope. Again, this is a stunningly beautiful setting although its rather precarious clifftop location was responsible for the cycling events being stopped some years ago, as a cyclist who had fallen skidded across the turf to a halt perilously close to the edge of the cliffs. The Games get under way after the parade from the village centre, led by the pipe band and Chieftain and his retinue, reach the Park. Bill often competed here for and won the Rispond Cup, awarded to the best heavy. This trophy, named after a local area, was donated in the early 1970s by Lord Rootes of motor car fame, who owned a nearby estate. Because of the travelling distance involved, it meant either leaving home the previous night and camping overnight in the Park, or a very early morning drive, taking care to avoid the many deer sleeping on the road.

The next day, Saturday, Games took place in a number of places – **Halkirk**, **Airth**, **Dufftown** and **Auchterarder**. The latter were at one time a very popular Games with the heavies, particularly with Arthur Rowe who achieved some excellent performances there, but they have been defunct since the late sixties.

If Bill and others had gone to Durness they normally competed the next day at Halkirk, six miles south of Thurso in Caithness, and stayed overnight in the area. Halkirk Games were one of the biggest in the north, often drawing crowds of six thousand, and benefitted from the hard work and enthusiasm of their thirty six strong committee. Prize money was always good, at times appearance money was said to be paid to athletes and there was a full programme of nine heavy events, including tossing the sheaf. The Games were first held in 1886, in a field next to the Gerston distillery, and from then till 1920 were held in a field next to Hoy railway station. Local landowners, the Sinclairs, had been patrons of the Games since their inception and in 1921 gifted Recreation Park, the current Games venue, to the community. Always a well run Games, with an efficient and innovative committee, they succeeded in attracting top heavies and athletes from all over Scotland despite their distant location. Brothers Alistair and Murray Gunn, two of Scotland's top heavies over the past twenty years, are from nearby Gerston, site of the original Games, and have a long family association with the Games stretching back to 1912 when forebear James Gunn first competed in the heavy events prior to becoming a long serving Secretary of the Games in 1924.

Airth Games, which take place in the village of Airth about six miles from Stirling, evolved from an annual fair held on the last Tuesday of July. The fair was an important occasion for the hiring of farmworkers but also featured sideshows, jugglers and music. The Games began in 1871 and continued to be held on the last Tuesday of July till 1939. Then they benefitted from the Glasgow Fair and attracted big crowds of over ten thousand whereas now average attendance is about three to four thousand. They are held in the North Green Park and are well supported by local businesses.

Dufftown Games, like nearby Tomintoul Games, take place in the heart of 'whisky country' in Speyside. They were first held in 1892 after two gatherings, the Dullanside and Fiddichside, held on the banks of the rivers Dullan and Fiddich, amalgamated to form the Dufftown Games. Although the age of those two gatherings is not known the Fiddichside one had been in existence since at least 1851. This has been vouched by the recent discovery of a beautiful silver medal with 'Fiddichside Gathering' inscribed on its face while on the other side there is engraved' Awarded to Charles McPherson of Scalan, heavy events champion 1851-1853'. Scalan is a hamlet between Dufftown and Tomintoul.

The first Dufftown Games attracted a crowd of six hundred who each paid 6d ($2^1/_2$p) for admission. Nowadays they attract a crowd of about four thousand and are held in the Mortlach School field in the village. Till recently their Honorary President was the now deceased Burke Nicholson, Baron of Balvenie, who had been vice chairman of Coca Cola in the USA and had been very supportive of the Games.

Believed to have started as informal sports on the pier at **Mallaig**, the Games themselves date back to about

1926. Traditionally they were held on a Monday as no landings of fish took place on that day as boats did not then go out on the Sabbath. Since their inception they have been held at a number of venues but, now known as the **Mallaig and Morar Games**, are held in the Lovat Memorial Field on the first Sunday in August. Competing here meant a round trip of over four hundred miles for Bill.

On the first Saturday in August a number of Games were held – **Aberlour**, **Fort William**, **Inverkeithing** and **Aboyne**. Aberlour Games, in Speyside, were begun in 1943 by the local Home Guard as a fund raising activity for the Welcome Home Fund for returning servicemen. After the war a committee took over responsibility for the Games, which are held in the Alice Littler Park.

The **Caol Games** at Fort William were held under the shadow of Ben Nevis. Fort William will always be associated with the champion heavy, AA Cameron, who was born and lived near here and whose wonderfully ornate world championship heavy events belt is on display in the West Highland Museum in the town.

Inverkeithing Games trace their roots to the first Lammas Fair held on 1st August 1652 when a variety of goods and livestock were on sale in the Main Street. More recently the Games were held before World War I at Kirkgate Park, Bellknowes, where they continued till 1967. After a break of five years they were restarted at the Ballast Bank arena in the town where they continue to thrive. A full programme of heavy events, trade events, cycling, dancing and piping usually attracts crowds of between four and five thousand.

Aboyne Games features separately.

The following Friday usually saw Bill at **Dornoch Games** which began in 1871 and are held in the town's Meadow Park which was gifted to the community by the Duke of Sutherland. These Games, which usually attract crowds of about two and a half thousand comprise the whole range of Games' events – piping, dancing, running, jumping, heavy events and cycling. Two novelty events are also included, 'tilt the bucket' involving a wheelbarrow, a pole and a suspended bucket of water and the other involves a ten foot high slippery board at a 45° angle which contestants run at to scramble to the top and try to pull themselves over the other side. Apart from the usual cash prizes Dornoch awards three gold medals each year, to the champions in piping, athletics and heavy events. These were originally donated by the famous philanthropist Andrew Carnegie who owned the nearby Skibo Castle, now a luxury hotel. Both his daughter and granddaughter have continued the tradition of awarding these gold medals annually and recently his granddaughter became the first lady Chieftain of the Games. These medals were much prized by Bill who, despite many close contests here, particularly with Arthur Rowe, succeeded in winning seventeen of them.

Often on the same day, in north west Sutherland, the **Assynt Games** were

Bandsmen's Race at Atholl Gathering 21st century

held in the Culag Park at lovely Lochinver. These Games were first held in 1904 and feature a colourful opening ceremony. Prior to midday a brightly decorated Chieftain's Barge, carrying the Games Chieftain, his piper, former Chieftains and guests, visit islands nearby while hospitality is enjoyed. They then disembark at the pier where they are met by a pipe band which leads them to Culag Park to open the Games. Sandy Sutherland still judges the heavy events here as did Charlie Simpson till recently, while Arthur Rowe still holds the light and heavy hammer records since 1970 (148' 1" and 119' 5"). The famous Scottish poet Norman MacCaig who had an association with Assynt regularly attended these Games.

On the Saturday Games took place at **Strathpeffer**, **Aberfeldy** and **Cortachy**. Strathpeffer Games were first held in 1882 following an impromptu games the previous year

Atholl Gathering 1859

held by the tradesmen engaged in building the famous spa facilities in the town. They are held in a beautiful tree-lined setting in the grounds of Leod Castle, with a backdrop of heather covered mountains. Bill recalls these Games being well patronised by local landed gentry whose banners were displayed in the arena, adding a slightly rarefied air to the proceedings. When he first went there in the early sixties the Games also featured horse racing and in the early seventies were attracting crowds of over seven thousand. Next to the castle is a wonderful Spanish chestnut tree, reputedly planted in the year of the Spanish Armada, 1588.

The **Atholl and Breadalbane Gathering** at Aberfeldy first took place in 1843 but was discontinued after 1934. They were restarted in 1972 as part of the Atholl and Breadalbane Agricultural Society and Cattle Show. The Show takes place over the Friday and Saturday with the Games on the Saturday. Although at one time Games often ran alongside agricultural shows, Aberfeldy is one of the few left, **Echt** in Aberdeenshire and **Strathardle** near Kirkmichael in Perthshire being others. The games are held in the lovely setting of the town's Victoria Park, looking out on the well known local landmark of the Weem Rock, site of the games' hill race. One of the main attractions is the Clan Menzies Manhood Stone event in which this stone, weighing about two hundred and fifty pounds, has to be lifted and carried as far as possible. Till 2006 the record was held by well known heavy, Stephen King of Inveraray, at one hundred and sixty eight feet but that year John Davidson of Glenshee extended it to nearly one hundred and eighty feet, a remarkable achievement. This Stone was located at the entrance to Castle Menzies where it had lain for many years by well known games' athlete, John Robertson, and a colleague, Duncan McDiarmid, and is believed to have been the Clan Menzies Stone of Manhood. It is distinctive, being very round and smooth and quite small for its weight, all of which make it extremely difficult to lift.

Cortachy Games, held in beautiful surroundings on the Earl of Airlie's estate next to the River Prosen and within sight of Cortachy Castle four miles north of Kirriemuir, are a small family-oriented Games held now on the same Sunday as Crieff. They are believed to date back to 1885 and in addition to the usual events also feature a flower show and an 'industrial show' involving baking and sewing competitions, as well as a dog show, kids' events, a duck race on the river and at the close of the afternoon an auction of produce to raise funds. The atmosphere is relaxed and friendly and a visit here is like a trip back to yesteryear.

The next stage on the circuit for Bill consisted of three Games on successive days at **Ballater**, **Glenisla** and **Crieff**. The first was on the following Thursday, about mid August, when Ballater Games took place in the lovely tree-lined setting of Monaltrie Park amid the surrounding Deeside hills. They were first held in 1864, on 27th July, at the Church Square in the town. The earliest Chieftains were the lairds of Glenmuick while the current Games Chieftain, Captain AAC Farquharson of Invercauld recently completed sixty years in that post. Bill competed here regularly although was always uncomfortable throwing the hammer in such a tight arena.

The next day, Friday, the Games of the **Glenisla** Highland and Friendly Society took place in the tight confines of The Haugh at Forter, about fifteen miles north of Kirriemuir, in the heart of the glen. These are one of the country's most picturesque and traditional Games. The Haugh (or Meadow) is reached by single track road from Kirkton of Glenisla, following the meandering River Isla which borders one side of The Haugh. On the opposite side, below the road down to the field, is terraced banking which forms a natural amphitheatre for spectators, placing them close to the action in the arena and giving the venue an intimate air. The nearby undulating heather-clad hillsides of Glenisla provide a perfect scenic backdrop to The Haugh. These are one of the oldest Games in the country, having first been held in 1856, and their Committee are keen to maintain the old traditions. In 1856 they were held in a field called Dalonnach, above Forter bridge. The Highland and Friendly Society was formed the following year and in 1858 the Games were moved to today's site at The Haugh. Since then they have been held continuously, apart from 1900, when both Secretary and Patron died, and breaks for the two World Wars. As shall be seen with Braemar Games, these Games were started by the local Highland and Friendly Society, one of whose stated objects in hosting Games was, 'to preserve the Language, Music, Games and Dress of the Highlanders of Scotland.' To this end the programme once featured a Gaelic language competition. A hint at the traditional association of these Games with local landed gentry is Regulation No. 7 of the Society, that 'Noblemen and Gentlemen are respectfully invited to become Honorary Members'. The heavies compete for the Forter Castle Cup, won many times by Bill and as recently as 2004 all the heavy event records there were still shared between him and Arthur Rowe, created between 1964 and 1973, a remarkable achievement.

The next day, Saturday, was the competitive highlight of the season, the annual Scottish Heavy Events Championship at **Crieff Games**, which will be dealt with separately. Although Crieff was usually Bill's

third Games on successive days, that did not detract from his level of performance. The accepted approach in any sport is to expend minimal energy in the days preceding a major championship and although Bill's performance levels did not appear to suffer because of competing on two successive days prior to Crieff, one wonders what he might have achieved with appropriate rest.

On the same day as Crieff, Games were also held at **Glenfinnan**, **Helmsdale**, in Caithness, and **Kinloch Rannoch**. Some consider Glenfinnan Games, near Fort William, as the most attractive in Scotland because of their setting, their emphasis on the traditional aspects of the Games and corresponding lack of commercialisation. They are held in a field at the head of Loch Shiel, near the Memorial commemorating Bonnie Prince Charlie's raising of the standard there to signal the start of the 1745 Jacobite rebellion. The heavy events and other competitions are restricted to locals only, ie those from the surrounding parish and these Games have remained true to their origins.

Kinloch Rannoch Games, in Perthshire, are another delightful small Games which usually have none of the major heavies competing as they are normally all at Crieff. Although entry is not restricted to local athletes, local heavies tend to make up the greater part of the field, some doubling up that day by competing in the local events at Crieff in the morning and then skipping up to Kinloch Rannoch to compete in the afternoon.

The **Skye Games**, held in Portree, used to take place on a Thursday near the end of August but now are held on a Wednesday in early August. They were first staged on Thursday 6th September 1877 due to the initiative of a committee of well-established locals who thought a Skye Games would complement the Skye Gathering Ball, the leading social occasion on the island. It was envisaged the Games would rival the successful Games at Oban and Inverness. Harry McDonald of Viewfield and Donald MacDonald of Tormore were the leading members of this committee and are due much of the credit for first establishing the Games and then keeping them going. To attract the best athletes, and consequently a good crowd, extremely generous prize money for the time was offered. For instance, in 1877 each of the two hammer events carried a prize of three guineas which, in today's terms, equates to almost one hundred and sixty pounds. Their formula worked, as the first Games at the Home Farm,

Portree, apparently attracted a crowd of just under three thousand. Many of them surely went to watch the great Donald Dinnie compete, himself undoubtedly lured there by the amount of prize money on offer. It was a profitable afternoon for Dinnie who earned £11.19.6, or £11.98, for his efforts, about £650 in today's terms. But his participation was not without incident as, following his defeat in the first race by the local exciseman Macaulay, he protested that his rival had cut in front of him on one of the bends. The Committee, anxious not to upset the great man, ordered a re-run of the race, much to the annoyance of Macaulay who refused to compete.

In 1893 the Games moved to their present venue, known as The Lump or 'The Fancy Hill'. Situated above Portree, overlooking Portree Bay and offering excellent views of the Cuillins, this had been the site of an old quarry which was grassed over and formed a natural amphitheatre for spectators to position themselves. It can also lay claim to being one of the most picturesque Games settings in the whole country. Through the years the Games have prospered, attracting all the great heavies from different generations, including, apart from Dinnie, AA Cameron of Spean Bridge in the early twentieth century, George Clark from 1925 to 1960 (actually winning several events in 1959 at age fifty two), down to Bill and Arthur who had many close contests here.

Another big Games held on a Thursday in late August regularly frequented by Bill was the **Argyllshire Gathering** at Oban, presided over by the Duke of Argyll. This often entailed an overnight stay for Bill the previous night at Lochearnhead Hotel, where the famous heavy Ewen Cameron was a generous host. Bill sometimes wondered if in being such a generous host Ewen had an eye on his own prospects on the field the next day!

The Games came into existence after a meeting was held in the Argyll Arms Hotel at Inveraray on 25th August 1871 at which it was agreed, 'that it was desirable there should in future be an Annual Gathering of the Gentry of the County of Argyll for social purposes. . .' It was further agreed that 'a small acting committee composed of landowners in the county be formed for promotion of the Gathering. . .' In 1872 it was decided that a Ball be held annually for which gents' tickets would cost a guinea (£1.05p) and ladies' half a guinea. The Marquis of Lorne was elected President of the Gathering in 1872, since when there have been only four other Presidents including the present one, all Dukes of Argyll from the tenth to the thirteenth Duke.

The first Games were held in 1873 and recorded a profit of £34, about £1800 in today's terms. By 1878 the best heavies in Scotland were competing at Oban, with Dinnie, George Davidson of Drumoak and Kenneth McRae of Beauly all featuring in the prize lists. By 1880 the railway had reached Oban making the Games more accessible to tourists. Maintaining appropriate etiquette, however, was important as it was recorded in 1895 that 'a Mr Bullough

March to the Games 2006

The Duke of Argyll leads the March to the Games at Oban

was requested to leave the Ball as he had on a jacket instead of a tailcoat'! It appears that after World War I the Games were spread over two days, with events open to servicemen and local amateur athletes on the first day, and the second day devoted to events for professional athletes. In the 1930s top heavy Ed Anderson, the Dundee policeman, broke a number of records for which he was awarded a special medal by the Committee. The Gathering continues to have strong associations with the county's landed gentry and the Annual Ball remains an important fixture in the Argyllshire social calendar. In the late sixties and early seventies Prince Charles and Princess Anne attended the Gathering. At one end of the Games field a marquee and enclosure area is reserved for Members of the Gathering whose heraldic banners fly overhead, sixteen in total, representing old Argyllshire families. The hill on the adjoining side, which is always covered by spectators on Games day, houses a flagstaff flying a banner which is a reproduction of the clan rallying standard of the Dukes of Argyll and their predecessors as head of Clan Campbell.

Three important Games were usually held on the last Saturday of August – **Invergordon**, **Lonach** and **Birnam**. At different stages of his career Bill competed at all three of them although latterly he did so more at Invergordon as there were eight heavy events there and they were therefore more attractive financially. Held in the lovely grounds of Invergordon Castle, courtesy of the Games' Chieftain of many years, Colonel HAC MacKenzie, they were inaugurated in 1921 and were noted for being extremely well run Games.

The heavies competed for two cups, the Robin MacKenzie Cup for caber tossing and the Colonel MacKenzie of Dalmore Cup for the heavy events championship. George Clark's record here at the 56lb weight for distance set in 1933 lasted for forty years before Bill broke it.

The **Lonach Games**, held at Bellabeg Park, Strathdon, Aberdeenshire are one of the oldest and most colourful Games on the calendar. In 1823 the Lonach Highland and Friendly Society was formed, among its principal objects being '*inter alia* the preservation of the Highland Garb and as far as possible of the Celtic language; the support of loyal peaceable upright and manly conduct; and the promotion of social and friendly feelings among the inhabitants of the District.'

The Society was formed as part of the celebrations of the coming of age of John Forbes of Newe and Edinglassie, son of the most important local family of Forbes, whose war cry in the days of skirmishing clans was 'Lonach', the name of the hill overlooking the village. The first Games took place in 1836 at nearby Castle Newe, the then seat of the Forbes family, and thereafter they were held at the Haugh of Colquhonnie and for about the past fifty years at Bellabeg Park which was gifted to the Society by Mrs Thesinger of Tornasheen. Initially only Society members could compete but by the 1860s, in common with other Games, they were open to all. In 1845 the Society built its own Hall for meetings and functions and this was extended in about 1900. It has been regularly used to hold the Games' night dance which some years ago once attracted over a thousand people.

Lonach is particularly noted for 'the

traditional March of the Clansmen' – the Men of Lonach, in full Highland dress, armed with pikes and Lochaber battleaxes, and counting Forbeses, Wallaces and Gordons among their number— which begins at about 7.30 in the morning and visits each of the houses of the Gathering's main patrons in a six mile loop. In accordance with long standing custom they receive a dram at each house before making their way, mostly upright and to the accompaniment of pipes and drums, into Bellabeg Park at about one o'clock to signal the opening of the Games. This is the biggest and most colourful Clansmen's March at any Games in Scotland and is a very popular sight for tourists.

As a result of the Games' close association with the Forbes family, a deputation from the Clan Forbes Association in the USA attended in the late 1990s. Lonach was always well supported by good crowds of up to ten thousand but their profile has heightened recently through support from the well known entertainer Billy Connolly, now a local landowner. This has led in recent years to the attendance of a number of celebrities at the Games, one of whom, the actor Robin Williams, even took part in the hill race.

The **Birnam Games**, by Dunkeld in Perthshire, are the third to be held that Saturday. First staged in 1864 in a field belonging to Mrs N Campbell, they took the place that year of the nearby Dunkeld Games which were cancelled as a mark of respect for the death of the sixth Duke of Atholl. Over the following years they proved more popular than Dunkeld Games, which led to the demise of the latter in 1872. They had been established in 1822, making them one of Scotland's oldest

Games after St Fillans. An 1867 poster advertising Birnam Games listed the heavy events of, 'Putting 22lb stone, Throwing the Sledge Hammer and Tossing the Caber', each with a first prize of £2, which equates to about £110 today. The Highland Railway Company ran special trains on Games day, with the timetable being advertised on the Games posters and in 1892 an attendance of over five thousand was recorded. The venues have changed from Mrs Campbell's field to Birnam Home Park to Jubilee Park and, from 1976 onwards, the Recreation Park, the current venue. It was here in 1967 that Bill achieved one of his best ever throws with the light hammer of 147' while competing for the Rattray Cup for champion heavy.

The 'Blue Riband' of the Games season, the **Braemar Games**, always take place on the first Saturday of September and is described in the next chapter.

On the Sunday a relatively new Games are held at **Blairgowrie**, in Boyle's Field at the south end of Glenshee, which often attract a large number of the competitors from the previous day at Braemar.

On the second Saturday of September **Pitlochry Games** always took place. They were first held on 10th September 1852. This is verified by the existence of a prize of a brooch of semi-precious stone with the following inscription: 'Presented by Lady Feilden at the First Pitlochrie Games to Mr Charles Duff of Dunavourdie as the Best Player on the Highland Bagpipes, 10th September 1852.' They take place on the Recreation Ground by the river Tummel, in a pretty parkland setting.

In the figure of Sir David Butter, KCVO, MC of Cluniemore they have the longest serving Chieftain of any of the Games – he has occupied that office for sixty two years since 1946. His wife, Lady Myra, was related to Pushkin, the famous Russian author.

Bill also competed regularly here with considerable success, at one time sharing all the heavy events records with Arthur Rowe. As the last Games of the season in central Scotland they always provide a fitting finale, with massed pipes and drums, good crowds and a full programme of dancing, athletic and heavy events. It is customary for competitors to linger on the field after the end of the games having a drink and socialising together as, for many, this represents the end of the season.

It was at these games in the early 1970s that an infamous mishap occurred to well known local heavy and colourful character, Ian Brown, a farmer from Murthly. Known to his friends as 'Steptoe', due to his frequent dealings in second hand goods, Ian competed in a 'kilt' which had seen much better days. Another well known local heavy, Donald Ross, helped Ian put his 'kilt' on and assured him with a straight face that the belt keeping it up was well and truly fastened. However, after a few swings of the hammer the kilt fell to the ground, confirming Ian to be a true Scotsman, whereupon an American tourist leapt from the crowds and exclaimed, 'Say, can you do that again and I'll catch it on camera!'

That excellent all-round athlete, John Robertson of Logierait was recently honoured for having competed here for forty consecutive years, as he also did at Crieff Games. He competed in the heavy events with distinction at local level and indeed once won the Scottish under-23 caber tossing championship. But it was as a sprinter and jumper he particularly excelled, finishing runner-up on one occasion in the famous Powderhall Sprint and twice winning the 90 metre sprint there. The Games are in the family genes, his wife being Jean Swanson, the famous Highland Games dancer, and their sons Craig and Scott, noted Games runners.

The final Games of the season were the **Invercharron Games** which took place at Balblair Park, a few miles north of Bonar Bridge, usually on the third Saturday of September. These Games were first held back in 1888 but were not held during the years of the Boer War and became defunct. In their early years soldiers from the Royal Scots Greys used to attend as a special attraction, one of the events they participated in being the 'Cleaving of the Turk's Head'. This apparently involved soldiers on horseback riding past a platform with objects on it representing Turks' heads and swiping at them mightily with their swords. The Games were re-formed in 1981 and feature an opening ceremony where the Chieftain beats the targe (shield) to rouse the athletes for competition. This is said to derive from the ancient custom of the clan chief doing so prior to leading his clansmen into battle. These are small Games, usually attracting a crowd of about one thousand, but always have a good relaxed atmosphere. There is a full programme of heavy events and the champion heavy is awarded the Frew Shield.

Halkirk Games Committee 1954

Aboyne Games Committee mid-1990s (Bill's brother Edward 5th from right, front row)

6. Aboyne, Crieff and Braemar Games

Aboyne Games

The pretty village of Aboyne lies at the eastern end of Royal Deeside, largely on the north side of the River Dee, about thirty miles west of Aberdeen. Its centrepiece is the Green of Charleston, an open recreation ground in the middle of the village which hosts the annual Games. Pine and spruce clad hillsides stretch away into the distance, complementing the pretty picture Aboyne paints. It is thought its name derives from Gaelic and means 'ford of the current of running water' although it is also contended it meant 'ford of the white cattle'. Whichever version is correct it is clear the original settlement was closely linked with the River Dee, and was strategically placed at a crossing point of the river.

Although today's village dates back only to about 1670, prehistoric relics testify to human habitation here over many thousands of years. These include the nearby Tomnaverie Stone Circle, the Balnagowan 'necropolis', a collection of about one thousand cairns, and the Formaston Stone.

By the late fifteenth century Aboyne was the property of the Gordons of Huntly whose link with the community today has been perpetuated through the Chieftain of the Games since their inception, always being the Marquis of Huntly. For some years the front cover of the Games programme featured the emblem of the Gordons, a stag's head above a crown featuring the family motto, 'Bydand' ('Stand Fast'). In about 1670 Charles Gordon, the first Earl of Aboyne and son of the Marquis of Huntly, rebuilt Aboyne Castle and about the same time began to construct what became the Aboyne of today, originally known as Charlestown of Aboyne, in his honour. Gradually the village grew as a church, school and markets were established. It served the agricultural hinterland and became a regular stopping place for cattle drovers heading to markets in the south. By about 1800 an annual fair was being

Aboyne Games 1871 as depicted by the *Illustrated London News*

held and in 1859 the most significant event in its development to date occurred – the arrival of the railway. In that year the Deeside Extension Railway was built from Banchory to Aboyne and on 2nd December 1859 was opened to the public. The parish benefitted greatly. Travel became much easier, trade improved and the village expanded as commerce developed. Hotels were built to cater for tourists attracted by Deeside's royal connections. In 1866 in turn the line was extended from Aboyne to Ballater, after which it was due to be extended to Braemar but objection from Queen Victoria, protective of her privacy, put an end to that.

Many celebrities were to pass through Aboyne Station en route to nearby Balmoral including, in 1896, the ill-fated Tsar of Russia. Sadly the government of the day in the mid 1960s saw fit to dispense with the Deeside line, another victim of the infamous 'Beeching cuts'.

Sir William Cunliffe Brooks MP was a major player in the development of Aboyne into a large village and minor resort in the late nineteenth century. He was a millionaire Manchester banker and one time MP for Cheshire who, between 1888 and 1899, bought several local estates including Ferrar and Glentanar after his daughter married the eleventh

Bill Anderson throws the hammer at Aboyne Games, early 1970s

Marquis of Huntly. Latterly he resided at Glentanar House on the south side of the Dee.

Braemar Games were first held in 1832 and were given the Royal seal of approval in 1848 when Queen Victoria and Prince Albert attended, marking the beginning of continuous Royal patronage to this day. The Queen's acquisition of the Balmoral Estate, her support of the Games and her declared fondness for 'the Scottish landscape, people and culture' gave not only Deeside but Scotland a tremendous boost and helped make Scotland and all things Scottish very fashionable. As a result, tourism began to develop and patronage of the Games began to be considered highly worthy among the landed gentry, following the Royal Family's example.

Lonach Games at Strathdon had begun in 1836 while Banchory and Kincardine O'Neil (next to Aboyne) had both held Games since before 1850. Ballater, some twelve miles to the west of Aboyne, had founded their Games in 1864. It seemed that only Aboyne, among the important Deeside villages, did not have their own Games, a matter of concern to their sense of local prestige.

A public meeting was held in the Huntly Arms Hotel on 27th July 1867 which, according to the minute 'was numerously attended, Lord Provost in the chair, at which a unanimous wish was expressed to set up athletic games on the Market stance at Aboyne'. The committee formed to run the Games included 'Donald Dinnie, Birse' as well as 'Luban Dinnie, Birse', a younger brother of Donald. The Marquis of Huntly promised his full support and donated prizes to be competed for by his tenantry.

The Games were held on 3rd August 1867 with events including light and heavy hammers, light and heavy stone, caber, high and long jumps, pole vault, wrestling and four races – boys' race; 100 yards; 450 yards and a hurdle race. First prizes ranged from 15/- (75p) to £1.5/- (£1.25). The star of the first Games was Donald Dinnie, by then established as Scotland's best heavy and best all-rounder. He is credited with nine firsts and a second which earned him prize money in excess of £11, a small fortune at the time when a farm labourer's wage was about 10/- (50p) per week, and equivalent nowadays to a sum in excess of £550. His 'firsts' included the light hammer (107' 10"), the light stone (45' 7") and heavy stone (35' 5").

While some of his performances may not have made much impression today it has to be remembered that, for example, in the hammer events it is not known if the old sledgehammer head was still being used, as opposed to today's spherical head, and whether the old pendulum technique was being used as opposed to today's method of throwing with back to the direction of throw preceded by preliminary swings of the hammer in the widest arc possible. Nor did Dinnie then have the advantage of spikes on the sole of his boots to give him a solid anchored base from which to throw. However, despite all these reservations, many a heavy today would be content with an effort of 107' in the 16lb hammer which as recently as 1990 at Aboyne would have secured third place in the competition. Nor should much weight be placed on his height in the high jump (5' 1") – it was common then for Dinnie to do just enough to win to enable him to set a new record the next time, to earn more money. But his stone putting was excellent and his distance with the light stone 45'7" would have earned him first place as recently as 1984 at Aboyne, while his heavy stone mark 35'5" would have earned him runner-up spot the same year. There is no doubt this was world class putting. The AAA (British amateur) Championships did not begin till 1880 but Dinnie's light stone putt in 1867 would have won him the title by a margin of over seven feet!

There are some parallels in the background of Dinnie and Bill Anderson. Dinnie was one of ten children while Bill was one of eleven.

Dinnie was born in 1837 while Bill was born exactly one hundred years later, in 1937. Dinnie was born at Balnacraig, near Aboyne and both had manual working backgrounds, Dinnie being a stonemason while Bill was a farmer. Both turned professional in their teens and went to become, in Dinnie's case, the best heavy and all-round athlete of his era and beyond and, in Bill's case, the best heavy of all time. And they are the only Highland Games heavy athletes to be inducted into the Scottish Sports' Hall of Fame, albeit Bill is the only one in the category of Highland Games (Dinnie, for some reason, comes under the category of 'Athletics'.)

Dinnie's father, Robert, was a master mason renowned locally for his strength and all six Dinnie sons were powerful young men. In the 1851 census Robert Dinnie is recorded as living with his wife Celia at Wood Cottage, Balnacraig. He is described as a master mason employing five men. In the 1891 census he is still living at the same address with his wife, respectively aged eighty three and eighty one. Donald, like his father, became a mason and worked full-time at that career till nearly thirty. There is no doubt the heavy manual work involved developed a naturally impressive physique. At his peak Dinnie measured 6'1" in height, weighed over fifteen stones and boasted a 48" chest. He made his professional debut in the early 1850s by winning a prize of £1 in a wrestling bout. That launched a worldwide career in wrestling, heavy events and strongman events that would last till the early 1900s, despite his being well into his sixties by then.

First, he established himself as Scotland's best heavy athlete and best all-round athlete. Bearing in mind concern over the authenticity of some marks, he is credited with a best of 10.6 seconds for one hundred yards; he claims to have done a high jump of 6'1" at Turriff while there appears to be general acceptance of his having achieved 5'11" on several occasions; a best long jump of about 20' and a possible triple jump of about 44'; in the light putt he is generally credited with a putt of 49'6" on Lord Charles Kerr's bowling green at Kintoul, Perth in 1868 and, with the heavy stone, 37' at Aboyne; in the light hammer conditions regarding the implement and terrain were so variable it is difficult to gauge authenticity but there appears to be general acceptance of his having exceeded 120' while almost reaching 100' with the heavy hammer; and in the caber he was simply unbeatable. Such was his reputation he was immortalised in verse at the time:

> He's springy, elastic and light when he's running,
> Comes up to the mark in time and to spare,

His opponents can't match him or beat him in cunning,
They say, we were beat because Dinnie was there.

He also became a world renowned wrestler and stage strongman, recording outstanding dumbbell and barbell lifts, including the amazing feat when aged sixty of holding in the palm of his outstretched hand at right angles to his body a fifty six pound weight for forty five seconds. He became a full-time athlete when aged 30, undertaking several tours of North America, Australia, New Zealand and South Africa, competing in Caledonian Games and giving highly remunerative exhibitions. He was a genuine showman, well aware of his own worth, and while at his peak from about 1865 till about 1880 had a legitimate claim to be considered the world's foremost athlete. He was also a pioneer in marketing for sportsmen, his name being associated with the famous Scottish soft drink 'Iron Brew' (now 'Irn Bru'), whose label depicted him in athletic gear endorsing the product. His image also endured with soldiers in World War I nicknaming fifty pound shells as 'Donald Dinnies'. And Bill Anderson recalls in the early 1950s hearing an elderly aunt recite,

Donald Dinne frae Abyne,
Throws the hammer awfu' fine.

The Games at Aboyne appeared to go from strength to strength and their evergrowing popularity was due in part to the participation of Donald Dinnie and other top heavies of the time. Up to and including 1881 Dinnie competed on eight occasions at Aboyne; he won first prize in the heavy hammer each time, his best mark of 1867 lasting till 1896, when George Johnstone of Aberdeen beat it with a throw of 84'3"; he also won first prize in the light hammer each time, his best mark from 1867 lasting till 1890 when Johnstone again beat it with a throw of 109'6"; in the heavy stone he won first prize six times with a best of 37' in 1879. No heavy beat 37' till 1900 when the great AA Cameron from Spean Bridge threw 38'9"; in the light stone Dinnie won seven firsts; in 1876 he set a record of 46'9$\frac{1}{2}$" which stood till 1907 when Charles McLean of Fort William added a $\frac{1}{2}$". That record, in turn, stood till 1961 when Bill Anderson beat it with a heave of 47'8". But for McLean's $\frac{1}{2}$" improvement, Dinnie's record would have stood for eighty five years – a remarkable achievement.

In considering how such throwing figured in a British and world context, it should be appreciated that greater distance could usually be achieved with a spherical shot than the irregularly shaped Scottish stone used at Aboyne and other Games. In 1872 the British amateur record stood at 42'5" which increased in stages to 44'10$^1/_2$" in 1885 and to 45'3" by 1894. By 1893 a Canadian of Scots descent, George Gray, had increased the world record to 46'11$^1/_2$", marginally ahead of Dinnie's 1876 Aboyne putt but over two and a half feet short of the putt credited to him at Lord Kerr's bowling green. By 1904 Irish athlete Dennis Horgan had extended the world record to 48'10", still below Dinnie's best. It was not till 1909 that Dinnie's best was surpassed when American Ralph Rose increased the world record to 51', which would remain unbeaten till 1928. In terms of the Olympic Games, Dinnie's 1876 Aboyne putt would have secured him the gold medal in 1896, 1900 and 1908 while his 'Lord Kerr' putt would also have done so at the 1904 Olympics. The evidence therefore suggests that Dinnie was the best shot putter in the world of his era.

Donald Dinnie

Other top heavies also competed in the 'Dinnie era' at Aboyne, including his great friend James Fleming of Ballinluig, Kenneth McRae of Beauly and George Davidson of Drumoak. From then on all of Scotland's top heavies graced Aboyne with their presence, helping to maintain it at the forefront of Scottish Games up to and of course including the era of Bill Anderson. Their names read like a Who's Who of Scotland's top heavies – in the latter part of Queen Victoria's reign George Johnstone, in the early part of the twentieth century the outstanding AA Cameron and Charles McLean; in the inter war years Jim Maitland of Deskford, near Cullen; Bob Starkey of Crieff; Edward Anderson the Dundee policeman; Bob Shaw and George Clark (who spanned the Aboyne prize lists from 1926 to 1961, winning his first first prize in 1927 for throwing the 56lb weight for distance and his final first prize in the same event thirty four years later, in 1961); AJ Stuart of Glenlivet, whose 1934 light hammer record of 125' 3" endured for twenty five years till Bill Anderson broke it in 1959 and then, after World War II, still Clark and Shaw, Sandy Gray; Jack Hunter; Jock McLellan; Bob Aitken ; Jay Scott; Ewen Cameron up till the era of Bill Anderson and Arthur Rowe from 1959 onwards.

Bill Anderson's record at Aboyne Games was incomparable. In twenty nine consecutive participations between 1959 and 1987 he won the heavy and light hammer events on twenty six occasions each, creating six records in the former and seven in the latter; in the heavy stone he recorded twelve firsts and one record; in the light stone seven firsts and one record; in the caber, sixteen firsts (three being first equal); in the 56lb weight for distance, nineteen firsts and one record (in 1968 with 41'11" beating George Clark's 1932 record of 39'6"); in the 28lb weight for distance, seventeen first prizes and four records; and in the 56lb weight for height, first held in 1965, in twenty three participations, fifteen first prizes and two records. He won the Heavy Events Championship twenty three times out of twenty nine, 'losing' two to Arthur Rowe in the 60s, and four from 1979 when aged forty two and older, to Grant Anderson (twice), Hamish Davidson and Geoff Capes. Considering that he was aged twenty two in 1959 when he first competed and almost fifty on his last appearance in 1987 and that he had to compete against the best heavies of different generations over that period his was a truly formidable and, in all probability, unsurpassable record.

Apart from the period of the two World Wars, Aboyne Games have been continuously held since 1867. From their Victorian beginnings they have grown to become among the very best in the land, on occasion attracting crowds in excess of ten thousand crammed into the temporary grandstand and ringside seating. The importance of the heavy events and the heavies to their success cannot be underestimated. In the mid 1980s a survey of spectators was carried out, enquiring what was their favourite event. The majority responded, 'the heavy events'. A supplementary question asked who their favourite athlete was, in response to which the overwhelming majority stated, 'Bill Anderson'.

From initially playing host to Deeside athletes they have subsequently entertained athletes from all over Scotland, Britain, Europe and North America. For some time they have been widely acknowledged as the best Games from the athletes' perspective – even Braemar in its Braemar Annual of 1935 acknowledged that – in terms of the professional way in which they are run, the first class venue, the high standards of officiating, the meticulous record keeping and the excellent prize money on offer. And on the occasion of the first Games in the new millennium – August 2000 – they were rewarded with a world best mark.*

---

* Bruce Aitken of Auchenblae, Bob's son, threw the light hammer 156'8¹/₂", beating Stephen King's record of 153'2" at Inveraray in 1998. As observed elsewhere, an element of caution has to be exercised in the appraisal of games' records. A downhill slope at Inveraray favours the thrower while Aitken achieved his record out of competition with his own hammer which had a thin Malacca cane shaft, as opposed to the stiff unyielding Aboyne shafts. Bill Anderson's 1969 record of 151'2" at Lochearnhead was on level ground and during competition with the Games' hammer.

They have been fortunate over the years to have been served by a large, capable and experienced committee, some of whose members on occasion have exceeded forty years' service in the cause. The committee has also been flexible to change when required and on occasion innovatory. Tradition has always been a cornerstone of these Games which, for many years, were linked to the Braemar Games by being held the day before, Aboyne on the first Wednesday of September and Braemar the first Thursday. But in 1968 Braemar decided to change their date to the first Saturday of September, with the hope of attracting larger numbers, but Aboyne continued with their original date till 1979 when the date was changed to the first Saturday in August.

An important feature of the Games, still maintained, is the hoisting and flying of the various standards and banners representing, among others, the Chieftain and principal Patrons of the Games. At the opening of the Games, the national flag – the Saltire – is raised on a flagstaff at the rear of the grandstand while the long standard or 'Standing Flag' of the Chieftain of the Games, the Marquis of Huntly, is hoisted on the Green signifying, 'The Gordons hae' the guidin' o't', ie to identify the person in command, the Marquis.

The principal trophies awarded for the heavy events also underline the importance of tradition at Aboyne. The magnificent Dinnie Challenge Trophy is awarded annually to the heavy with most points in the Open Heavy events. It was presented in 1931 by his daughter-in-law, Mrs Edwin Dinnie of Brechin. Resembling a form of silver tankard it stands about eighteen inches high with a figure representing Donald on top, in kilt and vest, putting the stone. Engraved on the front of the trophy, in a column of Celtic design, is an excellent likeness of Donald and on the sides of the trophy he is depicted throwing the hammer and high jumping. Rising from its base are two silver cabers at either side reaching up to the figure of Donald on top of the trophy. The winner of the Open Heavy events also receives a replica of the Dyce Nicol medal, the medal having been donated by the Dyce Nicol family of Ballogie whose association with the Games stretches back to 1869. The Dinnie Stone Trophy, donated by Lieutenant-Colonel William Lilburn of Coull, another family with long association with Aboyne Games, is awarded annually to the winner of the light stone putt. This consists of a putting stone used by Dinnie at Aboyne from 1869 to 1881 which is mounted on a silver ring, on which hang small medallions carrying the name of each of the past winners.

The Games have played an important part in the life of the community as reflected in two features in the village, one old and the

Aboyne Games 1871 – Donald Dinnie is standing right side on to camera, left of centre, in trunks and dark top next to bearded athlete in white facing camera

other new. The old is a beautiful stained glass window in the Huntly Arms Hotel depicting a kilted hammer thrower on the Green, a most appropriate location given that the very first meeting to promote the Games was held in the hotel back in 1867. The new feature is the Millennium Gates on the Green, next to the granite fountain opposite the Huntly Arms. These were officially opened in September 2001 by the Earl and Countess of Wessex. They consist of four granite pillars, each with an ornamental granite top and two wrought iron gates fitted between them. A commemorative plaque is affixed to one of the pillars with the Gordon family crest attached to each of the gates, emphasising the link also between them and the Games. This is a community's tribute to the Games and the Green and a declaration of intent that the Games will endure for many years to come.

In which context, it is fitting to quote from a poem dedicated to the Games, written many years ago by the late Reverend David Hamilton, Honorary Chaplain to the Games:

> Then gentlemen! I give a toast
> To those who see that these are not lost
> Who revel in a homely boast o' honoured names;
> Aboyne's green sward will aye be host
> Tae Highland Games.

Crieff Highland Games

The town of Crieff, about fifteen miles west of Perth, sits on the southern slopes of the Knock Hill overlooking the Strathearn valley. It is a site of ancient settlement, vouched by the presence of prehistoric stone circles, hill forts, Pictish stones and traces of Roman camps. Nowadays it is the second biggest town in Perthshire, after Perth, with a population of about 6000 and has been an important tourist centre since Victorian times. The most likely explanation for the origins of its name is that it is derived from the Gaelic words *Croibh* (pronounce 'Cruive'), meaning a place of trees, and *Cnoc* a hill, hence 'The Knock' meaning therefore 'The hill of the trees'. But for a long period during medieval times it was known also as Drummond, in honour of the Drummond family, the Earls of Perth, who in 1491 built Drummond Castle about two miles to the south of the town, under licence from King James IV.

The name of Crieff was not completely restored till early in the eighteenth century by which time it had already acquired a rich and colourful history. What particularly defined Crieff in terms of importance was its strategic location on the boundary between Highlands and Lowlands, a natural stopping off point for travellers making their way through the numerous hill passes that lay to the north. Its location also made it a target for lawless Highlanders who would swoop down these same passes to carry off a selection of the local livestock, great numbers of whom were to be found nourished by the lush plains of the Strathearn valley. By the seventeenth century it had begun to resemble a frontier town. To combat such lawlessness a system of swift and exemplary justice had been put in place. Records show that as far back as 1443 King James II held a circuit Court of Justiciary outside the town, exercising his 'power of pit and gallows', sentencing convicted women to death by drowning in the pit and convicted men to hanging on the gallows. His power 'of pit and gallows' was later delegated to his nobles and clan chiefs who presided over courts. The famous historian Lord Macaulay, in his *History of England*, wrote of how one Highlander's cattle reiving raid had ended in failure with the arrest of the main participants and thereafter to the sight 'of a score of highland plaids dangling in a row from the gallows.' The Gallows of Crieff acquired a fearsome reputation.

Crieff's location was also important in the establishment of its cattle markets in the seventeenth century which grew to become the biggest in the country. The biggest market or 'tryst' of the year became the Michaelmas sale, held in October each year. A regular attender at that and other markets throughout the year was the legendary outlaw Rob Roy McGregor, whose principal occupation was cattle dealer – both legal and illegal. He it is who is given the 'credit' for devising the system of 'blackmail' and consequently the entry to the English language of that word. This was an early form of protection racket whereby Rob Roy and his followers would undertake not to 'lift' prized black cattle, in exchange for the cattle owner paying a tribute or 'mail' (tax) of black cattle, thus becoming known as 'blackmail'.

The famous military regiment, the Black Watch, has long association with Crieff and Perthshire. It was first raised by Charles II in 1667 and one of its principal functions then was to guard against cattle thieves, to prevent the blackmail. One theory, therefore, is that its name derived from its duty of 'watching' the 'black mail' racket.

While Crieff's cattle markets expanded and established the town as an important commercial centre they also brought problems of what would now be called 'anti social behaviour'. Such a periodic concentrated influx of Highlanders, weary from their long treks and keen to unwind before the return trek, and the company of their temporary hosts proved a combustible mix. Drunkenness, fighting and thieving were commonplace and the response of the justice system again was swift and merciless – the Gallows of Crieff were kept busy.

However, Crieff, which had been growing in importance thanks to its cattle markets, was dealt a dreadful blow in 1716. The previous year the Earl of Mar had initiated a Jacobite rebellion in Scotland, to restore the Stuarts to the throne in place of the Hanoverians, and in 1716 his troops met the Royalist army under the Duke of Argyll at Sheriffmuir, near Dunblane. Although the battle itself was inconclusive, afterwards the Jacobites retreated pursued by the Duke of Argyll. Passing through Crieff, on their way to Perth, the Jacobites set fire to the town to deny their pursuers the possibility of provisions and to delay them. As a result Crieff lay virtually in ruins till about 1731. Despite that, the cattle markets continued and it was reckoned that in the Michaelmas market of 1723, thirty thousand head of cattle were sold in one day, most of them being driven the five hundred miles south to Smithfield market in London.

The town was largely rebuilt under the auspices of James, the master of Drummond, starting with James Square, named after himself, and now the town centre. Shortly after that had been accomplished Crieff received another visit from more Jacobites, this time the supporters of Prince Charles Edward Stuart, 'Bonnie Prince Charlie', in whose name the 1745 rebellion had been instigated. On this occasion, the first day of February 1746, the Jacobites were in retreat, en route to Culloden after their ill-fated advance south to Derby, again emphasising the importance of Crieff's strategic location. Conscious of Crieff's lack of support for the cause, the Jacobites wished to set fire to the newly rebuilt town but were ordered not to do so by Bonnie Prince Charlie and his host, the Duke of Perth, formerly James, master of Drummond. Not only was he one of the few local nobles to have declared in favour of the Jacobites but he clearly had a considerable interest in denying the Jacobite troops' wish to set fire to the town he had painstakingly rebuilt.

After that near brush with disaster and the defeat of the Jacobites at Culloden, suppression of the rebels and their sympathisers was rapid and severe. As a result of the Duke of Perth's support for the Jacobites his Drummond Estates, which included most of Crieff, were forfeited to the Crown till 1784. Under Crown guardianship new industries developed: by 1750 there were five breweries and in 1763 a paper making factory was opened. In 1770 Crieff lost its major Michaelmas cattle market to Falkirk Tryst.

As with many communities, the arrival of the railway in 1856, via the branch line from Gleneagles, and in 1868, via the direct line from Perth, made a big contribution to the development and growing prosperity of the town. The latter was reflected in the founding of the prestigious Morrison's Academy in 1859. Its founder and benefactor, Thomas Morrison, had been born in Muthill, near Crieff, and after completing an apprenticeship as a mason made his way to Edinburgh where he amassed a fortune as a master builder. Also reflective of the town's increasing prosperity and importance as a holiday resort was the building of the Strathearn Hydropathic Establishment in 1868, now known as the Crieff Hydro Hotel. It was founded by Dr Thomas H Meikle whose initial prospectus stated, 'the cure of the suffering and the exhausted is specially aimed at.' Among its advertised attractions was the purity of its water supply from Loch Turret, four miles distant, and the 'Turkish, Russian and electric baths'. Crieff Hydro continues today as a prestigious hotel offering a high level of comfort and a wide range of

Bill Anderson with the Dinnie Challenge Trophy
and Bob Aitken with the Chieftain's Challenge Trophy at Aboyne Games

leisure facilities. Two years after the opening of its 'Hydropathic Establishment' Crieff held its first Highland Games, in 1870.

The first Games of the 'modern era' were held in 1819 in St Fillans, under the banner of St Fillans Highland Gathering Society, at the east end of Loch Earn, about ten miles west of Crieff. After some years they fell into abeyance and it was not till 1865 that thought was given to resuscitate them. But nothing happened till 1870 when St Fillans' neighbour, Comrie, a village several miles west of Crieff, made moves to revive the St Fillans Highland Society and to stage the Games again. This was the motivation Crieff needed to set up its own Games. Concerned that, with this move, its status as capital of Strathearn and as a growing health and holiday resort was under threat from Comrie, a number of leading citizens decided to take action.

The first Games were arranged to be held in Academy Park, Crieff, on Thursday 18th August 1870 with the associated rifle shooting competition at Bennybeg Shooting Range nearby. The Chieftain was Captain Henry E H Drummond Moray, Younger of Abercairney.

Twenty events were listed for competition including piping, dancing, running, jumping, pole vaulting, a sack race, a Best Attired Highlander competition and heavy events. The heavy events consisted of putting the heavy stone (22lb), throwing the sledge hammer and tossing the caber, with first prizes of £2 or £3 for each event. As previously noted, £2 was a sizeable sum of money then. 6d ($2^{1}/_{2}$p) entry money was required for each event and Highland dress had to be worn. The Committee showed remarkable foresight by holding 'juvenile' stone putting and hammer throwing events for those under twenty one years of age, obviously to encourage youngsters.

The Academy Park was an ideal venue, affording spectators in the grandstand, on the terrace and on the slope of Tomachrochter, known as the Knowe, an excellent view. Despite poor weather the inaugural Games appear to have been very successful. The Committee met at the Town Hall at twelve noon and, led by two pipers and the Crieff Volunteers, marched in procession to the park. It was estimated that a crowd of over four thousand had attended, who were kept entertained through the downpour by the Auchterarder Brass Band.

Bob Starkey, famous heavy of the 1920s

The 1871 Games were notable for marking the first appearance there of Donald Dinnie, who was the star attraction. He won first prizes in throwing the hammer, putting the stone, tossing the caber and high jump and was to go on to enjoy similar success at Crieff up to his final appearance in 1881. Those wins in 1871 earned him about £7.10/- (£7.50), then a very handsome sum. In 1879, as the Rector of Morrison's Academy refused the use of Academy Park for the Games, they were moved to the Market Park where they have been held ever since. A permanent grandstand was erected there in 1890 and was subsequently extended several times. This became the eye-catching focal point of the venue, spectacularly decorated with heather bunting and greenery, but sadly burned down in 1971.

Much of the success of Crieff Games can be attributed to the quality of the heavy events staged there. Everyone who was anyone in the world of Scottish heavies has competed there since 1870. Dinnie competed between 1871 and 1881 and he was followed by the other greats of the Victorian era, Fleming, MacRae, Johnstone, Davidson and thereafter, at the turn of the century, AA Cameron who dominated till the outbreak of World War I. In 1905 Dinnie re-appeared to compete in a veteran's hammer throwing competition, which he won with a mark of 101'10". If that distance is accurate it was a phenomenal throw by a sixty eight year old. In the 1920s Sergeant Major Bob Starkey, Jim Maitland ('The Deskford Giant') and police officer Edward Anderson of Dundee were the heavies who carried all before them. In 1925, for the first time at Crieff, there was held what was described as the 'Special Heavy Championship', which was the forerunner of today's Scottish Heavyweight Championship. In 1928 it staged the 'Heavywieight Championship of the World' won by Anderson with Starkey a close second. In 1930 Starkey presented the Games with the shot putt used in the 1924 Paris Olympics, scene of Eric Liddell's triumph. While there as a coach to the British team he befriended Clarence Houser the American shot putt gold medallist who gifted him the Olympic shot which the Committee still has. It was not surprising that Crieff hosted these self-styled championship events as for some years the heavies had recognised the Crieff Games events as an unofficial Scottish championship.

In 1937 a new name emerged as champion heavy – Bob Shaw – and he and Clark would dominate the heavy events till after the War. When Crieff re-started in 1950 another new champion appeared – Jack Hunter – and he went on to win it a further two years in succession. In 1950 no heavy was able to toss the first caber due to its weight – apparently it had been lying outside behind the grandstand since 1939, exposed to the elements, and had become waterlogged.

1953 was a notable year in the heavy events Championship as for the first time a local heavy won not only the local events but also the open events to secure the title. He was Ewen Cameron about whom more is written elsewhere. Sandy Gray of Leochel-Cushnie won his one and only title the next year, before Jock McLellan of Alness won the first official Scottish heavy events title in 1955. This status was achieved through Crieff's affiliating to the Scottish Games Association, the parent body formed in 1946 to promote and regulate the Games, and the Association granted a licence to Crieff to stage the championship, thus making official what had hitherto been unofficial. To maintain standards certain minimum distances were prescribed, which had to be attained by the' heavy' before he could be awarded points in the championship, eg 16lb hammer, one hundred feet and 16lb shot putt, thirty five feet, 28lb weight for distance, fifty five feet and so on.

1959 saw Bill Anderson's maiden Scottish championship victory and launched him on an unrivalled winning sequence that spanned twenty nine years, during which he never once finished out of the top three. He won it outright on sixteen occasions and shared the title twice, with Arthur Rowe. As seen elsewhere, the championship approached its zenith when Arthur Rowe appeared for the first time in 1963 and won the title. From then till about the mid seventies Bill and he engaged in a series of closely fought battles. During that period Bill won six, Arthur four and two were tied. The title changed hands only between them and only they created records during that sequence. Thereafter Bill Anderson dominated most of the 1970s with Hamish Davidson, Grant Anderson and Geoff Capes winning titles from 1979 onwards into the 80s. Bill however won in 1980 and in his last competitive appearance at Crieff in 1987, won his last title, to seal an incomparable Scottish championship record.

In the years following his retiral the title was claimed by some excellent heavies, including Capes, Eric Irvine of Edinburgh, Francis Brebner of Peterhead and George Patience of the Black Isle. But the heavies who have made most impression on the championship have been Alistair Gunn of Halkirk, with seven titles, Gregor Edmunds with four and Bruce Aitken with three.

Since 1989 Bill has been principal judge of the heavy events at Crieff. He describes his judging style as 'firm but fair', acknowledging being a stickler for the rules. And in 2003 he was greatly honoured by being invited to be Chieftain of the Games. He became only the second athlete ever so honoured, the first being his former fellow heavy, Ewen Cameron, Chieftain in 1975.

His contribution, with the other heavies, undoubtedly helped keep Crieff Games to the forefront of Highland Games in Scotland. As with Aboyne, an excellent and resourceful Committee has played a huge part in the success of Crieff. Imaginative Chieftain appointments have included not only Bill Anderson but former Prime Minister Sir Alec Douglas-Home (1965), the Duke of Atholl (1984) and Crieff native Ewan McGregor, the famous actor (2001), as well as a host of local celebrities and dignitaries. Their initiative in staging attention-drawing events began in late Victorian times and has continued to the present day with recent examples being the Golden Lions Free Fall Display team of parachutists, Lumberjacks' Displays, Eddie Kidd the World Stunt Motorcycling Champion and Medieval Jousting Pageants. While drama has been at the core of much of Crieff's history, that on offer at the Games has been of a more palatable kind than that associated with cattle thieving and the infamous Gallows of Crieff.

The formula that has served Crieff Games so well in the past – best quality heavy events, skilled organisation, a variety of special attractions, top pipe bands and an excellent arena – will undoubtedly continue to maintain Crieff as one of Scotland's premier Games.

Braemar Games at Braemar Castle, nineteenth century

Braemar Highland Games

It is no exaggeration to say that Braemar hosts the world's most famous Highland Games nor is it distorting the truth to accept that their fame is inextricably linked to their royal patronage. It is difficult to conceive of another major sporting event that has over a period of one hundred and sixty years been supported annually by its country's reigning monarch and family members.

But to ascribe Braemar's success solely to that length of royal association does not tell the whole story. Its location is ideal, sitting at over one thousand feet amid (on Games day) purple heather clad hills and mountains with the Cluny Water tumbling through the middle of the village on its way to the River Dee. It is situated at the western end of Royal Deeside and just beyond the eastern end of Glenshee over the Cairnwell Pass, the site of the formerly tortuous ascent of the infamous 'Devil's Elbow', graveyard of many a car radiator. It lies to the south of the spectacular Cairngorm mountains and to the north of the Mounth, the series of peaks stretching west from near Aberdeen that separate Deeside from the Angus Glens. Irrespective of the route taken to reach Braemar, a rewarding trip through some of Scotland's most beautiful countryside is guaranteed. Once there, the village, in its lovely elevated setting, exudes tranquillity, charm and spaciousness with its irregular dispersed layout, handsome granite buildings and immaculately tended gardens. Two large hotels, the Fife Arms and the Invercauld Arms on either side of the Cluny Water, impart hints of permanence, tradition and quality.

The Games field itself, the Duke of Fife and Princess Royal Memorial Park, near the middle of the village, is a most attractive venue, meticulously maintained, whose grass resembles a manicured lawn. It is the only 'custom-built' Highland Games field in Scotland used for no other major purpose than the annual Games. And on Games day, with some twenty thousand spectators present, it is a wonderfully atmospheric arena, with all these spectators close to the action. The intimate circular arena has a natural banking extending part of the way

Braemar Games at Invercauld House

Queen Victoria in the Royal
Pavilion at the Braemar
Games at Balmoral

Archibald Mackintosh & Alexander Mackintosh.

round, accommodating rows of ringside seating with spectators standing behind. Further round are two large temporary stands reaching skywards, next to which runs the old low covered enclosure with its wooden seats inside. Standing proudly on its own at the end of the old enclosure and on a small rise is the focal point of the arena, the Royal Pavilion. An ornate wooden structure, thatched in evergreens, garlanded with heather blooms and decorated with rowan berries, it is open fronted and surmounted by the Royal Coat of Arms, with the Royal Standard flying overhead.

Thus Braemar itself, its location and the setting for the Games, have all contributed to their success. Further explanation for this success reaches back beyond these factors and the relatively recent years of royal patronage, to draw on centuries of history and tradition. Braemar has been associated with royalty since about the eighth century when the King of the Picts, Hungus, built a timber fort called Doldencha near the site of Braemar Castle. It is believed he dedicated the first chapel to Saint Andrew in the same area where in 1241 St Andrew's Church was built, by the old cemetery near the Castle. Kenneth McAlpine, the first King of Scotland, had a royal hunting seat here, near Craig Coinnich (Gaelic for 'Kenneth's Hill') lying just south of the village. King Malcolm Canmore, who slew Macbeth at Lumphanan in 1060 some thirty miles east of Braemar in revenge for his father Duncan's murder, also had a royal hunting seat here to exploit the many deer in the nearby Forest of Mar.

Some commentators credit Malcolm with having held the first Braemar Gathering and Games. It is said that in the course of a gathering assembled for a deer hunt he staged a hill race up Craig Coinnich (1764 feet) to identify the fastest runner, in order to engage him as his royal messenger. It is even maintained that the young McGregor of Ballochbuie was the winner. Attractive though the story is, there is unfortunately no evidence to vouch it. Lending the story an air of authenticity was the fact that the original hill race in the nineteenth century did take place up Craig Coinnich till Queen Victoria put a stop to it, fearful of its possible fatal consequences for her retainers who took part. Latterly it has been revived but now takes place up Morrone (2891 feet).

Hill races certainly were held in medieval times and possibly up Craig Coinnich. Canmore did build a hunting seat, the first Kindrochit Castle (Gaelic for 'end of bridge'), near a wooden bridge over the Cluny Water, in the middle of the village. Later the second, stone built, Kindrochit Castle was erected, some of whose foundations can still be seen today near the banks of the Cluny. These date back to at least the fourteenth

Charles McHardy & John Michie, Forbes Men.

McHardy won the caber and hammer at Braemar Games held at Balmoral in 1859
for which Queen Victoria presented him with the sword and the dirk above.
Michie was a well known Lonach stone putter

century when there is record of Kings Robert II and III using the castle as a hunting lodge.

Great deer hunts continued to be popular through the centuries. They lasted several days and the noblemen and clan chiefs involved were accommodated in a number of lonchards, purpose-built lodges in the woods, equipped and colourfully decorated to the highest standards of the time. An account of a deer hunt in the early seventeenth century in the Forest of Mar demonstrates how this was a hunting trip on a grand scale,

> ... many kettles and pots boiling and many spits turning with a great variety of cheer, baked venison, roast and stewed beef, mutton, goats, kid, hares, fresh salmon, pigeons, hens, capons, chickens, partridge, moor-coots, capercailzies and ptarmigan, good ale, sack, white and claret, tent or Alicante, with most potent Aquavitae.

Braemar played host to one of the most momentous events in British history, the raising of the Standard on 6th September 1715, heralding the start of the Jacobite rebellion to restore King James Stuart, the VIII, to the throne of Great Britain. The final plans for the uprising had been hatched by a number of nobles and chiefs who had assembled under pretext of taking part in a great deer hunt at Aboyne. The Standard was raised by John Erskine, 24th Earl of Mar, known as 'Bobbin John' because of his fickle political loyalties. The Standard was raised in front of two thousand Highlanders on part of the site now occupied by the Invercauld Arms Hotel in the village, at a spot marked by a plaque opposite the hotel. During the ceremony the gilt ball fell off the top of the flagpole, which was considered a bad omen – rightly so, as it turned out. Because of the Rebellion's failure, Mar's estates were forfeited to the Crown who, in 1724, sold a large part of them, including Braemar Castle, to John Farquharson, the 9th Laird of Invercauld, ancestor of one of the Games' principal patrons of recent times, Captain AAC Farquharson of Invercauld.

Repression in the aftermath of the failed 1745 rebellion was brutal and severe and steps were taken to eradicate the Highland way of life by banning the wearing of tartan, bearing arms and holding Gatherings. Military garrisons were also posted at key strategic points across the Highlands and, in 1748, Farquharson leased Braemar Castle to the government for that purpose. The castle was rebuilt, with its star shaped defensive walls, and in addition to its military duties the garrison was also engaged in the control of illegal whisky distilling which was then widespread in the area.

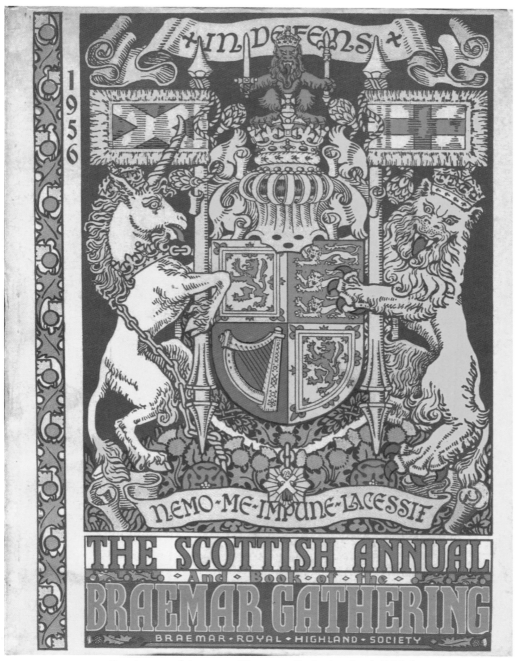

Front cover of the annual Braemar Gathering Book (1956)

In early July 1800 the first faltering steps were taken in the creation of the world famous Braemar Highland Gathering and Games. In the village on that date the first 'Wrights' Walk' took place, a procession of a number of 'wrights', whose uniform was the white linen apron worn at their daily work. These 'wrights', ie wheelwrights and 'square' wrights, joiners, had formed a loose association which met occasionally for social evenings in what was then still a very remote part of the Highlands. From that evolved the idea of an annual Walk through the village. This was a colourful occasion when the wrights wore their sashes and aprons and were accompanied by pipers. After the Walk they adjourned to a convenient spot where informal sports took place, including stone putting, as well as piping and dancing. These social gatherings and the annual Walks proved very popular and gathered momentum to the extent that it was decided to formalise matters by creating a mutual assistance society, a Friendly Society.

'The Braemar Wrights' Society' was registered as a Friendly Society in 1817. Its aims were the assistance of sick and aged members and provision of funeral benefits and annuities to widows of members and orphaned children. Early funds were used to buy oatmeal as in the three years following the Battle of Waterloo (1815) there had been extensive crops' failure, which had led to steeply rising prices. In 1822 the Society decided that all members wear Highland Dress at their meetings, which were now being held in Braemar Castle dining room. As its constituency widened, a decision was taken in 1826 to change the Society's name to the 'Braemar Highland Society', a change promoted by the Earl of Fife.

Informal sports had taken place following the Walks but in 1832 it was decided to formalise these and hold a Games. On 23rd August 1832 the first Braemar Games were held with total prize money of £5. Five events took place – putting the stone, won by John McGregor; throwing the hammer, won by Peter MacHardy; tossing the caber, won by William MacHardy; running, won by James Shevan and length of service competition, won by John Bowman. No other details were recorded.

By way of contrast, today the prize fund amounts to £12,000 while the number of events exceeds sixty. The Games may have grown tremendously since their inception but they have remained true to their origins. Today's athletics' events have evolved from that limited first programme. The guiding concept behind the first Games was the staging of a Gathering to celebrate and maintain Highland culture and traditional sports which is still the main purpose.

From such early records as survive, it is apparent in the early years that the MacHardy family dominated the heavy events. In 1838 John MacHardy of Ellenfearn, Braemar, won the 28lb stone putt with a heave of 25', as well as winning the caber. Peter MacHardy of Inverey won the fourteen pounds hammer throw, as he did in the first Games, with a distance of 87'. The 28lb stone putt event still figures in today's Games programme and is referred to as putting 'Braemar Style'. That entails the heavy having to putt the stone from a standing position behind the wooden trig board, ensuring both feet remain in contact with the ground prior to release of the stone. The size and weight of the stone make it difficult for the heavy to obtain a good hold of it and the lack of momentum from any prior movement across the throwing area, as is permitted with lighter stones, combine to make this an extremely demanding event. Another Games in Scotland where this event is held are the Glenisla Games. In 1844 Alex MacHardy is recorded as winning the stone putt, hammer and caber medals and in 1845 he set a stone putt record of 28'11".

Reflecting the ethos of celebration of Highland culture, in 1841 a new event was inaugurated at the Games of 'reading and translating of the Gaelic language'. By 1842 the standing of the Gathering and Games was such that the list of Honorary Members of the Society now included the Earl of Hopetoun, the Earl of Selkirk, the Earl of Suffolk, Lord Duncan and Lord MacDonald, among others. But within a few years a much more prestigious name than any of those was to become associated with the Gathering and Games and, in due course, contribute to putting the Braemar Games on a different plane.

On 14th September 1848 Queen Victoria, accompanied by Prince Albert and other members of the Royal Family, for the first time attended Braemar Games held at Invercauld House that year, home to the Farquharsons of Invercauld. The Society, knowing that she was due to spend a holiday at Balmoral, had invited her to attend and had fixed the date to accommodate her schedule. This was her first visit to Balmoral and she found it captivating. In her journal she recorded that on the 8th of September she had walked up a nearby hill to admire the view and 'all seemed to breathe freedom and peace and made one forget the world and its sad turmoils.' This was the start of what was to be her lifelong love affair with Balmoral and the Games. She returned to attend the Games again the following year, when she contributed to the prize list, and thereafter she attended virtually each year through the rest of her life. It can be fairly said that Victoria put Braemar Games and Deeside firmly on the map, setting a pattern of royal patronage of the Games that has continued to the present day.

1860 was also a significant year as that marked the first appearance of Donald Dinnie at the Games. He had become a member of the Society in July 1860, paying the then entrance fee of 18/- (90p) and was to remain a member for twenty years. On his first appearance he won the 28lb stone putt with a throw of 28'3", eight inches less than Alex MacHardy's 1845 record. He also won the Society medal for the same event, in a competition restricted to Society members. We next hear of him at the 1863 Games where he appears to have had a duel with yet another MacHardy, this time Charles. Dinnie won the 28lb putt with 26'3", MacHardy being third, and also the heavy hammer with 84', MacHardy finishing second. However, in the caber these positions were reversed, Dinnie only managing second to MacHardy.

In 1866 a significant change to the Society's designation occurred on 20th July, when the word 'Royal' was added to the title, which now became the 'Braemar Royal Highland Society'. This of course occurred with the full blessing of Queen Victoria. As an example of her interest in and affection for the Games, in 1869 she commissioned Sir Joseph Edgar Boehm, the famous Viennese-born sculptor, to make three solid silver figures entitled 'The Highland Games'. Each was twelve inches high and depicted local heavy athletes competing at different events: John Thompson, putting the stone; Archibald Brown, throwing the hammer and William Thompson, tossing the caber. Boehm, who obtained British citizenship in 1865, became the country's foremost sculptor and Sculptor in Ordinary to the Queen. These figures remain part of the Royal Collection in Balmoral. Apart from Dinnie other top heavies competed here in Victorian times including Fleming, Davidson and Johnstone.

The early years of the twentieth century saw the appearance of two renowned heavies, James Morrison of Glasgow, and the incomparable AA Cameron of Spean Bridge. By 1904 'AA' held three records, the light hammer at 117'10", the heavy hammer at 92'8$^1/_2$" and the 28lb stone at 32'11". That was such an outstanding putt that it endured till Arthur Rowe beat it in 1962.

After the Games had alternated between various local venues, the Society finally acquired a permanent base in 1906 when the Duke of Fife gifted the Society a twelve acre site in what was originally Auchendryne. After development work the site was named 'The Duke of Fife and Princess Royal Memorial Park' and the first Games held there on 6th September 1906 were the first to charge spectators admission.

Following World War I, Starkey, Maitland and Jock Nicolson are the heavies first to feature in the prize list. In 1926 Starkey won both the light and the 28lb putts; Maitland won both hammers with 112'10" in the light and 90'6" in the heavy. A young George Clark features for the first time in the list, with a third place in the light hammer. Maitland also won the 28lb and 56lb weight for distance events with 62'8" and 32'1" respectively. Jock Nicolson won the caber. Ed Anderson also began making his mark at this time and soon became the heavy to beat while the young Clark developed into his most formidable opponent.

About this time, first prize was £3 while a new record earned a further £1. In addition, the heavy with the most points in the heavy stone, heavy hammer, the 56lb weight for distance and caber received a gold medal.

After World War II Clark was still to the fore and in 1951 became the first man to toss the special Braemar caber, all 120lb and 19'3" of it. By comparison the Society's caber, for competition among local heavies measured 17'3" long and weighed 90lb. Apart from Clark, other heavies to enjoy success at Braemar through the 1950s prior to the emergence of Bill Anderson included Ewen Cameron, Sandy Gray, Jay Scott, Jock McLellan, Sandy Sutherland, Jack Hunter and Louis Stewart. By then prize money had increased to £6 for first while new records earned £2.

In 1952 Braemar's record attendance of 31,000 was set as spectators poured in to catch a glimpse of the new Queen Elizabeth II, who had acceded to the throne earlier that year.

Although Bill Anderson had competed at Braemar in 1956 at the beginning of his national service when he won two minor prizes, his first 'proper' appearance was in 1959. Then he made his mark by creating two new hammer records, 126'9" in the light and 102'7" in the heavy one, taking that record over 100' for the first time. He then went on to clinch his first Braemar heavy championship, thereby completing an excellent treble that season with the Scottish and Aboyne titles already won. Sandy Sutherland became the second man after George Clark to toss the Braemar special caber, thereby earning the sought after £10 special prize. The next year Bill broke Jay Scott's light stone record with a putt of 46'10" and extended his own hammer records to 109' and 130'7" in the heavy and light respectively. In so doing he notched up another championship as he was also to do in 1961 and 1962. But the headlines in 1962 were more concerned with the début of Arthur Rowe than they were with Bill's fourth consecutive Braemar title success.

Rowe followed his record breaking appearance at Aboyne the previous day with more records at Braemar, in front of a 25,000 crowd. The first record he took was the oldest surviving one at Braemar, AA

Cameron's 28lb stone putt of 1904 which had defied the attempts of many top Scots' heavies in the intervening years. Clark came very close on one occasion and others had creditable efforts but the record survived. With his third and final throw, Englishman Rowe beat it with a putt of 33'6½", 7½" beyond Cameron's mark. The announcer greeted the feat in measured tones as follows, 'Mr A Rowe who has come over the Border to show us how to putt the stone has broken the Braemar record with a putt of 33'6½". . .'

Considering Rowe's pedigree as a shot putter it may have surprised some that he could only beat Cameron's fifty eight year old record by a small margin, given that he enjoyed advantages in training, preparation and coaching alien to Cameron. On the other hand, the 28lb stone putt was extremely demanding, this was Rowe's début at the event and at that time practice throws were strictly prohibited. The following year he extended it to 36'8", a better reflection of his putting prowess.

Rowe went on to claim Bill's 1960 light stone record by putting the 16lb stone 52'10½". The press gave extensive coverage to these feats focussing on the irony of an Englishman claiming heavy records at Braemar, Rowe being the first high profile non-Scots heavy to compete and win at the Games. However, despite Rowe attracting most of the headlines Bill won his fourth successive championship, recording successes at both hammers, the 28lb weight for distance and sharing first place in the caber with Sandy Gray. From 1962 onwards Bill and Arthur were now set to lock horns each year at Braemar till 1973. In those years Bill recorded seven wins to Arthur's five. All the contests were very close and enthralled the crowds – during those twelve consecutive 'head-to-heads' at Braemar, Arthur set sixteen new records and incredibly Bill also set sixteen.

During that period only one other heavy set a new record and that was in 1973. Brian Oldfield of the USA, who had finished sixth in the Olympic shot putt final in Munich the previous year, set new records in firstly the 28lb stone, 40'7", breaking Arthur's 1970 record of 39'5", and then the light stone, 63'2", to shatter Arthur's 1968 mark of 57'9". Oldfield would go on in 1975 to set a professional world shot putt record (16lb) of 75'. Born in Elgin, Illinois, in 1945, he was persuaded to compete at Braemar by George Clark who wanted to increase competition. An excellent all-round athlete, he also won the high jump with a leap of just under six feet. Neither Bill nor Arthur knew he would be competing till he appeared at the Park to take part. The first sight Bill caught of him was from the changing tent and as he and Arthur peered out to watch Oldfield powering his way down the track in the one hundred yards sprint, 'seeming to occupy two lanes to himself,' as Bill recalls. On seeing Oldfield, Arthur apparently became rather muted as he knew his putting records would be broken and two first prizes would be heading across the Atlantic.

In both 1974 and 1975 Bill achieved a complete sweep of all eight heavy events as he decimated the opposition. In 1974 he became the first winner of the Norman Murray Challenge Trophy for winning the special Braemar caber. This was a trophy presented by the family of Norman Murray of Strichen who had been a noted local heavy in the inter war years. In subsequent years Bill often went to Santa Rosa, California, to compete in the US heavy events championship which often clashed with Braemar, reducing his Braemar appearances.

In the late 70s and into the 80s new heavies who made an impact at Braemar included Hamish Davidson, Grant Anderson, Laurence Bryce and Douglas Edmunds. Then Geoff Capes and Alistair Gunn made their marks through the 80s and in Gunn's case beyond. Latterly the Aitken brothers Bruce and Stephen, Bruce Robb and Gregor Edmunds have been well to the fore.

Although today there is no rivalry in the heavy events of the intensity that characterised Arthur and Bill's, there is still a very high level of performance. In recent years a number of participants have competed, from countries as far apart as North America, Iceland, Germany, Ukraine and Australia. There has been concern expressed about the risk of foreign heavies being seen to be taking over but unless they infringe regulations there is no way to stop them from competing, without making the event invitational only. The tradition at Braemar has always been that anyone who turns up on the day wanting to compete does so, unless in the officials' opinion he is a danger to himself and others through inexperience.

As has been seen, tradition is important at Braemar and the development of the Games over the years has been based on that sense of tradition. The Royal Family patronage has been part of that tradition and to some extent the Games have been characterised by that. But other forms of tradition have played their part. Many top heavies as far back as AA Cameron and Ed Anderson, once retired from competition, have gone on to become judges and to be appointed a judge at Braemar is considered a prestigious accolade. For the past twenty years Sandy Gray has been joined as a judge by Bill Anderson, thus maintaining Bill's long association with Braemar, while Bob Aitken and Alan Sim have also judged there.

Late 1970s –
Bill Anderson
receives the Ewen
Cameron Cup
from the Queen
as long serving
secretary John
Miller looks on

That continuing association has also been boosted by Bill's having generously gifted to the Society some one hundred and fifty trophies won by him throughout his career. It is intended that they will be put on permanent display at the Duke of Fife Park, in a centre which the Society is planning to build to house meeting rooms, displays of Braemar Games' memorabilia and an education area focussing on Highland culture and history. At present there is a small display of some Games' memorabilia in the Heritage Centre opposite the Duke of Fife Hotel, including some of Jim Maitland's cups, old Games' books and programmes and a replica of the famous Braemar special caber. But in pride of place in the centre of one room is a lifesize wax model of Bill in action throwing the hammer which succeeds in capturing his power and determination. Given his contribution to Braemar over the years it seems a fitting tribute.

Top heavy Bruce Aitken receiving a trophy from the Queen at Braemar

Alistair Gunn receiving the Norman Murray Trophy

Craig Sinclair (Drumoak) winning at Braemar

Father and son, Douglas and Gregor Edmunds

Brothers, Alistair and Murray Gunn

Arthur Rowe at Braemar, late 1960s, Geordie Charles partially visible seated behind

7. Anderson v. Rowe head to head
Bill's first games overseas

ARTHUR Rowe, having dipped his toe into the water in 1962, had submerged himself fully in 1963. Not only had he won the Scottish title but also had competed with great success throughout the circuit and it was clear that he was to become a fixture in the heavy events for years. His first full summer had been very rewarding not only financially but also socially. He and his wife Betty, whom he had first met at the Yorkshire County Sports where she competed as a sprinter, had never been to Scotland prior to Arthur's début in 1962. She recalled being impressed at how beautiful parts of Scotland were, particularly the settings of Games such as Arisaig, Lochinver, Glenisla, Durness as well, of course as Braemar and Aboyne.

By now he was earning his living as a self-employed jobbing builder in Barnsley during the winter months, which gave him the flexibility to devote his summer to the Games. In that sense he had an advantage over Bill who had to fit in his Games activity round work at his brother Andy's farm.

From his first full season in 1963 Arthur competed on the circuit effectively full-time till 1973 after which his appearances became sporadic till he stopped in about 1976, apart from a very occasional appearance thereafter. During that period to 1973 the Scottish title changed hands regularly between them with the contest regularly going down to the wire. Braemar was also the scene of great tussles, in front of enormous crowds, as was Aboyne. Elsewhere on the circuit it was a similar story. The pair of them repeatedly broke and set new records, often beating the other's mark by a small margin as the public responded to this intense Anglo/Scottish rivalry by turning up in numbers to witness their duels.

For example, prior to the Scottish championship in 1964, the two combined to set three new records at Aberdeen Games, five at Invergordon, six at Oldmeldrum and seven at Halkirk. On occasion when they competed at different games, they usually achieved clean sweeps of all the heavy events.

The stage was set for an engrossing contest at the Scottish Championship at Crieff in August and so it proved to be. The pair could not be separated and shared the title, for the first time in recent memory. Arthur won both putts, the weights for distance and height while Bill won both hammers and the caber, his better subsidiary placings in the other events enabling him to equal Arthur's points' tally. However, record breaking at Aboyne was more prolific with four being set, three by Arthur and one by Bill, with Arthur carrying off the Aboyne championship trophies.

At Braemar the next day the record breaking pattern was more even, two apiece, Arthur's in the light stone and 56lb weight over the bar, and Bill's in the two hammers. But Arthur's additional victories in the heavy stone, 28lb weight for distance and caber brought him success in the overall championship, thus enabling him to complete a tremendous clean sweep of the Scottish (shared), Aboyne and Braemar titles that summer.

Although eclipsed by Arthur in the field, nevertheless Bill had had a very good season. Thanks to the Games, he had spent six weeks in the Bahamas from early July onwards doing exhibitions of heavy events. This trip had been organised by Jay Scott and his actress wife Fay Lenore. In the party were heavies Bill, Charlie Allan and Jay Scott, two female dancers, a small pipe band and Glasgow student boxers Sandy McNeill, George McHugh and Douglas Edmunds, who were to take part in boxing exhibitions. The latter two were then also well-known amateur athletes as Scotland's top shot putters and Edmunds was later to go on to have a successful career as a heavy at the Games. (He is the father of current top heavy Gregor Edmunds.) Bill was delighted to take part as he was paid £100 per week plus all expenses to perform in this exotic location. Previously he had dabbled in minor commercial ventures, such as doing exhibitions at Oban and other holiday centres during the summer months. He had also done a television commercial for the Egg Marketing Board, showing him polishing off a plate of eggs at breakfast with clips of his lugging around milk churns on the farm and throwing the hammer at Braemar.

However, the Bahamas' venture was on a far grander scale than these previous forays into 'marketing' and was his first foreign trip in connection with the Games. Bill and colleagues were accommodated in the old grandeur of the Colonial Hotel, with its own sumptuous tropical garden. On their way in to Nassau from the airport they passed a twenty feet high billboard depicting Jay Scott in his kilt advertising their exhibition Highland Games. The format was that each evening for about an hour in an arena in Nassau, Bill, Jay and Charlie 'competed' at putting the shot, throwing the 56lb weight for height, tossing the caber and then lifting the 'manhood' stone from the ground on to a table. Good crowds, including large numbers of American tourists, attended each performance with members of the crowd being invited to try lifting the 'manhood' stone.

The trip was very successful and by the end of the six weeks Bill was in excellent physical condition, thanks to having competed daily.

This was demonstrated on his return when he went to compete at Dunbeath Games in Caithness and defeated Arthur by one point, to clinch the Achnaharish Cup for champion heavy, in the process setting three records. There was however no escaping the fact that over the season Arthur had gained the edge over Bill which made Bill even more determined. And this for the first time pointed Bill towards weight training.

Initially he received assistance from David Webster, well-known Highland Games' authority and enthusiast, and Alex Thomson, both then leading lights in the famous Spartans' Physical Culture Club in Aberdeen. Then he acquired a set of 'home-made' weights and began training with them at Greenferns. He concentrated on the large muscle groups by restricting his programme to leg squats, bench press and power cleans. Over time he built up his programme to doing repetitions with 600lb in squats while in the bench press he was doing repetitions of about 300lb. In the power clean he put the emphasis on speed of execution, to develop the power required in the heavy events, and did repetitions of about 250lb.

Gordon Forbes recalls joining Bill for these early weight training sessions at Greenferns. Their 'gym' was a cold damp farm bothy cluttered with various pieces of discarded farm equipment and without electricity, only a 'tilly lamp' for light. Using the home made set of weights at times augmented by farm weights, the two of them underwent their routines, refusing to be discouraged by what Gordon says could only be described as 'very basic' conditions. This was light years away from today's 'state of the art' gymnasia. In addition to weights he also devised a general exercise programme with skipping, burpees and other exercises which gave him an excellent general fitness base on which to build his conditioning and strength work with the weights. Bill was always conscious of the demands made on his body in the course of a full Games season when, on occasion, he could be competing several days in a row sometimes in as many as eight events per day plus, occasionally, wrestling. A good general fitness foundation was therefore essential and Bill found it stood him in good stead. Generally he used to finish the season stronger than Arthur which in part he attributed to this conditioning.

Another foreign trip beckoned before the year was over, this time to the USA and Canada. The offer to take part in this trip could not have been more welcome. One day in early May, as Bill was driving his brother's open tractor at Cowford in the pouring rain, soaked to the skin, David Webster, unannounced, appeared in the field and started waving his arms frantically to attract Bill's attention. He explained that he was invited to take part in a travelling sport exhibition in the USA and Canada later that year, called the 'Wonderful World of Sport'. That, in essence, would involve him demonstrating some heavy events in exchange for £70 per week plus expenses. As the rain lashed down and Bill sat drenched in the open tractor he reckons it took him all of two seconds to say, 'Yes!' The tour was to take place after Braemar Games for about six weeks. Other heavies also went – Jock McColl of Oban, Louis McInnes of Fort William, Jay Scott and Sandy Sutherland.

Given that all the exhibitions were in indoor arenas, the heavies were restricted to the shot putt, 56lb weight for height and tossing the caber. Apart from the heavy events, there was a wide range of sports and activities in the 'Wonderful World of Sport', from gymnastics to Thai foot boxing.

Their first show was in Utica in New York State, from where they moved on by bus to Baltimore, Montreal, Toronto, Rochester, Washington DC, Detroit, Chicago, Pittsburgh and finally Philadelphia. Bill thoroughly enjoyed travelling through North America and the sightseeing involved and was particularly interested passing through Amish country to observe their traditional agricultural practices. In Montreal they competed in an arena where George Clark had wrestled many years before and Bill chatted to some officials who could recall him wrestling with his money secreted in his trunks as he was loath to trust anyone with it. Jock MacColl considered it, 'the trip of a lifetime' in which 'Bill was a great advert for Scotland.'

For his part, Bill recalls going into some Irish bars in Baltimore with Jock, who proved absolutely unbeatable in arm wrestling competition.

Another positive from the trip was the financial aspect which, along with his earnings from the Bahamas, enabled Bill and Frances to purchase their first house later that year, in Mid Stocket Road, Aberdeen. That year also saw Bill leave farm work to go into the building trade as a 'concreter' which, apart from one brief period, he would work at till retirement in 2001.

The next two seasons saw Arthur wrest the Scottish title from Bill's grasp. In 1965 at Crieff five new records were set as Arthur pipped Bill by 25 points to 22 for the title while in 1966 two were set. But evidence that Bill's weight training was paying off came at Aboyne in 1965 when he broke his own heavy hammer record by seven feet on his way to winning the title. Meantime, three records fell at Braemar in 1965 as Bill claimed victory only for Arthur to win there the following year when one record was set.

Elsewhere, highlights of those two seasons included a compelling light hammer contest at Fettercairn in front of 6,000 when Bill eclipsed Arthur by 142'4" to 141', a series of 60 feet plus light putts by Arthur at Tobermory, Alva and Caol, a light hammer record of 145'7" by Bill at Birnam and a heavy hammer record of 118'11" by Arthur at Oban.

1965 and 1966 were Arthur's peak seasons at the Games. Many more outstanding performances were to come but these years were arguably the closest he came to 'dominating the scene'. As has been seen, the margin between success and failure was often minimal and to claim complete domination would be unwarranted. But in those years he began occasionally to beat Bill 'at his own game', ie the hammers (eg he now held both hammer records at Crieff) in addition to setting a number of records in the 28lb weight for distance event. Hitherto, he had been untouchable in the putts, as he continued to be, but had mostly had to play second fiddle to Bill in the hammers and 28lb weight events. That was now changing as he began breaking some of Bill's records in those events. Which probably explains why Bill received an anonymous letter marked 'URGENT', addressed to Bill Anderson, Athlete and Farmer, Bucksburn and postmarked 'Perth, 6th September 1966', in the following terms.

> Dear Bill,
> Thanks for all the records and entertainment you have given us for years. But please put a little bit more determination into your efforts – a little more surly, please, and less of the 'smiling boy'.
>
> You are a man now. It's been most humiliating to have a Sassenach

(Arthur Rowe) come to Scotland year after year and not only beat you but beat our records as well. <u>ALL</u> Scotland looks to you but you are <u>not</u> responding. Even the Queen and Duke are quitting. If you start beating him he will soon stay away. And other chaps (who are threatening to come from England) will stay away too. But you will only beat him if you train harder (<u>NO</u> liquor – <u>NO</u> tobacco – <u>NO</u> women) – give us a bit more of George Clark's determination and less of Henry Gray or <u>John McLennan</u> (who would have been <u>the greatest thrower in the world</u> if he put more 'devil' in it). Come on then 'Bill', 'Snap out of it'. You are a fine chap but you are also a Scot like us. And we are all watching you. Good Luck!

Arthur's progress was clearly making its mark on some Games' fans! Whoever the author he clearly had a sense of humour but also a good knowledge of the heavy events. Despite the admonitions in the letter Bill was sure that Arthur's current superiority was not attributable to any lack of training on his part or any supposed predilection for traditional vices!

The next year Bill received another of these anonymous letters, this one a poem,

Come on now Bill and show yer strength,
Wi' ilka' (each) heave and turn;
And fan (when) ye're like tae weaken, man,
Remember Bannockburn.

An' at the Hielan' Games next week
We'll a' be there, I trow (trust)
An' fat (what) a great cheer ye'll get,
For 'lickin' Arthur Rowe.

        Fae an admirer

As in 1964, Bill's Games' activities in 1965 were not confined to Scotland. He crossed the Border to Leeds and the Crystal Palace in London to give exhibitions of heavy events. And on 17th July 1965 he flew to Visby to take part in the 'Stangstorming' on the island of Gotland off the east coast of Sweden. 'The Stangstorming' was a Swedish caber throwing championship but unlike the Scots' event it was thrown for distance. The previous year Swedish caber thrower, Erik Heedin, and a colleague had been invited to Aberdeen to take part in the World Caber Tossing Championship, which Bill won. But the Swedish athletes failed to make much of an impression on the Scots caber. This was not perhaps surprising given that Swedish 'cabers' measured only about fourteen feet and were lighter and thinner than the Scots' ones. The throwing technique was also different as the athlete ran up to a trig board where he had to halt before throwing the caber almost horizontally but with enough of an angle on it to make it turn over. The throw was then measured from the trig board to where the caber came to rest. Despite having no experience of this style Bill beat off the challenge of Heedin and a number of other Swedish throwers to win their championship. Interestingly, caber tossing featured as a demonstration event at the Stockholm Olympics of 1912.

Whether or not the anonymous letters sent to Bill had anything to do with it, between 1967 and 1969 the balance of power between Arthur and Bill tilted back in Bill's favour although they were often separated only by the thickness of the metaphorical cigarette paper. In 1967 and 1968 Bill beat Arthur to the Scottish title at Crieff, on both occasions by a single point, while in 1969 the title was shared between them. A number of records again fell but mention must be made of Bill's 1969 heavy hammer of 123'5", adding 5" to Arthur's record. This was hammer throwing of the very highest order, so much so that forty years later the record still stands, the oldest surviving major Games heavy event record – a tremendous tribute to Bill especially when it is borne in mind that since then top heavies from all over the world have competed at Crieff.

During the same years at Aboyne 'normal service was resumed' with Bill emerging victorious in all three years. Although no records were set in 1967 Bill was particularly gratified to win as it was Aboyne's Centenary Games year.

However, 1968 was a different story as five new records were set up, three by Bill and two by Arthur. 1968 also was the first of three consecutive appearances at both Aboyne and Braemar of colourful American heavy, 'Big' Bill Bangert. Bangert, then well into his forties, was a millionaire who was mayor of the town of Champ, near St Louis in Missouri. He was the US national shot putt champion in 1941 and 1944 and was selected to represent his country in the 1952 Olympics at Helsinki but had to withdraw. He trained with Bill at the traditional Scots events at Greenferns before Aboyne. Despite being a veteran he performed creditably that year at Aboyne, winning prizes in the putts and the 56lb weight for height. He became a well-kent figure over these years, where his appearance always attracted much publicity.

At Braemar Arthur edged out Bill in 1967, creating a new light stone record, while both tossed the Braemar caber. That year when the Royal Party walked on to the arena to speak to some of the heavies Arthur introduced Sandy Gray to the Queen and Duke as 'the daddy of them all', referring to his having by then competed at Braemar since the early 50s. This scenario had an echo in 2006 when Sandy was being presented by the Queen and Duke with an award to mark his long association with Braemar Games when the Duke remarked, 'You've been coming here almost as long as I have.'

In 1968 and 1969 Bill prevailed. As at Aboyne, 1968 was a vintage year for records at Braemar, the first time the Games were held on a Saturday, with five new ones and one being equalled, to enthuse the 22,000 crowd. Unsurprisingly, 1968 proved a hard act to follow although two new records were managed in 1969 with Bill extending his heavy hammer record and Bill and Arthur sharing a new record in the 56lb weight for height.

Other notable performances throughout this period included Bill's light putt at Strathpeffer of 52'4"; his light hammer throw at Oban of 146'8" and 56lb weight for height at Birnam of 15'4" (all 1968). Arthur reached 15'4" in the 56lb weight for height at Luss; 83'5" in the 28lb weight for distance at Pitlochry (both 1967) and 85'6" in the 28lb weight for distance at Lochearnhead (1969).

But all those fine marks paled in comparison to Bill's performance at Lochearnhead Games on 26th July 1969. Competing against Arthur, Charlie Simpson, John Freebairn, Jim McBeath, Eck Wallace, Gordon Forbes and others in the British heavy events championship Bill achieved one of the greatest ever feats in heavy events' history when he became the first to throw the light Scots hammer in excess of 150' with a magnificent throw of 151'2". This was the culmination of a singular series of throws. First, Arthur broke Bill's existing record of 143' before Bill then responded by beating that with his next throw. Incredibly, Arthur then bettered that leaving Bill with one more throw to come. He recalls being utterly determined and (uncharacteristically) 'just going wild' with that final throw, which broke the mythical 150' barrier to reach 151'2", a new world record, the equivalent of baseball's 'shot that was heard round the world.' The impact on the turf was such that the hammer head broke off from the shaft as Bill improved his previous world best by over four feet.

Veteran judge, George Hally, not usually given to displays of emotion, was fulsome in his praise while the other judge, Charlie Balfour senior, an ex-heavy, commented, 'You'll never see the likes of that again.' Indeed, almost thirty years were to pass before Stephen King of Inveraray broke it at Inveraray in 1998, with a throw of 153'2". JJ Miller of Dollar, the famous Games commentator, repeatedly announced Bill's world record breaking feat. Not content however with that record, Bill also set a national record of 15'6" in the 56lb weight over the bar event, as well as ground records in the heavy hammer with a magnificent toss of 121'3" and in the 28lb weight for distance with 86'9". Not to be completely outdone Arthur set a new record in the heavy shot of 47'$^{1}/_{2}$" as Bill went on to clinch the title from him by three points, with Charlie Simpson third.

That afternoon ranks as Bill's greatest ever series of throwing performances at any time in his career. What makes it more remarkable is that the Lochearnhead Games were the ninth day's games in a row that he had competed in all over Scotland. The previous day's Games where Bill had competed were at Dunbeath in Caithness They finished about 5pm and that was followed by a drive of about two hundred miles to reach Lochearnhead, at a time when roads in the north of Scotland were not as good as now.

The Games the day before Dunbeath had been at Tobermory on Mull, where Bill had also competed and from Tobermory to Dunbeath involved another extremely long car trip. Conventional sporting wisdom recommended avoidance of such an exhausting schedule before championship events. Arthur, on the other hand, gave Dunbeath a miss, to rest up for Lochearnhead. Despite that, Bill thrived on lots of competition and had actually improved performance over the nine days in question, reaching his peak at Lochearnhead. One can only speculate nonetheless what he might have achieved with a more conventional build-up to that famous Saturday at Lochearnhead.

Although Lochearnhead had been the scene of intense rivalry over years between Bill and Arthur, on one occasion there they combined to great effect. At the end of one particularly wet day's games Doug Gillon, then a young reporter with the *Glasgow Herald* (now chief sports writer for *The Herald*), was unable to drive his car out of the car park as it was axle deep in mud. Bill and Arthur, with one at the front and the other at the back, lifted it clear of the mud and 'walked' it over several yards to a dry area. Doug had been convinced he was stuck there for the night.

Later that summer Bill edged out Arthur for the Glenisla Centenary Games title with new records in the hammer and 56lb weight for height.

Suitably impressed by Bill at Glenisla, a fan known only as 'Geordie' dedicated the following poem to Bill:

> Bill Anderson has everything
> Strength speed colossal size

He conquered all opponents
And collected each first prize
His back is like a barn door
His legs like oak tree trunks
He tosses heavy cabers o'er
As if they were but spunks.

During this period Bill had three foreign trips: in 1967 to Nova Scotia, Canada; in 1968 to Stockholm, Sweden, and in 1969 to Tokyo, Japan. On the 1967 trip to Canada Bill was accompanied by Arthur and Sandy Gray, the three of them staying together in a hotel in Halifax. The trip lasted a week during which they all took part in the Nova Scotia Centennial Highland Games on 27th August 1967 which were being held as part of Canada's centenary celebrations. The Games were held at the Wanderers' Ground in Halifax which were bordered by Citadel Hill, a natural amphitheatre housing thousands of spectators. Local Canadian heavies also took part but provided little opposition for Bill, Arthur and Sandy even though the caber event there was different as it was thrown for distance. Many of the local people being of Scots' descent there was a lot of interest taken in the Games and the visiting Scots heavies.

The Stockholm trip in 1968 was a promotional trip sponsored by McVitie's Biscuits, to coincide with a British export promotion there. Arthur again accompanied Bill and this time they were joined by Jay Scott and Englishman Dave Prowse, better known as a weightlifter, who had dabbled in the heavy events. Another member of the party was Scottish wrestler 'Wild' Ian Campbell. Over ten days they took part in five Games, some of which featured Swedish heavies including Erik Heedin. Apart from the usual heavy events Bill also wrestled Dave Prowse and the main Games at Solna, near Stockholm, were presided over by Princess Alexandria. Various promotional activities and sightseeing trips also took place to complete a very successful ten days.

By 1969 Bill had had the good fortune to have visited and competed in a variety of countries but the trip to Tokyo that year was a very special one. If it was not exactly a venture into the unknown, it was certainly completely different from anything Bill and his colleagues had ever previously experienced. It involved a 24,000 mile round trip, flying over the North Pole on the way out and returning via Honolulu and San Francisco. The trip was to last thirteen days, with nine being spent in Tokyo. As part of a promotional British week in Tokyo, again supported by McVitie's Biscuits, a Highland Games was to be staged on the 27th and 28th September. Accompanying Bill were fellow heavies Charlie Simpson, Charlie Allan and Dave Prowse, wrestlers 'Wild' Ian Campbell and Clayton Thomson of Glasgow, some dancers and pipers including Ian Blair from Aberdeen. David Webster was also present as an official. Their hosts were dignified and lavished good will on Bill's group but language difficulties were a barrier. In a contemporary newspaper interview Bill was quoted to the effect that they had been treated like royalty, that breakfast consisted of five courses including steaks a foot long as the 'Japanese had been told in advance of our visit that we each ate four pounds of meat a day.' While it was true that heavies did have prodigious appetites, that amount of meat was beyond even them. As on all foreign trips the heavies went everywhere in their kilts, which attracted much attention, and engaged in a number of public relations' activities aimed at promoting the Games and their sponsors.

The Games themselves took place over those two days in a central Tokyo arena, the Toshimaen Green Park, in front of members of the Japanese Royal Family including Princess Chichibu, sister of the Emperor, and Princess Margaret and Prince William of Gloucester representing the British Royal Family. A full programme of heavy events took place, with Japanese heavies competing in the shot putt, as well as highland dancing, wrestling and piping. The hosts ran the event with clockwork precision. At one stage, just as Charlie Allan lifted the caber, the pipes and drums of the Royal Highland Fusiliers were nevertheless instructed to enter the arena. As Charlie veered in their general direction with the spectators anticipating disaster, the command was heard, 'Drum Corps, Mark Time,' while the pipers continued their march and Charlie's caber landed by extreme good fortune between the pipe band and the drum corps. The whole exercise was a great success.

Prior to leaving Tokyo, Bill and his colleagues were privileged to receive an invitation to visit the leading Sumo wrestling academy of Grand Champion Wakanohama who was the holder of the sport's most prestigious trophy, the Emperor's Cup. The Sumo wrestlers not only trained at this academy but also lived there according to the very strict lifestyle enshrined in the principles of their sport. Having been shown around, one of the hosts suggested a wrestling bout between one of the Sumo wrestlers and one of Bill's party. Although the obvious candidates were Campbell and Thomson, Bill recalls wryly neither seeming particularly keen which led to Charlie Simpson volunteering. Charlie, although game, was no match for his opponent, who quickly threw him. Bill stepped forward next to take on the same opponent, all twenty seven stones of him, at Cumberland wrestling. Bill reckons he was outweighed by about eight stones but stuck manfully to his task. His opponent's bulk made lifting him difficult – giving rise to Bill's famous quote that, 'he was lifting the mannie on the outside but the mannie on the inside wisnae movin.' Just as the opponent was beginning to become complacent, Bill succeeded in tripping him and sent him crashing to the floor. Bill's upending of their man did not go down well in this centre of excellence, with the result that a bout at Sumo was proposed between Bill and their best man in an effort to reclaim loss of honour. As they lined up in the Sumo circle Bill correctly anticipated an attempted headbutt by his opponent and took evasive action. Despite the Japanese's best efforts he was unable to dislodge Bill from the circle. As his frustration grew he became noticeably bad-tempered even attempting at one stage to remove Bill's kilt. By then officials realised matters had gone far enough and stepped in to stop the bout, in the interests of all concerned. The Sumo wrestlers had not expected the level of opposition Bill had provided. However, Bill was an accomplished wrestler who won the Scottish Cumberland Wrestling Championship six times but it was an activity he was always wary of because of the risk of injury

By the end of the 1960s Bill Anderson was thirty two and in his prime as a heavy athlete. The balance of power had shifted back in his favour from Arthur. Many more good seasons lay ahead of him. That was due in part to his fierce competitive spirit but also to his rigorous training programme which now, as has been seen, included not only throwing practice but winter weight training and general physical conditioning. However it is questionable if his career was ever again to scale such heights, in terms of level of performance, as it did at the end of the sixties.

Yet Bill and Arthur's rivalry was set to continue unabated. In 1970 a marker was set down at Halkirk Games. That July afternoon a six thousand strong crowd thrilled to a classic Bill-Arthur duel in which each set three new records. As had so often been the case the outcome of the championship depended on the caber which on this occasion Bill won, to secure victory by the narrowest of margins. Other outstanding performances by Bill that summer in the lead-up to the Scottish championship at Crieff included heavy hammer throws of 122'1$^{1}/_{2}$" and 121'1" at Oban and Luss respectively while at Lochearnhead and in an exhibition at Meadowbank Stadium, Edinburgh, he reached 15'7" in the 56lb weight for height. The stage was set for an intriguing encounter at Crieff for the Scottish title.

As this was Crieff's centenary Games, Bill was especially keen to win. He did so but only after the closest of contests, his winning margin being one point. Although no records were broken they managed to break five between them at Aboyne and Braemar. Bill again clinched the Aboyne

Australia 1973 (l to r) David Webster, Gordon Forbes, Colin Mathieson, Arthur Rowe, Bill Anderson, John Freebairn and Charlie Allan

Glenisla Games, early 1970s (l to r) Ed Weighton, Charlie Allan, Hamish McDiarmid and Bill

Anderson v. Rowe head to head

Stockholm 1968
(l to r) Bill Anderson, Arthur Rowe, Jay Scott, a dancer, Dave Prowse and David Webster

Nassau 1964
(l to r) Jay Scott, Charlie Allan, Bill with 'manhood stone' and cabers

title setting a new 56lb weight for height record and also won at Braemar with new records in the heavy hammer and 28lb weight while Arthur set a new 28lb stone record and the two shared the 56lb weight for height record. That completed a highly successful summer for Bill with a clean sweep of the major titles.

Arthur was determined to restore the balance the next season and put in a hard winter's training on the weights. This paid off with some excellent performances in the lead-up to the Scottish Championship. Once more the destination of the title came down to the caber which Arthur won, to secure his first title outright since 1966. Meanwhile, Bill won again at Aboyne for the fifth year in a row but Arthur pipped him at Braemar to win for the first time since 1967. The balance had tilted back in his favour in terms of the major titles but Bill was far from despondent and been heartened by two highly enjoyable trips that year.

From 6th to 20th March he went on a promotional tour, sponsored by Grant's whisky, to Singapore, Hong Kong and Australia. For this Bill's fee was £225 plus out of pocket expenses and he had to agree to give interviews, do demonstrations and wear the kilt at all times. After a few days in Singapore and Hong Kong it was on to Australia where most of Bill's time was spent in the area of Geelong, near Melbourne. Again promotional work was involved for the purposes of which a company representative was 'allocated' to Bill to co-ordinate activities. This particular representative exhibited a significant fondness for the company's own product and took his duties to mean that a night without a bellyful of whisky was a night wasted. What was even more alarming from Bill's perspective was his insistence on driving, whatever the circumstances. However, the focal point of the trip was the Geelong Highland Games held at Queen's Park on 14th March. This incorporated the Australian Heavy Events Championship and had been organised by a Scottish émigré, Colin Mathieson. Mathieson, who had been born in Tighnabruaich and brought up in Tulliemet, Perthshire, emigrated in the early sixties to become a successful sheep farmer in Australia. He only took up the heavy events once in Australia, having been a hill runner as a youngster in Scotland, but soon progressed to become a formidable all-round heavy athlete whose strongest events were the caber (he was world caber tossing champion in 1975) and hammer. A crowd of 11,000 gathered to watch Mathieson, Billy Binks and other top Australian heavies contest their championship as Bill gave an exhibition of heavy events.

The other trip that year also took place out of season, to San Francisco for the McVitie's Games on 2nd and 3rd October. The Games were part of

Arthur Rowe, Olympic shot putter Brian Oldfield and Bill Anderson at Braemar 1973

1970s Heavy Events Rivals

Charlie Allan was another from Aberdeenshire farming stock, from Methlick, although he was the only heavy with a first class honours university degree (in economics). A noted amateur Scots hammer thrower Ian McPherson of Lairg also held that distinction. Charlie grew up in the heart of Games country, Gight Games being on his doorstep and Arnage Games nearby. There were sports held at New Deer Show and Ellon Show, both also nearby, and Oldmeldrum Sports was but a cycle ride away.

Charlie naturally started taking part in such events, winning the sum of five guineas in light events in 1954. Shortly after he also took up the heavy events and initially became known as a talented all-rounder. He recalls the ethos at the time placing emphasis on being an all-rounder at the games, youngsters being encouraged to try all the events. One afternoon he won the grand total of thirteen prizes for light events, heavy events, wrestling and the pillow fight. Generally, there was a congenial atmosphere among the competitors which he thinks declined once former amateurs and strength athletes started competing in the mid 1970s. He attributed this to their background being more single-minded about winning whereas generally the games' athlete enjoyed participation for its own sake.

Following a rugby injury he took up heavy events more seriously, making his mark by the early 60s and becoming one of the top heavies from the late 60s through to the mid 70s, winning the World Caber Tossing Chamionship in 1972. Another career highlight was winning the Chieftain's Challenge Cup at Aboyne in 1969 for the best all-round light and heavy events athlete. That latter period coincided with his doing heavy weight training for the first time. Charlie stopped competing in 1975 but has maintained a close interest in the games since then and now contributes a regular column in The Herald on agricultural matters.　　●

British Week there and featured film star Rex Harrison as special guest while Princess Alexandra and her husband, Angus Ogilvy, were present in an official capacity. The Games were held at the Polo Park at Golden Gate which had been created by an immigrant Scot, John McLaren from Bannockburn, who had reclaimed the land from wilderness. A crowd of twenty five thousand turned up to watch Bill achieve a clean sweep of all the heavy events from his rivals Charlie Allan, Charlie Simpson, Dave Prowse and a number of American heavies, including John Ross. Also present in the party from Scotland were dancer Billy Forsyth and wrestler Clayton Thomson. In the evenings on occasion Bill and his fellow heavies, in traditional dress, went down to the world famous

John Freebairn had a slightly different background from most games' athletes. John played professional football as goalkeeper with Partick Thistle while a civil engineering student at Glasgow University between 1958 and 1962. Initially he was capped by Amateur Scotland but later signed professional forms with Partick to help finance him through university. Handed a free transfer by Partick in 1962 he concentrated his sporting energies on the games' circuit from then on, competing through to the eighties and thereafter as a veteran till the present day. As a former professional sportsman the world of amateur athletics was effectively closed to him. He soon became one of the leading heavies and best all-rounders on the circuit.

John was another heavy who scarcely touched weights, only training seriously with them over the winter prior to going to Australia in 1973 with Bill and the others. Despite that, he lays claim to some excellent marks in the heavy events; about 48' in the light putt; about 120' in the light hammer, and 97' in the heavy hammer; about 74' in the 28lb weight for distance and 14' in the 56lb weight over the bar. In the light events he lays claim to 12'4" in the pole vault; over 6' in the high jump; 23' in the long jump and about 48' in the hop, step and jump. John subsequently became heavily involved in coaching amateur athletics and competing in veterans' athletics. •

Gordon Forbes, born in 1946, was one of the best hammer throwers on the circuit during the years he competed between about 1969 and 1979. Despite weighing only about the fourteen stones' mark (at his heaviest he was fifteen stones) he succeeded in generating tremendous speed which he combined with an explosive delivery. His best with the light hammer was about 140' and about 115' with the heavy hammer. Perhaps it is not surprising that he was so adept at the hammer as he began throwing a small version of it aged ten at Dalrachie, his family's farm high in the hills at the far end of Glenlivet. This consisted of a 7lb farmyard weight attached to the end of a piece of rope which he and his brother used to swing round as they played at throwing the hammer. Living conditions then at the farm were fairly Spartan and in their remote location there were few competing distractions in terms of outside interests for the boys.

As he grew up, Gordon knew of the great 1930s hammer thrower from Glenlivet, AJ Stuart of Chapelton Farm. The Tomintoul Games nearby were a major annual attraction and his father was a friend of George Clark. With that background it was inevitable that Gordon felt attracted towards the games. Gordon was also very good with the 28lb weight for distance, reaching a best mark of about 75 feet. He was one of the top heavies during his time on the circuit, which was brought to an abrupt end in 1979 after a bad shoulder injury when attempting the pole vault at Dunbeath Games.

Perhaps of all the contemporary heavies he was the one closest to Bill. They met in about 1968 through work in Aberdeen. They began to train together and thereafter travelled together over ten years to games throughout the country. Gordon's recollection of weight training with Bill has already been mentioned. He also did throwing training with him at Greenferns where he recalls throwing the hammer in a field next to the milk cows' steading. 'The grass was over knee height and often wet but eventually we trampled some of it down, walking back and forth through it. Bill used to throw the hammer in his 'wellies' there and time and time again reached between 140' and 145' with the light hammer and 120' and 125' with the heavy one. One wet night he got over 125' with the heavy one,' reminisced Gordon.

While on the circuit, their routine never varied. If staying away they always booked into the same bed and breakfast each year. If travelling on the day, which was mostly the case, they would stop at Forfar on the way back to Aberdeen for fish suppers. Once he had the temerity to beat Bill at the hammer at Drumtochty Games when he was due to stay the night with Bill in Aberdeen prior to going to another games the next day. As they left the games park, Bill turned to him with a glint in his eye and said, 'You were an embarrassment out there today, it's the camp bed for you tonight!' And as Gordon recalls, it was indeed the camp bed for him that night, with the predictable effect on his performance the next day. •

Geordie Charles was another of the farming heavies. His farm, Redmyres, was virtually next door to Greenferns and on occasion he

joined Bill and Gordon there for throwing training. A powerful man, he had built up his strength through years of work on the farm. Although not the most athletic he was a good all-round heavy whose strengths were the weights for distance and hammers. •

James McBeath of Dunbeath was an outstanding all-rounder who, as already seen, enjoyed huge success with the Chieftain's Challenge Cup at Aboyne. Born in Lewis in 1944, the film 'Geordie' caught his interest as did the local Dunbeath Games where his father competed. Local Games and Young Farmers Sports led to his participating on the circuit all over Scotland, travelling with twin Tom, local sprinter Angus Wares and cyclist Victor Polanski. From the late 1970s he placed more emphasis on the heavy events and claims best throws of 49'6" in the light putt, 138' in the light hammer and 78' in the 28lb weight. In the light events he claims best efforts of 22'6" in the long jump, 45' in the triple jump and 5'11½" in the high jump. He also competed with distinction in the USA, Australia and Indonesia and still competes today in veteran athletics. •

Fishermen's Wharf. One evening while in a German bar there, Charlie Simpson, also a talented musician, took over from the resident accordionist and proved a huge success with the clientele, earning his group free beer all night.

1972 saw Bill regain the Scottish title although again it was very close, with Arthur upstaging Bill by winning Bill's 'speciality', the light hammer, with a fine heave of 140'11$^1/_2$". As in the previous year, it all came down to the caber again but this time Bill was adjudged the winner, to clinch the title. Aboyne again fell to Bill who set a new record in the 28lb weight. This time Bill upstaged Arthur by beating him in his 'speciality', when he putt the 22lb stone 43'4" to Arthur's 42'10", to record one of his few wins at the putt over Arthur. Braemar was another classic confrontation between the two of them with the outcome hanging on the last event, the 56lb weight for height. With his last throw, Bill again rose to the occasion to beat Arthur with a heave of 14'6".

Before the 1973 season started, Bill went on his second trip to Australia, firstly again to Geelong to take part in the South Pacific Highland Games on 18th March. As these Games also incorporated the World Caber Tossing championship a number of top heavies made the trip – Arthur, Charlie Allan, John Freebairn and Gordon Forbes. David Webster went as an official and 'tour manager'. The Right Honourable Lord Aberdeen and Lady Aberdeen had been invited to be the Games' Patrons and to perform the official opening ceremony. Again Arthur's winter of hard work paid off as he won the all-round championship as well as the world caber tossing championship. The trip incorporated two other Games at Canberra and Sydney and Bill and the others did appearances for the sponsors including visits to Burns' Clubs, Caledonian Societies and the like.

With the benefit of that out of season competition behind him Bill got off to a great start on the circuit by achieving a clean sweep of all seven heavy events at the opening Games of the season, at Blackford, including an impressive light putt of 50'11". In Arthur's absence, Charlie Allan secured seven second places.

At Aboyne Games for the first time in eleven years Arthur was absent but a highly impressive debutant more than compensated although possibly his presence would not have been appreciated by Arthur himself. That debutant was American Olympic shot putter, Brian Oldfield, who had placed sixth at the Munich Olympics the previous year before turning professional. Oldfield was a tall, striking, blonde-haired individual with an enviable physique and every inch the athlete. As with

Arthur, George Clark had been instrumental in persuading Oldfield to compete at Aboyne. Oldfield, who was born in Elgin, Illinois, in 1945, went on in 1975 to set a world professional shot putt record, using the rotational technique, of 75'. The records he set on his début at Aboyne had both belonged to Arthur, the light and heavy stones. Despite no prior experience of stones as opposed to putts, he propelled the heavy stone out to 49', adding 2'2" to Arthur's 1968 record. With the light stone, he reached the phenomenal distance of 61'7", adding 3'9" to Arthur's 1966 record. This was truly world class putting. Oldfield also secured second places behind Bill in the 28lb and 56lb weights for distance events. He then turned his attention to the light events, winning the high jump with an excellent leap of 5'11" and placing in the long jump and hop, step and leap to cap a magnificent afternoon of all-round athleticism. As for his high jump it has to be kept in mind that in those days there were no landing pits provided – the athlete jumped from grass and landed on grass. However, the overall heavy events' title again went to Bill for the seventh successive year and twelfth time in total.

At the Scottish championship at Crieff Bill prevailed again over a sub-par Arthur whom he beat into second place in all the heavy events as he achieved a clean sweep. At Braemar Oldfield re-appeared, much to Arthur's chagrin and broke Arthur's two stone putting records. That sense of foreboding Bill had seen on Arthur's face as he peered out the changing tent at the awesome sight of Oldfield sprinting at full pelt had been understandable. Oldfield also won the high jump as well as placing in the sprint. Bill meantime was quietly amassing points in all events to clinch his tenth outright Braemar title.

Pitlochry Games the following Saturday brought the 1973 season to an end. Much more significantly, in real terms, it also brought to an end Bill and Arthur's rivalry. After 1973 Arthur did continue to make occasional appearances at the Games but he was no longer competing full-time on the circuit, with the result that his appearances were much reduced, his commitment less, his own level of performance down and the close rivalry with Bill to all intents and purposes was over.

It is worth examining the level and quality of that rivalry. It is no exaggeration to say that the Bill Anderson-Arthur Rowe era was the golden period of Scottish heavy events. As is commented on elsewhere, the heavy events have been graced through the years by a number of outstanding exponents who of course all had rivals. The likes of Dinnie, AA Cameron, Edward Anderson and George Clark were for the most part comfortably ahead of their rivals although the latter two, for a spell in the 1930s, had a number of close head-to-head confrontations. But their rivals in general could only inflict damage on them in one or two of the range of heavy events and such rivals did not endure long.

The rivalry between Bill and Arthur was much closer and sustained over a longer period. At their peak at any given Games each was capable of beating the other. One of the distinguishing aspects of their rivalry was that each was an extremely accomplished all-rounder, capable of top performances in all the events. Within that generality Bill had his particular strengths, the hammer throws, and Arthur his, the putts, but there was little to choose between them in the other events. Such was their quality that they were well ahead of their rivals, who it should be emphasised, nevertheless were all accomplished heavyweights. However, indicative of that gap is the fact that between 1963 and 1973 the only heavies who broke records at the major Games, Aboyne, Crieff and Braemar, were Bill and Arthur, with one exception. And that exception was Oldfield who, as we have seen, arrived at the Games with an already sparkling CV.

Of the other heavies mentioned earlier, Gray, Aitken, Simpson, Wallace and McColl continued competing throughout most of this period while Sutherland and Scott had tailed off previously. Others who came to the fore during this time included Charlie Allan, John Freebairn, Gordon Forbes, Geordie Charles and Jim McBeath. Another who showed promise was George Mackie of Laurencekirk later capped by Scotland at rugby.

In spite of such competition, during that period the Scottish championship, and the Aboyne and Braemar titles, were the monopoly of Bill and Arthur and it was a question of who was going to be third. And during that period their domination of the individual events was also virtually complete. Illustrative of that superiority are the Aboyne Games' results for 1963-1972.

In the two stone putts, Bill and Arthur occupied the first two places each year; in the hammers it was the same except in 1969, when Gordon Forbes split Bill and Arthur, and in 1971 when Arthur failed to place. In the 28lb weight again the two were first and second each year, apart from 1969 when Arthur did not place; in the 56lb weight for height, which began there only in 1965, again they were first and second each year apart from 1965 when Sandy Gray won, with Bill second; in the 56lb weight for distance again they were first and second apart from when Sandy Gray split them between 1963 and 1966 and Charlie Allan did so in 1972; and in the caber again they occupied the first two places except when Sandy Gray again split them in 1963, 1965 and 1966. All of which means that for the programme of eight heavy events over the ten years between 1963 and 1972 a maximum of one hundred and fifty six first and second places were available, of which Bill and Arthur availed themselves one hundred and forty three! That is a remarkable achievement particularly when it is borne in mind that the Crieff and Braemar statistics were very similar.

A comparison of their best Scottish Championship marks at Crieff with the winning marks there in 2008 lends perspective to the quality of their throwing. The 22lb putt was won by Aaron Neighbour of Australia with 46'7" (Arthur's record was 48'9"); the 16lb putt was also won by Neighbour with 55'6" (Arthur's record was 57'10"); Bruce Aitken won the light hammer with 138'2" and the heavy hammer with 114'6" (Bill's records were 141'8" and 123'5" respectively); Gregor Edmunds won the 28lb weight with 79'2$\frac{1}{2}$" (Bill's record was 87'2") and Neighbour won the 56lb weight for height with 15'6" (Bill's record was 15'3").

It is almost invidious to assess who of the two was better but, taking into account that whole period, there is little doubt that Bill does emerge ahead, although not by much. Arthur had particularly good years in 1963, 1965, 1966 and 1971 whereas Bill mostly had the upper hand in the other years. Of the eleven Scottish titles contested between 1963 and 1973 Bill won five, Arthur four and two were shared between them. At Aboyne Bill won nine, Arthur two, while at Braemar Bill won six and Arthur five. As has been seen, they regularly broke each other's records, often by the smallest margins. Bill thinks that their rivalry was both good and bad for the Games. The good being obvious – higher profile and increased interest in the Games. The bad he thinks was that they were so ahead of their rivals that youngsters would have been discouraged from participating. Both he and Arthur were great competitors, especially Bill, and were capable of coming from behind to pull off a winning final throw when necessary. But the fierceness of their rivalry remained firmly on the Games field and never spilled over into any form of rancour. Their mutual respect however did not extend to giving tips to each other on how to improve technique. No doubt Bill could have benefited from some advice from Arthur on shot putting and *vice versa* on hammer throwing but none was expected nor given. As Sandy Gray put it, 'Arthur coming up gart (made) Bill try a bittie harder.' Bill's presence no doubt had the same effect on Arthur.

For long spells during his time on the summer circuit Arthur had made Scotland his home. At various times he had lived near Stonehaven, at Tarland near Aboyne; in bed and breakfast accommodation with Ms Dolly Buchanan at Lochearnhead, where he was also on occasion provided the use of a caravan by Ewen Cameron. At other times he brought up his own caravan and toured it round the Games. As the years passed, work and family commitments made it more difficult for him to spend his summers full-time in Scotland which he grew to love. Arthur was a popular figure on the circuit, a gregarious *bon viveur* who enjoyed the social life after the Games. Andy Brown, stalwart Aboyne former heavy, knew Arthur well and recalls evenings after Aboyne Games being in his company in the Huntly Arms Hotel there as Arthur relished a porterhouse steak and trimmings, washed down appropriately.

Arthur's absence from the circuit was missed inevitably and for a while the heavy scene went a little flat. His occasional forays north soon dwindled to none at all as he concentrated on his family (he had three children) and developing his small building business. He remained keen on all sport and at one stage developed a particular interest in cycling. So much so that when the mountain stages of the Tour de France were on television he would station his exercise bicycle in front of the set and proceed to sweat buckets as he tried to emulate the participants. He was always wholehearted in everything he did.

Sadly, he died as a result of cancer on 13th September 2003 at the age of sixty seven.

8. History of the Games and heavy events

IGHLAND Games, in the form in which they are known today, can be traced back to 1819 when the first Games of the 'modern era' were held at St Fillans, in Perthshire. But the original roots of the Games extend back many centuries, to dates unknown. In this area fact and fiction intertwine, making it difficult to provide positive assertions.

For example, one of the folk tales from the Western Highlands describes how Conall Gulban left his home there to go off in search of adventure and the High Ruler of the place he came to asked about feats of strength of the people from whom Conall came. Conall then, according to the tale, gave an exhibition of stone throwing and hammer hurling which easily beat all the assembled company.

According to the *Book of Leinster*, published in 1150, Tailteann Games existed in Teltown, County Meath, north of Dublin, from about 1829 BC till the twelfth century AD. In addition to running, wrestling and jumping, stone throwing and a primitive form of hammer throwing took place at these Games. Legend has it that the mythical Irish warrior Cuchulainn was responsible for the development of the latter event by swinging a chariot wheel round his head before throwing it. There exists the possibility that when people from Ireland settled in the west of Scotland in the fifth and sixth centuries they brought these athletic activities with them.

It is often maintained, as seen earlier, that the Games here attribute their origin to a hill race staged by King Malcolm Canmore near Braemar, in the eleventh century. Another claim advanced is that Ceres in Fife is host to the oldest continuous Games staged in the country as they were first held in 1314 to celebrate the triumphant homecoming of their archers from the Battle of Bannockburn. Unfortunately, there is no documentation available to vouch either the Braemar or the Ceres claim. But it is known that Malcolm Canmore did have a hunting seat near Braemar and the possibility exists he did organise a hill race to enable him appoint a fleet footed messenger. Certainly hill races are a common feature of many Games and have been since at least the early nineteenth century. And it is perfectly feasible that the Ceres archers' return was celebrated with, among other things, traditional sports but which were still some way removed from being a Highland Games.

What is certain, however, is that by about this time, early fourteenth century, stone putting was a popular pastime, so much so that Edward III in 1335 issued an edict banning its practice as it was causing people to neglect archery! Walter Scott in *Lady of the Lake* (1810) Canto V, wrote,

> When each his utmost strength had shown
> The Douglas rent an earth fast stone
> From its deep bed then heaved it high
> And sent the fragment through the sky
>
> A rood beyond the furthest mark
> And still in Stirling's Royal Park
> The greyhaired sires who knew the past
> To strangers point the Douglas cast
>
> And moralise on the decay
> Of Scottish strength in modern day.

This describes how 'the Douglas' (a leading Scots noble of the time) pulled a stone from the turf and heaved it beyond the best mark of the others competing. He goes on to narrate that this occurred in Stirling's Royal Park where the mark of his throw was still visible to those who knew and such was the length of his throw that it made current Scots long for the days of yesteryear, when men of 'the Douglas' strength could be found. This as least illustrates that prowess at stone putting was highly valued. King Henry VIII was also a noted stone putter and hammer thrower and sent an envoy and party of athletes to Scotland to take on Scots in a series of contests at these events – the outcome of which is unknown.

The Scottish Highlands in medieval times were in many ways a land apart. The physical characteristics of the terrain made communication and transport difficult. Society was clan-based and the language was Gaelic. The King's writ did not run strong in these parts. Poverty was widespread and inter-clan feuds were frequent. Cattle stealing was prevalent and encroachment by clans on each other's territory was common. In this society each member of the clan was theoretically related to each other and the clan chief was the head of this extended family, with powers akin to those of an absolute monarch. The clan members owed their occupation of their property directly to him. In turn, they owed him allegiance which meant that when called to arms by him they had to respond.

The rigours of the Highlands' climate and its rugged mountainous terrain required the clansmen to be physically fit and strong in order to survive and go about their daily business. But such qualities were also very important from a military point of view as each chief wished to keep his men in a constant state of readiness for battle. One way in which this was done was the regular holding of clan gatherings – the chief would regularly summon his clan to assemble, all at the one venue. This in part would be to facilitate the conduct of clan business through meetings and discussions. Another purpose to it would be to keep the clansmen on a footing of battle readiness by engaging them in various forms of physical activity and quasi military training. Contests in running, wrestling, archery and feats of strength, such as putting the stone and throwing the hammer, would take place.

On occasions these Gatherings would involve a number of clans coming together with the various chiefs' champions competing against each other in these disciplines. The best runners would be required as messengers; accomplished archers were in obvious demand; wrestling was a useful skill for combat and the strongest men were often engaged as chiefs' bodyguards. The clans had to be in a state of constant alert to be able to deal with any threat, as alliances often shifted. As one commentator put it,

> Whensoever the clans entered into league with their enemies they would not live in such security that thereby they would suffer their bodies and forces to degenerate but they did keep themselves in their former activity and nimbleness of lives either with continual hunting or with running from the hills unto the valleys or from the valleys into the hills or with wrestling and such kind of pastimes whereby they are never idle.

In fifteenth century Lochaber there was apparently a gymnasium for teaching all sorts of athletic exercises including stone putting, hammer throwing and wrestling. This appears to have been highly structured for the time, with regulations requiring scholars to eat together at communal tables.

Deer hunts, or tainchels, as alluded to, took place frequently and provided another pretext for a clan gathering or a gathering of clans. These were often great social occasions as well as having the pragmatic aim of securing food supplies. And at some of these hunts, sporting activity took place in the form of an early version of the Games, as can be seen from the following extract from the 'Wardlaw Manuscript'. This was a social commentary of the times by the Reverend James Fraser of Phopachy, minister of Wardlaw or Kirkhill in Inverness-shire, which he began writing in 1666,

> ... in 1655 Seaforth... went to visit his friends the length of Kintail; and resolving to keep a hunting be ther way in the Forrest of Monnair, be prevailed with the Master and Tutor of Lovat to goe along with him, Captain Thomas Fraser, his brother, Hugh Fraser of Belladrom, Alexander Fraser, barron off Moniack, and with them the flower of the youth in our country, with a 100 pretty fellowes more. We travelled through Strathglaish and Glenstraffar to Loch Monnair. Next day we got sight of 6 or 700 deere and sport off hunting fitting for kings then country gentlemen. The 4 days we tarried there what is it that could cheere and recreat men's spirits but was gone about, jumping, arching, shooting, throwing the barr, the stone, and all manner of manly exercise imaginable and every day new sport; and for entertainment our baggage was well furnished of beefe, mutton, foule, fishes, fat venison, a very princly camp, and all manner of liquors. The 5 days we convoyed Seaforth over the mountain in sight of Kintail and so returned home...

In addition to the Reverend Fraser, two English gentlemen from the Inverness garrison also went on the hunt. Later they stated, 'that in all their travels they never had such a brave divertissement and if they should relate it in England, it would be concluded meer rants and incredible.'

Another type of communal gathering where sporting activity also took place was the hairst kirn or celebration held once the harvest had been safely gathered. This normally took place in autumn and was marked by a ceremonial thanksgiving, dancing, eating and drinking as well as sporting contests. This form of harvest celebration continued into the nineteenth century and one English visitor to the Trossachs, Percy Yorke, has left us this account relating to 1820,

> The ceremony over, the whole marshalled themselves into a line of procession and one of the Highlanders being a piper, of which there is almost always one with every band of mountaineers who descend at harvest time to the Low Country, he struck up a

'pibroch' of triumph. On arriving at the barn door they separated and. . . betook themselves to various amusements to pass the interval from dinner till the hour of six o'clock, the time of assembling to the kirn-supper. A party of Celts amused themselves and me, among others, by their extraordinary feats in 'putting the stone', hopping, leaping and running.'

It can, therefore, be seen that a number of the constituent events of today's Games took place centuries previously in the informal sports held as part of these various forms of gathering. What are known today as heavy events, putting the stone, hammer throwing and tossing the barr (caber), were developed and maintained through their being staged in the informal context of these gatherings. However, their practice was not confined to the context of such gatherings but also took place in more informal settings. Putting stones were often located near churchyards in order that men could practise with them on Sundays before and after the church service. However this did not always go down well with the local minister as events one Sunday in an Inverness-shire parish demonstrated. There, a new minister who was noted for his physical strength and enthusiasm for the Gospel, was displeased at members of his congregation indulging in this practice and reportedly 'pitched the stone an immense distance into the river after which he herded the men into church.' This episode may have occurred during the period when the influence of Puritanism was growing in the early seventeenth century and any form of enjoyment on a Sunday was considered Sabbath-breaking. There are echoes of this in the words of William Lithgow who wrote in 'Scotland's Welcome to King Charles',

> For manly exercise is shrewdly gone
> Football and wrestling, throwing of the stone.

Famous Victorian games' athlete and historian, W McCombie Smith (brother-in-law of Donald Dinnie) researched his family tree and discovered a forebear, John McComie of Forter, known as McComie Mor (the great McComie) who was a noted strongman and stone putter in the 1650s. Armed with private family records, he set off to trace the location where McComie Mor was known to have competed against fellow clansmen. High up on the slopes of the Mayar peak which stands 3043 feet high at the north end of Glen Prosen he found the place in question, in a flattish meadow-like area. Here there was a putting area with a stone trig and several old putting stones and indications the area had once been a small athletics arena. One of the stones weighed about thirty five pounds and Smith considered that the distance attributed to McComie

Mor with this stone of twenty six feet was realistic. Recently Gregor Edmunds and his father Douglas with others undertook a search for this area and stone for the purposes of a television programme. Using the detailed account in Smith's book they remarkably located both. Gregor had a makeshift putt with the stone reaching about 28'.

Further proof that these early forms of heavy events continued to be practised is provided by the Reverend Alexander Johnson, minister of Monquhitter in Aberdeenshire, who, writing of the mid eighteenth century, stated, 'Farm servants frequently met to exert their strength in wrestling, casting the hammer and throwing the stones.' And the Old Statistical Account for Kilchoman, Argyllshire, covering the period at the end of the eighteenth century, records that 'putting the stone was a chief amusement.'

In addition to the practice of such events, it is clear the Highlanders had for centuries held a deep appreciation of feats of strength and prowess in them was valued highly. Lying at the gate of every chieftain's house was the Clach-Na-Feart, the putting stone. The custom was that guests would be invited to throw before entering the house and the distance achieved went some way towards assessing the prestige of the guest, almost a type of initiation test. Once the guests had entered the house their servants who had accompanied them would pass the time putting the stone along with some of the host's servants.

Another variant of this was the Clach Cuid Fir, or Stone of Manhood. This was a much larger stone, often weighing about two hundred pounds, which required to be lifted and placed on a wall about four feet high. If a youth succeeded in doing this he was entitled to consider himself a man and wear a bonnet, to signal that status. Of course, the Manhood Stone was also used commonly in general feats of strength competitions but also on occasion for other purposes.

About the end of the eighteenth century in the Parish of Kilmun, Argyllshire, there was a 'testing stone', known as the 'Clachabhoisgaen', on the farm of Dergachy occupied by the Brown family, a number of whom were noted athletes. This was made of granite and was highly polished from constant use, hence its being known as the 'flashing stone' or 'shining stone'. The test required a young man to be able to lift it and throw it a certain distance and only if he succeeded in doing so was he considered fit for matrimony.

Perhaps the best known 'Manhood Stone' is the Inver Stone, so called as it came from the hamlet of Inver on Deeside, which weighs two hundred and sixty five pounds. Over the years it has been the object of much competition including a famous occasion in the early 1960s, in the Kelvin Hall in Glasgow, when during an indoor Games festival it defied all attempts by members of the crowd to lift it over a two week period. But when it featured in the Braemar Games' programme later that same decade, all the competing heavies succeeded in lifting it. Another well known Manhood Stone was 'The Puterach' which lay at the entrance to the kirkyard at Balquhidder, Perthshire, which required to be lifted chest high. A more daunting task is presented by the 'Dinnie Stones', or 'Dinnie Steens', which weigh in at about seven hundred and forty pounds. These are named after Donald Dinnie in memory of his feat in having carried them, by means of iron rings attached, across the width of the Potarch Bridge in Deeside when he was assisting his father, a master mason, carry out work on the bridge in about 1860. The stones remain at the front door of the Potarch Inn next to the bridge and again have featured in a number of staged attempts to lift them, including Sandy Gray's excellent effort, as has been noted, at the Music Hall in Aberdeen. And in 1973 a Belfast policeman, Jack Shanks, succeeded at Potarch in lifting them over a distance of seventeen feet, equivalent to Dinnie's feat, one of the very few to have succeeded in moving them. That tradition of lifting heavy stones is reflected in the programme of a number of today's Games which include this as a special event.

Therefore, for a long time before the first Games of 'the modern era' at St Fillans in 1819, Highlanders had exhibited a love of and enthusiasm for a number of different types of feats of strength. These varied feats, which incorporated the practice of some of what we know today as the heavy events, provided the template for today's Games.

But the question arises why did the Games resume then? To answer that one has to go back to the failed Jacobite rebellion of 1745 when some of the Scottish clans, for the fourth time in fifty six years, rose in support of the attempt to restore the Stuarts to the British throne, this time in the person of Prince Charles Edward Stuart, known as Bonnie Prince Charlie. Despite initial success that led to an advance as far south as Derby, the Jacobite cause died on the moor at Culloden, near Inverness, when the Hanoverian troops convincingly defeated Bonnie Prince Charlie's men in April 1746 in the last battle on British soil.

Many of those living south of the Highland Line considered the Highlanders to be little more than barbaric savages who lived in a different way, dressed in a different way and spoke in a different way while posing a continual threat to the stability of the monarchy and thus the country. In the aftermath of Culloden a wave of brutal repression followed in what were perceived to be the Jacobite strongholds, enthusiastically enforced by the Hanoverian army leader, the Duke of Cumberland, who would become known for obvious reasons as 'the Butcher'. The estates of Jacobite loyalists were forfeited and the clan system was dismantled, the chiefs being stripped of many of their powers, including their right to 'raise the clan' for military action, and converting the relationship between chief and clansmen into something more approaching the conventional landlord and tenant one. The Hanoverians had set out to smash a culture and with the passing of the Disarming Act 1746 the last piece of the jigsaw fell into place. That draconian piece of legislation prohibited the Highlanders from carrying arms, gathering in any numbers, the wearing of kilts or tartan in any form and the playing of bagpipes. As the Act made its way through Parliament a government minister described it as one 'for undressing and disarming those savages.' Breaking the law led to six months' imprisonment for a first offence and transportation for seven years for a second breach.

After a period of about twenty years the strict enforcement of this law became relaxed. One factor was that the perceived threat of the Highlanders had lessened. Another factor in part related was that many Highlanders had entered specially formed Highland Regiments in the army, which were exempted from the provisions of the Disarming Act, and had acquitted themselves particularly well in Europe and were to continue to do so throughout the American War of Independence and the Napoleonic Wars. It is reckoned that between 1740 and 1815 some eighty six Highland Regiments were formed and that in total 100,000 Scots were serving in the army.

By about the 1770s the wearing of tartan had begun to be fashionable and an appreciation of 'things Highland' was developing. An important step in this process was the formation in 1778 of the Highland Society in London whose stated aims were the preservation of ancient Highland tradition and the repeal of the law forbidding the wearing of Highland dress. Reflecting the relaxation in enforcement of the law, a Highland Gathering was held at Falkirk Tryst in 1781 and the following year the repeal of the Highland dress law was achieved when the Marquis of Graham successfully saw the repeal enacted in Parliament. That news was greeted gleefully in the Highlands when the following proclamation in Gaelic was posted at various places in the north:

Listen Men!
This is bringing before all the sons of Gael that the King and
Parliament of Britain have forever abolished the Act against the
Highland Dress that came down to the clans from the beginning of

the world to 1746. This must bring great joy to every Highland heart. You are no longer bound down to the unmanly dress of the Lowlanders. This is declaring to every man, young and old, single and gentle, that they may after this put on and wear the trews, the little kilt, the doublet and hose along with the tartan kilt without fear of the law of the land or the spite of enemies.

Soon after that, tartan became even more fashionable to the extent that in 1789 (when Bonnie Prince Charlie died an alcoholic in Rome) three of the King's sons were gifted full Highland dress outfits. More Highland Societies were formed to preserve and promote what was considered the ancient Highland culture. It was ironic that some of the symbols of the Highland way of life should be rehabilitated at a time when the old way of life itself had been destroyed in the Highlands. It was doubly ironic that those in the vanguard of this promotion included Lowlanders, who had previously despised all forms of Gaelic culture and Highland landowners who were no longer chiefs but commercial landlords.

The campaign also received substantial support from Walter Scott who wrote romantically about the Highlands and Highlanders, extolling the virtues of both. As a result tourism in the Highlands, previously considered virtually a no-go area, began to open up, at least for the well-to-do. The deeds of the Scottish regiments in the Napoleonic Wars, bedecked in tartans and kilts, also influenced public opinion heavily in favour of these Highland symbols.

All of these factors combined to create conditions apt for the staging of the first Games 'of the modern era' at St Fillans in 1819. These Games, and others that soon followed, combined in the one structured competitive setting the disparate facets of gatherings of various types that had taken place over previous centuries – piping, dancing, wrestling, running, leaping, heavy events, marches of clansmen, rifle shooting, Best Dressed Highlander contests and sometimes Gaelic recitals. From here on the Games were to follow substantially that format. The St Fillans' Games were hosted by the Highland Society of St Fillans which had been established by Lord Gwydin on his Drummond Estate for the purpose of encouraging 'games peculiar to the Highlands'. The annual Games were 'held in a romantic spot' believed to be by Loch Earn on the south side of the village and were attended by 'numerous noblemen, gentlemen and ladies with a large assemblage of Highlanders. . . while prizes of bagpipes, dirks and snuff mulls sent competitors home in high delight.' They were held at the end of August and after the Games a procession led by the champions and pipers marched to the Society's Hall (now the Drummond Hotel's dining room) where much wining and dining followed.

One of the ladies present at the first Games in 1819 was a Miss Wright who wrote that 'a kind of stage was erected for the dancers and forms round for the ladies to sit. We did watch some great grunting Highland men throw the putting stone.' (Some may observe little has changed.) There is what purports to be a contemporary etching of those Games and its detail is broadly in accord with Miss Wright's account.

Three years after the St Fillans Games in 1822 the transformation in attitude towards the Highlander and his culture was sealed with the visit of King George IV to Edinburgh, the first by a British monarch since King Charles II in 1651. The occasion was stage managed by Sir Walter Scott who organised a number of pageants full of tartan and Highland symbolism. At Scott's insistence, groups of 'clansmen' were brought to Edinburgh, including MacGregors, MacDonnels, Sutherlands and Campbells, and paraded before the King. The King's corpulent figure was clad in Highland dress, featuring a short kilt and pink silk tights for the occasion causing one wag to comment, 'As his visit was so brief, it was kind of His Majesty to show so much of himself to his loyal subjects.'

The King's visit and public approval of Highland dress and customs meant the wheel had now turned full circle in terms of attitude towards Highlanders and their culture. Landowners and the aristocracy were thus given more impetus to embrace tartan and other symbols of the old Highland way of life, which they did with enthusiasm.

One way in which they demonstrated this was in organising and staging Highland Games which began to proliferate. For example, the Northern Meeting incorporated Games held in Inverness in 1821. The Meeting was a form of Highland Society which had been formed in 1786 for the purpose of an 'annual week of social intercourse' among the gentlemen classes of Invernessshire and area. Dining and participating in balls as well as hunting formed the core activities. In 1822 the Games of the Meeting were held at Duncancroy in Inverness, one of the events being the 'lifting of a boulder of eighteen stones (about 250lb) over a bar five feet in height', clearly a 'stone of manhood' contest. On a more macabre note, another event consisted of the tearing of three cows from limb to limb after they had been felled and stunned by a sledge hammer.

Dunkeld Games were held for the first time in 1822 and Bridge of Tilt Games at Blair Atholl in 1824, but Games were not confined to the Highlands as in the mid 1820s 'Border Games' were held at Innerleithen in Peebleshire, the St Ronan's Games. They were Highland Games in all but name as they featured among other events, 'leaping, racing, wrestling, stone heaving and hammer throwing, which took place opposite the noble old castle of Traquair'.

And in 1828 a Highland Games took place on the island of Inchkeith, in the Firth of Forth, where events included despite 'unfavourable conditions', rifle shooting, throwing the hammer, putting the stone and the hop step and leap. The engraving on the prize medals read 'The Highland Club of Scotland/*Amor Patriae*' (Love of the Native Country), an expression of the type of cultural nationalism espoused by Scott.

1832 saw a very significant event in the history of the Games with the first staging of the Braemar Games and in 1848 these Games were given the seal of royal approval with the first attendance of Queen Victoria and Prince Albert. The effect of royal patronage was very significant. Not only did it make them even more fashionable and encourage more of the landed class to support them but it began to convert them into effectively a 'British institution'. Coinciding with large chunks of the Highlands being converted into estates which catered for the British aristocracy to indulge in shooting fishing and hunting, support of and attendance at the Games came to be considered a highly desirable activity. The year after Queen Victoria's attendance at Braemar, the Scottish Society staged Games in Holland Park, London.

New Games continued to be staged and by 1855 in Aberdeenshire and Buchan alone, Games were being held at Auchterless, Banchory, Cruden, Cullen, Fiddichside (near Balvenie), Glenbuchat, Insch, Logie Coldstone, Lossiemouth, Lumphanan, Midmar, Oldmeldrum, Peterhead, Strathdon (the Lonach Games) and of course Braemar. Alongside these formal Games informal recreational activity took place in many small communities, eg in Lochgilphead, Argyllshire. where an account exists of what local men there used to do on Saturday evenings – some forty to sixty would go to 'the Wee Green' and strip to take part in a number of events, including putting the stone; the long jump; the hop step and jump and jump or shift the three stones.

There also took place at about that time in Argyllshire and elsewhere in Scotland a number of local informal type of Games. For example, in Argyllshire there were the Port Askaig Regatta and Sports (Islay); the Cullipool Gymnastic Games, connected to the Easdale Slate works; the Glenforsa and Killiechronan Games, which were restricted to tenants on the two estates and the Iona Games and Regatta. Putting the stone and throwing the hammer featured in all these Games and tossing the caber in some. Also in Argyllshire some Games began to be held as part of the

New Year celebrations incorporating the same events as the summer Games, eg at Campbeltown, Kilberry, Dunoon and Kilmartin. It was claimed that New Year Games had been held at Cot House, near Sandbank, since 1852. At the opposite end of the country, in Kincardineshire, New Year Games had been staged at Redhall near Fordoun by Carnegie of Redhall since the late 1840s and included all the heavy events, jumping and wrestling.

Meanwhile the number of formal Games continued to grow. Local nobility and landowners continued to be patrons and benefactors of the Games much to the benefit of their reputations socially. Large crowds were attracted to some Games with reports of a crowd in excess of ten thousand at Games in Montrose in the 1850s and in excess of five thousand at Oban in 1876 when Donald Dinnie was the main attraction.

The expansion in the number of Games, the advent of the railway and the availability of then substantial prize money meant that by the second half of the nineteenth century there was an established circuit of Games featuring professional heavies like Dinnie and others. Although all the Games had begun as local affairs with competitors from the neighbourhood only, competitors soon began to appear from outwith the area and from about 1860 onwards most Games were open to all comers. Conscious that professionals would dominate and discourage local participation most Games began to cater for two categories of competitor – local and open. Usually the local programme of events was more restricted and the prize money lower but it did ensure a 'level playing field' for the locals and provided incentive to participate.

So far as the heavy events themselves were concerned, they were the centrepiece of the Games from the beginning and continued to grow in popularity throughout the nineteenth century, particularly the special attraction of the caber. Putting the stone, as has been seen, had been practised for centuries and became one of the staple heavy events.

Apart from stones, a cast iron spherical shot putt, as in the standard Olympic event, was used at some Games. These were all of standardised dimensions and weight. Nowadays most Games use the latter although a number of the more traditional Games still use stones, eg Lonach, Glenisla, Aboyne and Braemar.

McCombie Smith, writing in 1891, stated there were three styles of putt, the Scottish style, the Braemar style and the Border style. The principal feature of the latter was that follow through after delivery of the putt was unrestricted, ie the athlete could cross over the trig without penalty, whereas the Scottish style required the athlete not to cross over the trig. Both these styles involved gliding across the measured area of 7'6" to the trig board before delivering the putt to build up momentum. The Braemar style was effectively a standing putt, where the putt had to be delivered without either foot losing contact with the ground prior to delivery. That style of course is still in use at both Braemar and Glenisla for putting the 28lb stone but the Border style has vanished. Nowadays some putters use a rotational technique whereby they effect a turn in the throwing area, not unlike a discus turn, prior to putting.

McCombie Smith cautioned about comparing throwing marks due to the variable ground conditions, uncertainty over exact weights of implements and variable judging – all of which are still applicable today. He also pointed out that the different nature of the implement affected the length of the throw, eg from a smooth round stone, as used at Inverness, a rough surfaced iron ball at Luss and a lead ball, with indentations for fingers, then in use at Aboyne, declaring that from throwers of equal ability the greatest distance possible would be at Aboyne, then Luss and finally Inverness, because of the stones' characteristics.

Another staple heavy event is of course the hammer throw which, like the putt, soon evolved into the light hammer (16lb) and heavy hammer (22lb). Again, like the putt it had been practised for centuries and its origins can be traced to the blacksmith's yard where traditionally young men would gather in the evenings for recreation and throw the smith's forehammer or sledgehammer. That type of hammer was still in use at the Games till about the mid 1860s but as the handles were often broken on landing, the round ball hammer, as used today, soon became universal. Through the nineteenth century a number of different styles were used. The earliest style involved turning in the throwing area before releasing, the number of turns employed seeming to vary. The last Scots heavy proficient in this style was John Tait, from a famous athletic family. However, safety concerns accelerated the demise of this style due to the number of accidents and near misses that occurred. One commentator of the time recorded,

> In throwing the hammer the practice of springing round with the body should not be allowed, more strength and address are required in the straight throw than in the dangerous display of mountebank agility which but too frequently sends the missile in the midst of a group of spectators.

There then followed the pendulum style where the heavy stood side on to the stance or trig, effected two or three swings pendulum style then released the hammer. A modification of this was the Figure of Eight style where the swings taken instead of the up and down pendulum style, described a figure eight before the hammer's release.

From that there then evolved what is essentially the modern style whereby the heavy stands with his back to the trig and swings the hammer several times in a circle round his head before releasing. It is reckoned that this style was introduced about the late 1860s. Its introduction combined with the slightly later use of longer, more flexible and slender shafts, led to a great improvement in distances as was demonstrated in particular at Aboyne from 1890 onwards.

The last significant development took place in the 1930s when AJ Stuart of Glenlivet was credited with being the first to use metal plates or spikes attached to the soles of his boots to anchor himself more effectively in the turf and secure a stronger throwing base. This innovation soon spread since when all hammer throwers have used it. The benefit has been calculated as yielding up to an extra 10% on the throw. It certainly worked for Stuart who, despite being only 5'8" and reputedly weighing only 12 stones, set a light hammer record at Aboyne in 1934 of 125'3" which lasted for twenty five years till Bill Anderson added just over three feet to it.

The caber needs little introduction as the most spectacular of the heavy events and the most iconic event of the Games. It is emblematic of them and instantly identifiable as Scottish. However, there appears to be no definitive answer as to how it started but there are several plausible explanations. One is that it was begun by forestry workers either as part of their work activity or as a recreational by-product. From the early seventeenth century, there was a considerable increase in forestry especially in Speyside. One theory is that it derived from the practice of the woodsmen having to negotiate tree trunks on to rafts to float them down river while another is it arose from woodsmen having on occasion to throw them across streams in the course of transporting them. The other theory in this context is that it began simply as a recreational activity among foresters during their breaks and developed into today's event. Another different theory is that during clan gatherings, some of which would take place in forest clearings or near forests, lifting tree trunks and throwing them started as a form of strongman exercise as part of the quasi military training. And the final theory relates to the use of tree trunks in the construction of traditional Highland houses and the manoeuvring required to put them in place.

Well known writer and Highland social historian, Isobel F Grant, writing in 1961 expressed the opinion that the origin of the event was the raising of the 'couples' in the roofs of traditional Highland houses. From medieval times to the late 1800s, the traditional Highland house was thatched, often with layers of turf. The cabers were the equivalent of roof rafters but were positioned contiguously to support the thatch material. Lending support to this theory is that these 'rafters' were actually referred to as cabers.

In similar vein the late Alec Valentine, former Scottish rugby international, wire hammer international and a top amateur Scots hammer thrower, writing in the Castle Gordon Games' programme of 1976, said, 'Caber is the name given to a strong part of a cabin as built by the Highlanders, the foundations for the floor were several layers of tree trunks interlocked at the corners as in North American log cabins – a style taken there by the Highland Clearances.'

All these theories have their advocates but perhaps the one considered most likely relates to the activities of woodsmen. Whatever the true origin a Games without a caber toss is unimaginable.

One of the most popular misconceptions about the caber is that it is thrown for distance but, as already seen, that is not so. However, in North America it was in the Victorian era thrown for distance and indeed in Nova Scotia in 1967 when Bill Anderson competed there the caber was thrown for distance. Indeed Bill remembers it featuring in some Fife Games at the start of his career and it is still thrown for distance at Ceres. McCombie Smith described throwing the caber for distance as taking place at one Games in Perthshire and as the style used in Leith (Edinburgh) 'a generation ago' although interestingly at the Highland Society of Edinburgh's tenth annual Highland Games in 1890 at Powderhall Stadium there the event was throwing the caber for distance and featured some of the country's top heavies of the time, GJ Johnstone from Aberdeen, Charles MacLean from Fort William and Alex McCulloch from Oban.

Taking advantage of a dip in the ground to land the heavy end of the caber and to do so on a piece of soft ground, in order that the caber would 'bite' and turn more easily are legitimate tactics in caber tossing. What was not legitimate and was known as a 'Fifer' (presumably as its exponents were from Fife) involved the following. Just before tossing the narrow end, which was in his grasp, the heavy slewed it out slightly to the side so that it was easier to turn because it was not perpendicular when it landed prior to turning over, as it should be, but would still fall over apparently correctly and thus give it the appearance of a legitimate throw when it was actually a foul. As this could be done quite subtly, judges had to be vigilant.

The final staple event of the heavies is weight throwing, the 28lb for distance and the 56lb for height, and at some Games such as Braemar, Aboyne, Glenisla and Mallaig, for distance. This was the last of the heavy events to be incorporated into the Games' programme and again its origins in a strict sense cannot be vouched. However, it is extremely likely that these events began in and around farms where box weights, the original type used in the Games, were readily available and farmworkers and others in the neighbourhood would challenge each other at throwing them as a recreational activity.

Bill Anderson remembers men on the farms doing 'tricks' with 56lb weights – lifting them with one finger and throwing them up in the air and catching them. And John Robertson of Logierait recalls another competition between men on the farm with 56lb weights where they would stand with two weights in front of their feet and then bend down to lift them and edge them out as far in front of them as possible.

It appears the 56lb weight for distance was the first of the three events to figure at the Games about the 1860s or 1870s. The standard box weight initially was used and heavies like Dinnie and Davidson are described as standing 'with their right foot at the stance, swinging the weight pendulum style and releasing it backwards with the right hand', an extraordinarily difficult feat. In some places two hands were permitted to be used while in Aberdeenshire a turn, probably a three quarter turn, was initially permitted. Then, as the event evolved, a full turn became the norm and a little later, mostly in Aberdeenshire and Banff, a double turn, as in the current technique, was permitted.

Writing in 1908, JJ Miller noted that the 56lb weight for distance event took place at Haddo House and Drumblair in Aberdeenshire, at Kirkcudbright, in the counties of Ayr, Perth, Fife and some places on the west coast but it was still an event whose 'adoption by (Games') Committees is very slow'. He also noted that in Aberdeenshire, Banffshire and Morayshire the 28lb weight for distance was as common as the 56lb event.

The 56lb weight for height (as a Games' event) only began in the early twentieth century and indeed at Aboyne Games not till 1965. This was probably due in the case of some games to the difficulty associated with acquiring the appropriate equipment to hold it. At Aboyne, the 56lb weight for distance began in 1924 while the 28lb started in 1925. The 56lb weight for distance featured in two Olympic Games, 1904 in St Louis, USA, and in 1920, Antwerp, where P McDonald of the USA won it with a distance of 35'10$\frac{1}{2}$", two handed style. Bill Andrson's record, single handed style, was 41'11" at Aboyne. And the event figured in the Scottish Amateur Athletic Association annual championships between 1921 and 1947, during which time the best mark was credited to D Campbell in 1933 of 34'4$\frac{1}{2}$", again two handed style.

As the nineteenth century drew to a close and the twentieth began, the popularity of the Games was ever increasing. By the start of World War I most towns and villages in the north of the country had their own Games and the annual Games Day was a huge event for the local community. For example in Buchan alone by this time, there were Games being held at Fyvie, Delgatty, Gamrie, New Pitsligo, New Blyth, Bonnykelly, New Aberdour, Rosehearty, Peterhead, Mintlaw, Maud, Ellon, Auchingatt, Slains, New Deer, Fraserburgh, Hatton, Turriff, Garmont, etc. Taking into account that at least a similar number of Games, and more in some cases, were being held throughout each of Aberdeenshire, Perthshire, Invernessshire, Cromarty, Ross-shire, Sutherland, Caithness, Angus, Fife, Argyllshire, Lanarkshire, Galloway, Dumfriesshire, the Lothians and Banffshire, several hundred per year were being staged through the country. Yet, difficult though it may be at this remove to accept, not all heavies wore the kilt while competing then and it only became universal after World War I, except at some Fife games.

In the 1930s crowds of up to 10,000 were common at Airth Games, a well established although not particularly high profile Games but one which benefitted from being held in the first week of the Glasgow Fair holiday. During that first week at least twenty Games took place, including those at Banchory, Gifford, Auchterarder, Kippen, Aberfoyle, Bannockburn, Auchtermuchty, Burntisland, Torryburn, Luss, Culross, Kirkcaldy, Taynuilt and Thornton.

Press coverage was commensurate with the level of Games' activity and most of the heavies of the period such as George Clark, AJ Stuart, Ed Anderson, Bob Shaw, Jim Maitland and George Mitchell were household names.

A critical note was struck by the famous Scottish author Neil Gunn from Dunbeath in Caithness. Writing in 1931 he lamented what he perceived as the professional or mercenary attitude of competitors that was in evidence at the Games, trailing in its wake 'cynicism and wrangling'. He thought something of the original local ethos of the Games had been lost through the number of travelling participants who appeared to be focussed more on potential winnings at the expense of upholding the finer traditions of the Games. He felt more encouragement should be given to local participants and more emphasis placed on the local identity of the Games and their importance to the local community and its way of life.

At this time rural depopulation was common as a lot of people were leaving the country to live in towns. Gunn's warnings did not affect the Games for the rest of the decade as they continued to flourish. But within a few years of the end of World War II the number of Games began to decline significantly despite the formation of the Scottish Games Association in 1946 by Tom Young. As its name suggests, this was a national association to which individual games affiliated and which acted as a loose national governing body. It enacted rules and regulations for the conduct of the heavy events and sought to introduce an element of uniformity. It soon began to publish an invaluable annual booklet containing its rules, the previous season's results, the dates and venues of the current season's games, records' lists and much other relevant information.

Perhaps, as Gunn said, failure to foster the local aspects was a factor in their decline at this stage. There were also other factors at play. A lengthy and arduous war had obviously marked a lot of people whose attitudes, outlooks and tastes had shifted. The advent of the motor car provided people with different outlets and continuing rural depopulation had a negative effect on the Games. Also, an entertainment tax on professional sport was introduced which hit a number of Games badly causing some to fold and others to turn amateur to avoid the tax, eg Strathallan Games at Bridge of Allan.

As Bill Anderson made his début in 1956 they were undoubtedly in decline but his arrival on the scene gave them a boost and raised heavy event performances to new levels. Within a few years the Games began staging a comeback. By the time he and Arthur Rowe were locked in rivalry in the early 60s healthy crowds were again the norm. Over a hundred Games are now held each year, which attract total crowds in excess of four hundred thousand. The heavy events have played a central role in that continuing success story.

9. The post-Rowe Era
foreign trips and notes on the history
of Games in North America

FROM 1974 on, with Arthur Rowe's appearances becoming very limited, Bill again enjoyed a period of great success, dominating the circuit and prize lists week in and week out. Between 1974 and 1978 he won five consecutive Scottish titles at Crieff. In addition, he also won five consecutive British and European titles. The British championship had first been staged at Lochearnhead in the mid sixties while the European championship was first held at Dundee several years later and both continued to be staged at these venues. Although they did not carry the same prestige as the Scottish championship they were still worthy titles and to complete a hat trick of all these titles in five consecutive years was not only an outstanding and unique achievement but again served to demonstrate Bill's utter dominance.

Underlining that dominance were his successes at Aboyne during those years when he won the championship each year. In 1974 and 1977 he had a clean sweep of all the heavy events while in 1975 and 1976 he won seven out of eight and in 1978, six out of eight. At Braemar in 1974 and 1975 he achieved a clean sweep of all the heavy events including the special Braemar caber, thereby becoming the first winner of the Norman Murray Memorial trophy awarded for that event. Doubtless his overriding success at Braemar would have continued had he not gone to the United States from 1976 onwards to compete in the US heavy events' championship at Santa Rosa, California, whose staging usually clashed with Braemar. Not content with sweeping the boards in Scotland, Bill proceeded to do so in America where for each of the years to 1978 at Santa Rosa he won the US heavy events title.

In terms of accumulation of titles, this was the most prolific period of Bill's career, despite the fact that by the end of the 1978 season he was

Heavies at Newburgh Games 1978 (rear l to r) W Henderson, Charlie Balfour, Ed Weighton; (front,l to r,) John Freebairn, Willie Robertson and Laurie Bryce

approaching the age of forty one, a stage at which most top sportsmen are happy to settle for some leisure. Even for a young man the heavy events were extremely physically demanding, not only because of their very nature but also because between six and eight took place at each Games. If one factors into the equation that a heavy athlete on the circuit would compete in about thirty Games per year and, in Bill's case had been doing so for twenty years by 1978, then some insight can be gained into the accumulative physical demands and the wear and tear imposed on the body.

While the heavy events could never be considered a young man's game, and there were a number of examples of heavies competing well into their forties, there was little doubt, in general, that by the age of forty, the heavy's peak had passed and the body was emitting tell-tale signs. Therefore, the level of performance attained by Bill during those years makes it even more commendable. Particularly when it is taken into account that he was not spending his life away from the Games' field sitting behind a desk but instead was engaged in heavy manual work for construction companies, mostly involved in concrete laying. During this period his best performances did dip a little but were still highly creditable. He achieved over 140' in the light hammer; over 120' in the heavy hammer; over 50' in the shot putt; over 15' in the 56lb weight for height; over 80' in the 28lb weight for distance and dominated in the caber, winning the world caber title in 1974.

Critics may ask whether this purple patch of success for Bill was due to Rowe's effectively no longer being a presence and consequently there being no real competition. The answer to that would be a resounding negative. As already seen, Bill had already begun to edge clearly ahead of Arthur before 1974 and continued to do so in their occasional meetings during 1974 and subsequently. And indeed, far from there being less competition, Bill was having to deal with increased and quality competition, at any rate from 1975 onwards.

1975 was to prove a pivotal year in the history of the development of the heavy events. It formed a bridge between the old and the new as that year three Scottish amateur heavy athletes of considerable pedigree turned professional at the same time, to join the Games' circuit. They were Laurence Bryce of Perth, Douglas Edmunds of Glasgow and Willie Robertson of Kirkliston, West Lothian. What made this development particularly significant was that previously only one noted amateur had 'switched codes' to join the professional circuit, Arthur Rowe, and now three were doing so at the same time. What also made this significant was that these three in a sense were pioneers whose example led other amateurs to follow by switching in years to come. And the final significant factor of this development was that it heralded in a new breed of heavy at the Games, those who came from a strength athletics' background and in general from a different social background.

All three were athletes who had trained systematically with weights for years, with Bryce and Edmunds in particular having won a clutch of weightlifting titles. All had had the benefit of top level technical coaching and had applied themselves diligently over a period of time to the improvement of their technique. All had graduated through a structured system of club athletics to compete in regional and then national championships as their performance level improved. And then each tasted international competition to develop them even further.

Bryce and Edmunds were both university graduates and PhDs, although Bryce did originally come from a farming background. Robertson was a college lecturer although a stonemason by trade who also originally had a farming background. Traditionally the majority of heavies either had a farming connection or were members of the police force. Traditionally none trained with weights, their manual occupations providing ample exercise, and out of season training was an unknown concept although latterly that had changed with the advent of Arthur Rowe leading to Bill and one or two others doing weight training.

By contrast, Bryce, Edmunds and Robertson trained all year round and this in 1975 represented the beginning of a sea change in the world of the heavies. Excellent heavy and all-rounder John Freebairn thought that at about this time the atmosphere among the heavies began to change from one of general congeniality to one which was more competitive and had more edge, without ascribing responsibility specifically to any of these particular three individuals.

Ironically, with the presence of former amateurs, the Highland Games' scene was now to become more professional where out of season conditioning and training would become the norm for many. The days of the strong local farmworker turning out to compete in the heavy events at a few of his local Games, and picking up prizes, were for the most part being consigned firmly to the past. Such figures could now realistically only aspire to participating in local confined events and the prospect of a previously unknown debutant suddenly appearing in the open heavy events to claim a number of prizes, as Bill did at Alford in 1956, had now receded firmly into the past.

Of the three, Bryce had the most distinguished pedigree, having represented Great Britain several times in the wire hammer, an event in which he also represented Scotland at three Commonwealth Games in 1966, 1970 and 1974, finishing fifth, fourth and eighth respectively. He also won five consecutive Scottish titles between 1965 and 1969 and set several Scottish records. Also a useful shot putter, he was one of many prominent Scottish hammer throwers to benefit from the coaching expertise of Bob Watson, the Edinburgh University groundsman at Craiglockhart. Bryce's older brother, Hamish, was capped by Scotland at rugby at which Laurence had also apparently shown some potential. There was a games' connection in his family background. His great uncle was JJ Miller, the famous games' wrestler and heavy, while his father used to run Glenfarg games where the family farm was. In fact, Laurence as a youngster could recall the farmworkers talking in the fields about Bill's record breaking hammer throw of 1959 at nearby Crook of Devon.

Edmunds had phenomenal natural strength which he built up by systematic weight training and competitive weightlifting from an early age. He went on to concentrate on shot putting and discus throwing in which he won four Scottish titles at the former in consecutive seasons from 1965 to 1968 and three in the latter. He reached fifty two feet in the putt and one hundred and fifty one feet in the discus, winning several Scottish international vests in the process. But even he would concede he never fully succeeded in channelling his great strength to its maximum effect in the throwing circle.

Bryce and Edmunds were good friends who, some would say, misspent much of their younger days together in university athletics and who each went on to have sons who made their mark at the games' heavy events, Colin Bryce (who also represented Great Britain at bobsleigh) and Gregor Edmunds.

Willie Robertson began his athletic career as a sprinter but his natural strength soon saw him gravitate towards heavy field events. He also undertook a programme of heavy weights, becoming a very accomplished wire hammer thrower and won Scottish international vests in that event. Apart from his hammer throwing he was also a well regarded prop forward for Corstorphine Rugby Club. But his highest sporting achievement was reached in another sport – wrestling – at which he represented Scotland in two Commonwealth Games, in 1974 and 1986, his most celebrated bout being against Gary Knight, then a formidable All Black front row forward, in 1974. Willie was also a decent shot putter, having reached about 45' before turning professional.

It has to be remembered as well that Bill's competition this time was not restricted to these three former amateurs. John Freebairn, Gordon Forbes and Jim McBeath were still very much to the fore while other 'newcomers' to the heavy events who had arrived by the more conventional route included Alec McKenzie of Garve, Les Ferguson from Muir of Ord and George Donaldson of Kirriemuir. McKenzie was a very good weight thrower, both for height and distance, as well as being a good caber tosser. Both Ferguson and Donaldson were good putters and caber tossers, in addition to being decent all-rounders.

Another formidable heavy who competed here occasionally at this time was the previously mentioned Colin Mathieson from New South Wales. Colin was an outstanding caber tosser and very good hammer thrower. He employed an unusual technique at the caber, holding it high under his chin and running with it while his back was bent forward almost at a right angle. However, it was a technique that worked as he demonstrated by winning the world caber tossing championship at Aberdeen in 1975 and succeeding in becoming one of the few heavies to toss the Braemar special caber the next year.

1977 saw another former amateur turn professional, to compete at the heavy events. Grant Anderson from Dundee (no relation to Bill) had not been a field events' athlete like the other three but an international weightlifter who had represented both Scotland and Great Britain, winning a bronze medal for Scotland at the 1970 Commonwealth Games in the superheavyweight class. As a town planning officer, his background was also different from that of the traditional heavy. Standing 6'5", weighing in at about nineteen stones and being immensely strong meant he came equipped for the job. As his weightlifting career had been curtailed by injury he was glad to accept his new sporting challenge, having been persuaded by Douglas Edmunds, then living in Dundee, to give it a try. The less charitable among some heavies figured this was a deliberate ploy by Edmunds to introduce a new face to the circuit whose presence would weaken Bill's position and thereby indirectly advance Edmunds' cause. Whatever the truth of the matter, Anderson was soon to demonstrate his potential to be one of the very best. At one of his first games that summer, at Oxton, he set a new national best mark for the 56lb weight for height event by hoisting it 16'0", breaking the record previously held by Bill at 15'10". As the season progressed he became more adept at the techniques of the various events and began to win a number of prizes. He would go on to develop into a formidable performer.

The following year yet another former amateur of distinguished pedigree also turned professional. Hamish Davidson, aged twenty four, from Cawdor near Nairn, had been Scottish amateur shot putt champion three times, in 1973, 1975 and 1978, the first time when still a junior. He was the holder of the SAAA's best championship performance, with a putt of 57'2$^1/_2$", and had gained several Scottish international vests. That summer he had represented Scotland in an amateur international contest in Greece and performed well with an excellent putt of 56'10". Like Grant Anderson he soon demonstrated he was going to be a force to be reckoned with, particularly when later that summer he set what was considered a new world's best mark with the 28lb weight for distance of 88'10$^1/_2$" at Inverkeithing Games. He was also winning virtually all the shot putt events and, with increasing familiarisation at the hammers and caber, he began to pose a real threat. Davidson was not only a formidable performer but one whose occasional off-field exploits meant he thoroughly merited the description, 'a colourful character'.

It can be seen, therefore, that by the end of the 1978 season and for several seasons before, that Bill, far from lacking rivals, was contending with a considerable number of them, some of whom had arrived at the games' field with excellent pedigrees.

Between 1974 and 1978 Bill competed abroad a number of times. In spring 1974 he accompanied a party of one hundred and ten oil industry executives from Aberdeen to Houston, Texas, where the annual Offshore Technical Conference and Exhibition was taking place. Kitted out for the whole week in Highland dress, Bill gave exhibitions of heavy events in association with the conference, aimed at strengthening links between the Aberdeen oil industry and the American one. One of Bill's exhibitions involved a head-to-head challenge against the same Bill Bangert who had appeared some years previously at Aboyne and Braemar, which Bill comfortably won, including the one hundred yard sprint!

Two years later Bill was back in the States competing, this time at the US heavy events championship in Santa Rosa, California. Although Bill had competed in the States in 1964, 1971 and 1974 these had really been in the nature of exhibitions, whereas the national heavy events championship was a serious competition. He was initially reluctant to go as the dates clashed with Braemar which apart from being the most celebrated Games on the circuit, was one where he had been an ever present for almost twenty years. However, Gordon Varnedoe, an American heavy who was a noted caber tosser and member of the committee of the Santa Rosa Games, had been at Braemar Games the previous year and subsequently spent an afternoon at Bill's house in Aberdeen trying to persuade him to commit himself to compete in 1976. Bill was persuaded, encouraged by the potential financial rewards on offer and the fact the organisers were prepared to invite his wife Frances along as well. Bill did feel a wrench missing Braemar but doubtless his rivals were not too downhearted, given his domination there.

Any regrets Bill may have had were soon overtaken by the warmth of the welcome received, the abundant hospitality extended and the high level of winnings. On arrival at Oakland Airport, San Francisco, a jet-lagged Bill and Frances were taken aback and not a little embarrassed to be piped off the airplane by a pipe band assembled in their honour on the tarmac. When asked if this welcome was repeated when he returned the following year, Bill grinned as he recalled, 'Aye, but there were only two pipers then!'

The Games were held at the Sonoma County Fairground where two arenas were used for the heavy events. One, with a grandstand with a capacity of 5,600 along one side, was used to stage the caber and 56lb weight over the bar events directly in front of the stand, while an adjoining arena was used for the other heavy events. Apart from the heat the other thing which caught Bill's attention was the number of spectators wearing kilts, far more than were seen at home on games day. Otherwise the format of the Games was traditional, with numerous pipe bands, dancers, runners and jumpers, with a crowd of about thirty thousand present. There was a full programme of heavy events staged over the two days of the Games and about fifteen heavies, amateurs and professionals, took part. Bill won his first US heavy events' title by six points from Brian Oldfield (38 points to 32) and, in the process, prize money of $820, a far greater sum than was available at Braemar.

He had been the first top Scottish heavy to compete seriously in the United States since the days of Donald Dinnie, in the Victorian era, and the Americans took to him in a big way. As a result he was invited back to compete and did so each year till 1986 (apart from 1979 when injury prevented him), repeating his 1976 success in 1977, 1978 and 1980. Bill Bangert, Arnold Pope and Brian Oldfield had all competed at different times in Scotland but there was now two way traffic of heavies across the Atlantic. When Bill was busy securing his first US title in 1976 three American heavies were competing at Braemar: Ed McComas of Baltimore, Fred Vaughan of South Carolina and Ron Short of North Carolina. Their visit prompted a succession of other American heavies to follow, such as Kazmaier and McGoldrick, a tradition that has continued to the present day.

The 1976 Santa Rosa Games were the one hundred and eleventh held by the Caledonian Club of San Francisco. They were first staged on Thanksgiving Day, 29th November 1866, and are the oldest surviving Games in the country. At the opening of the second Games on 28th November 1867 the President, Donald MacLennan, stated in his address to the crowd of four thousand,

> 'We are assembled here this morning to participate in the sports so dear in the memories of our native land. Though transplanted. . . to the shores of the Pacific many thousands of miles from Bonnie Scotland, still the hearts of her children warm at the recollections of their youth and beat more strongly at the mention of her name . . . in these fond recollections we harbour our national Games to celebrate which we are met here today.'

The third Games, held on 25th July 1868, were reported in the *Illustrated London News*, which carried pictures of them thanks to woodcut artists, and therefore became the first American Games reported in a foreign journal.

Scottish Games had been held in the States before these Caledonian Club of San Francisco's Games. It is reckoned the first such Games were held in New York in 1836 when the Highland Society of New York staged its 'first sportive meeting' to 'renew the Sports of our Native Land'. In previous centuries Scottish emigrants had formed various types of mutual aid societies, the earliest being in 1657 in Boston when the Scots Charitable Society was founded. Thereafter over the next century and half or so many St Andrew's Societies were formed in parts of the States, with the aims 'to relieve indigent and unfortunate Scotchmen and their families; to foster and encourage a love of Scotland, its history, literature and customs and to encourage the national athletic games.' Among other places, these societies took root in Philadelphia, Savannah in Georgia, New York City and Baltimore and then proliferated across the country throughout the nineteenth century, latterly mostly describing themselves as Caledonian Societies and placing emphasis on social and cultural activities. They referred to their 'national sports' as Caledonian Games and prior to the Civil War, Caledonian Games were being held at Boston, New York City, Philadelphia and Newark, New Jersey.

The San Francisco Caledonian Club's games of 1866 were the first to be held after the Civil War, soon followed by the Detroit Games of 1867. That same year a 'Great International Caledonian Games' was held in New York, involving Canadian as well as American athletes, and in 1870 a convention was held in New York involving representatives from Canadian and American Games to discuss a system of governance of the expanding Games' scene. From this emerged the North American United Caledonian Association, a governing body in charge of Caledonian Games in North American for member clubs. Affiliation to this body required a club to have a membership of Scots or people of Scots' descent and which had as one of its aims 'the encouragement of Scottish Games'.

The games continued to spread and by 1880 were being held across the whole country. The 'boom time' for Caledonian Games in America was certainly the period of about twenty years after the Civil War. But in a sense they became victims of their own success as amateur track and field clubs began to spring up inspired in part by the example of the Caledonian Games and in part by the development of amateur athletics in Britain, at Cambridge and Oxford University athletic clubs. The first club was the New York Athletic Club, formed in September 1868, which held its first games on 11th November that year. Caledonian Club members took part, winning the heavy events, and the influence of Caledonian Club members was strong in the development of the Athletic Club. Its first Director of Athletics was George Goldie, appointed in 1885. Goldie was a native of Edinburgh who had been Princeton University's Gymnasium Director and was a pivotal figure in the development of amateur athletics in America. He was the first to introduce the pole vault to America and held records in the standing high jump and long jump. As a result of his and others' influence, the growth of amateur athletics' clubs increased and as a result Caledonian Games began to fall away. There were a number of reasons for this.

People's sporting interests began to change as not only did amateur athletics emerge but also boxing, baseball and football became popular. An amateur athletics' meeting was simpler and less expensive to organise – there was no need for pipe bands, dancers or equipment such as hammers and cabers. And with the drop in crowds attending their Games many Caledonian Clubs experienced financial problems and could not afford to continue staging Games. By the end of the century there were few Caledonian Games left and it was not until the 1920s and 1930s that tentative steps were taken in the re-establishment of the Games, with some being held at Round Hill, Connecticut, Los Angeles and Central New York.

However, the major step in the resuscitation of the Games took place in 1956 with the staging of the Grandfather Mountain Games at Linville, North Carolina, a marvellous Games in a beautiful and inspiring setting, which were to be a catalyst for a number of new Games. Another important step in the 'rebirth' of the Games was the staging of the Games in San Francisco in 1971 in which Bill and other Scots heavies took part. That attracted huge interest and helped put the Games back on the map to the extent that they are nowadays held across the whole country. As a consequence of that growth a number of outstanding heavies have emerged. Reference has already been made to Bangert, Pope and Oldfield. Others include Gordon Varnedoe, John Ross, Ron Short, Keith Tice, Ed McComas, Fred Vaughan, Tom Carmichael, Jim McGoldrick, Larry Brock, Dave Brown and Ryan Vierra, most of whom have also competed in Scotland. Thus the Highland Games' scene in American, having almost expired and then lain dormant for years, is now thriving and is set to continue that way.

1978 was a busy summer for Bill because in addition to competing on the home circuit, he fulfilled an engagement in New York, competed in the Grandfather Mountain Games and then the Canadian Heavy events championship in Fergus, Ontario. The whisky company Hiram Walker, flew Bill and his wife and daughter across to New York in July for Bill to undertake promotional activity. Bill did a series of newspaper, radio and television interviews about the art of caber tossing and his games' career, while plugging sponsors, Ballantine's Whisky, as much as he reasonably could. He also gave two caber tossing exhibitions, the caber having been shipped from Santa Rosa, in Central Park for television to the accompaniment of a piper. Bill and his family were taken sightseeing, including a visit to the Statue of Liberty, and saw a number of shows. Then after a hectic week they were flown down to North

Carolina to enable Bill to compete at the 32nd Grandfather Mountain Games the next day.

On arrival, Bill was shattered and at the pre Games' reception that evening some of his rivals made optimistic noises about their prospects given Bill's apparent state of exhaustion. But a good night's sleep for Bill put paid to their hopes as he completed a clean sweep of all the events next day, setting four records. Excellent competition included Fred Vaughan, Ron Short, Keith Tice and Ed McComas. These are perhaps the most iconic of the American Games, held in a lovely setting known as MacRae Meadows high up on the slopes of the 6,000' Grandfather Mountain. This rugged terrain is said to resemble Kintail in Wester Ross with lots of rhodendrons, mountain ash trees, wild heather-like plants and thistles. The occasional mountain mist reminds the visitor even more of Scotland. A welcome banner in Gaelic (*Failte gu Beinn Seanair* – Welcome to Grandfather Mountain) is extended above the main entrance to the arena, which is encircled by some one hundred and fifty clan tents, with a profusion of tartan everywhere. On Bill's visit he was slightly bemused to be taken into the Clan Anderson tent and introduced to the Chief of the Clan in America. Nowadays about forty thousand people attend the Games, which also act as the centrepiece for a number of Scottish-themed activities that take place in the vicinity.

The Games were founded in 1956 by Mrs Agnes MacRae Morton of Linville and Donald F MacDonald of Charlotte. Mrs Morton's predecessors in the MacRae family had established in 1892 the nearby resort town of Linville and for some time she had contemplated setting up some form of Highland Gathering. Donald MacDonald, who was then a journalist on the *Charlotte News*, had visited Braemar Games in 1954 which inspired him greatly and he determined to try to create a similar Gathering in North Carolina. Mrs Morton contacted him in 1955 and the two set to work. The first Grandfather Mountain Games were held on 19th August 1956, deliberately chosen as the anniversary of Bonnie Prince Charlie's arrival at Glenfinnan and the raising of the standard in the 1745 Jacobite rebellion. Since then the Games have gone from strength from strength, modelling their programme of events on Braemar.

Bill's final trip that year was to take part in the First Canadian Heavy Events Championship at the 33rd Fergus Highland Games in Ontario. Fergus, which is located on the scenic Grand River about fifty miles from Toronto, was founded in 1834 by the Honourable Adam Fergusson, a member of the Executive Council of Upper Canada. Most of its settlers were of Scots' descent, attracted by the fertile soil for agriculture and water power for mills. Extremely aware of its Scottish roots, it is also very proud of its Games and has permanent posters depicting scenes from the Games at the main entrance points to the town. On 16th August, in front of a crowd of thirty thousand, against a strong field, Bill achieved a clean sweep of all events, including tossing the 22' long Challenge Caber, to claim the inaugural Canadian championship and $850 prize money. This made 1978 an outstanding year for Bill because in addition to the Scottish, British and European heavy events' titles won in Scotland, he had also added to his collection the American and Canadian titles.

Highland Games were not new to Canada. As with the United States, they had been taken across the Atlantic by Scots emigrants who formed various types of Scottish societies. Compared to the United States, Scottish influence in Canada in general was much stronger. The Scots controlled most of the fur trade, banking and financial institutions, major educational institutions and, to a large extent, the government. In the Canadian Pacific Railway Company the Scots had the top jobs although most of the labourers and contractors were Irish. Examples of early Scottish societies were the North British or Scots Club of Halifax, founded in 1768, and the St Andrews Society of St John in New Brunswick, formed in 1798.

The first Highland Gathering appears to have been held in 1819 by the Glengarry Highland Society, with games taking place as part of the Gathering. They were followed by games staged in 1835 by the St Andrews Societies of Montreal and Quebec and, in 1838, by the Caledonian Club of Prince Edward's Island's games. Then in 1840 Lancaster, near Montreal, held games while in 1847 the Toronto Games took place. By the middle of the nineteenth century, Canadian athletes were crossing into the United States to compete and prior to Confederation taking place Highland Games were being held across Canada from Cape Breton Island in the east to Vancouver in the west.

In 1861 the Antigonish Highland Society, Nova Scotia, was formed and two years later they held their first Games at nearby Apple Tree Island. These Games are still held today, the oldest continuous Games in the country. At each entrance to the town there are wooden carvings depicting different figures in the Games while in the town centre there is a permanent mural of a Highland Games' scene. Canadian athletes participated in the Great International Caledonian Games at New York in 1867 and Canadian representatives were at the 1870 Convention that gave rise to the North American United Caledonian Association.

By the 1870s the Games were well established in Canada and despite objection from some athletes worried about the competition, Dinnie and his fellow heavy Fleming toured Canada during that decade. Later in the century, amateur athletics did begin to take hold but unlike in the United States, the Games and amateur athletics co-existed in a spirit of co-operation and often jointly hosted events. As a result, the Games in Canada continued successfully and do so to the present day.

One fascinating character from the Canadian Games' scene was Scots Canadian athlete Walter R Knox. Despite being coach to the Canadian Olympic team of 1912 and being appointed coach to the British team for the ill-fated 1916 Olympics, he was anything but an establishment character. He had a reputation as a rough tough hombre who had toured North America and Europe as a professional athlete with great success, frequently adopting false identities for betting purposes. He had toured the Highland Games' circuit in Scotland since 1911, the year he set a long jump record of 22'3" at Braemar, which was to stand for over sixty years. He was also an accomplished shot putter, with a best throw of over 45'. Out of season he spent time in gold mining camps in the Klondike, living rough and buying and selling claims and shares.

In 1979 Bill was beaten in the Scottish championship for the first time since 1971, the title being won by Hamish Davidson although Bill was hindered by the effects of a back injury sustained earlier that summer while in Nova Scotia. Having won a gallon of whisky as part of his prize, Hamish apparently wasted no time in sampling it at the same time doling out generous measures to members of the crowd. Willie Robertson recalls that his promised lift home from Hamish had to be aborted due to Hamish's condition, the two of them having to spend the night in Crieff. Davidson had been steadily improving since joining the circuit the previous season and had built on a successful Braemar at the end of that season when he and Grant Anderson had vied for the main honours, in Bill's absence in Santa Rosa. Grant Anderson similarly had made great progress and he and Davidson were now Bill's major rivals. That same summer Grant Anderson wrested Bill's Aboyne title from him, the first time since 1966 he had not been champion there. Again, Bill's injury handicapped him. And at Braemar, albeit in Bill's absence, Davidson came out on top despite the presence of the awesomely powerful American Bill Kazmaier, who set a new 56lb weight for height record with 16'2".

But in 1980, in his forty third year, Bill returned to top form, regaining his Scottish title at Crieff, regaining his Aboyne title to record his nineteenth win there and winning again at Braemar for the fifteenth time. For good measure, he also added the world caber tossing championship and the European heavy events title, won at Dundee Highland Games. Later that season he returned to Santa Rosa to compete in the US heavyweight championship, which for once did not clash with Braemar, and won it for the fourth time from a strong field featuring Grant Anderson, Vaughan, Tice, Harrington of Canada and Ross, among others. In so doing he won all eight events and set three records, two in the hammer events, including an excellent heavy hammer throw of 117'5" and the 56lb weight for distance. This caused rival Grant Anderson to exclaim in mock complaint, 'You didn't even let me win one first prize.'

The only title which eluded him that year was the British title at Lochearnhead, won by Grant Anderson. Again, these were truly remarkable performances by Bill, who ascribed part of the reason for his success to being injury free. He also felt he was still enjoying the benefit of the increased weight training programme he had undertaken over the previous two years, to compete in the Britain's Strongest Man and World's Strongest Man Competitions. The former took place at a Sports Centre in Woking, Surrey, in April 1979 over three days and was televised. Bill faced opponents including Geoff Capes, Andy Drzewiecki, a British international discus thrower, and a number of weightlifters. The events included pulling a 2 ton truck over 100 feet, lifting a 1400lb car, bending steel bars, racing a 700lb wheelbarrow over 90 feet, tearing telephone directories and other similar events. Bill did well, finishing second to Capes and earning the sum of £991.

The World's contest was held in June the same year at the Universal Studio Tour Centre in Los Angeles, with competitors accommodated at the nearby Sheraton Universal hotel. The principal officials included Hal Connolly, former Olympic hammer champion whom Bill found it hard to warm to, Parry O'Brien, former double Olympic shot putt champion, and Tommy Kono, triple Olympic weightlifting champion. Each participant was guaranteed a minimum $2,000 with Bill contending with nine opponents, including Bill Kazmaier, who had bench pressed 590lb, Swedish strongman Lars Hedlund, who had bench pressed 612lb, American Don Reinhoudt, a world powerlifting champion weighing over 24 stones, and other weightlifting champions and two American football players. Only one weighed slightly less than Bill, while the others comfortably outweighed him with the bulkiest being Cleve Dean, a strongman and arm wrestling champion who tipped the scales at a 'mere' 33 stones.

The format was similar to the British competition although some events were different – there was a 'Girl Lift' involving a number of girls on a platform, a hoist lift, a refrigerator race, barrel lifting and a form of caber toss, among other events. The wheelbarrow race was uphill over 100 feet and involved a 750lb barrow, which caused Bill to pull a muscle and damage his prospects. As he had arrived late in Los Angeles he had not been able to take advantage of the day set aside for orientation with the equipment used for the different events, which did not help his cause. Despite those drawbacks, he did well to finish fifth against a much younger field. In reality, he thought he had become too old to give of his best in this type of event and quietly made a mental note to do no more.

The man to whom Bill had finished second in the Britain's Strongest Man competition was Geoff Capes, well known shot putt champion, television celebrity strongman and budgerigar breeder. He had now decided to follow in the footsteps of the other amateurs and turn professional for the Games' circuit. As this decision was made by him after the end of the 1980 season, he was unable to make his début in Scotland before summer 1981.

Capes was undoubtedly the highest profile 'convert' to the Games since Arthur Rowe in the early sixties. An immense man of about 6'6" and weighing in at over twenty stones, and now aged thirty one, he had had a dazzling career in amateur athletics. A record seven times winner of the shot putt title at the Amateur Athletic Association's Championships, he also secured two Commonwealth Games' titles in 1974 and 1978, a bronze medal in the European Championships in 1974, a fifth place in the 1976 Olympics and a sixth in the 1980 Olympics. In 1972 he broke Arthur Rowe's long standing British record with a putt of 66'2$^1/_2$" and in 1974 became the first Briton to putt over seventy feet, with a heave of 70'1$^1/_2$". The British record of 71'2", which he set in his final season as an amateur, 1980, was set to last for twenty three years and at that time he held the record for the most capped British athlete with sixty seven international appearances. As a teenager he had been an excellent all-round athlete showing considerable ability as a sprinter, high jumper, footballer and basketball player, not to mention having run a mile in a very respectable 4 minutes 48 seconds when aged seventeen.

Near the end of his amateur career, Capes, when weighing about twenty two stones, even beat the noted distance runner Brendan Foster in a 200 metres race in a time of 24.9 seconds which for somebody of his bulk who had spent his athletic career in the shot putt circle was remarkable. His bulk and strength belied an impressive natural athleticism. He first came to national prominence during a television programme in 1967 which had been staged for the express purpose of finding a successor to Arthur Rowe, to give Britain a top shot putter. Numerous strength and power tests were held, from which a young Geoff Capes emerged triumphant.

But whereas Arthur Rowe was a popular gregarious figure who integrated himself well into the Games' scene, Capes was different. He tended to be domineering and authoritarian, perhaps to some extent due to his having been a police officer, and could behave in a bullish and confrontational way. He was perceived as bullying judges at times to get his own way and was reckoned to be responsible for one long serving judge at Crieff retiring prematurely. It was also claimed that he bent the rules to his own advantage, eg in throwing the 28lb weight for distance it was said that he began his movement inside the prescribed circle but would then take a step out of the rear of the circle to increase the area of his turn and thus gain an advantage.

Geoff Capes

He did have some history of brushes with authority in the amateur ranks, the best known being the incident at the 1978 European Championships in Prague when he was favourite for the gold medal. Because apparently he was not wearing the appropriate numbers on his vest, an official in the muster room, who was screening the athletes before they went out to compete in the final, told Capes he could not compete. Capes refused to accept this and as he made his way towards the arena became involved in a pushing match and altercation with officials, as a result of which he was disqualified.

Despite almost being temperamental opposites, Bill and Capes got on alright. Capes respected Bill for his achievements and gave him the credit he was due while Bill respected Capes for his athletic pedigree. The first time they met was by chance in a hotel in Paris in 1977 and Capes, who recognised Bill, shouted to him across a busy room, 'So you're the man who makes the most money at the Scottish Games.' Bill had of course heard of Capes but did not recognise him. After that rather abrupt beginning they struck up a reasonable rapport.

For all that Capes could be loud, brash and domineering Bill tended to be reserved, self-effacing and discreet. While not a shrinking violet, some mistook his quiet demeanour for introspection. Although a fairly self-contained character who was quietly self-assured and very capable of asserting himself when required, he also had another, lighter, side to his nature. When competing he stuck to the rules, seldom fouled and never gave officials any problem. But winning and giving of his best was of supreme importance to him and that called for a high degree of focus and intensity on the games' field. For him the games' field was not a venue for frivolity or somewhere to indulge in idle chatter. He was very driven by a desire to win and excel.

Brian Oldfield's nickname for Bill Anderson was 'The Rhino' – because he thought once Bill got going, he was unstoppable. In Laurence Bryce's opinion, Bill was the 'ultimate competitor'. He recalls at Alva Games one year he and Edmunds leading Bill in the putt with one round to go. Bill who till then had been using his new 'rotational' style reverted to his old style for his last throw and passed them both by over three feet!

Grant Anderson was particularly impressed by the way Bill dealt with new challenges. He recalls how in his first season he cleared 16' with the 56lb weight over the bar, literally taking the event to new heights. However, before the season was over Bill also had cleared 16' for the first time ever, despite then being forty. Bill always rose to the occasion, he thought. He remembered in particular one games in Santa Rosa when Bill had a duel with Keith Tice for the championship – each time Tice threw, Bill would edge past him just by a few inches, to maintain his lead and claim the title. Grant thought Bill an excellent technician, prepared to innovate if he thought it advantageous, eg adopting the 'rotational' style shot putt.

Because of Bill's all embracing will to win on the field some formed the impression he was rather dour and uncommunicative but that was wrong. Off the field he enjoyed socialising with fellow athletes particularly on trips abroad and during the Glasgow Fair week when with games nearly every day he was on the road all the time. Most of the time he competed he had a fairly young family and once a games had finished he made his way home to Aberdeen and did not linger to socialise. He had been convincingly the most successful heavy of not only his generation but of any generation and it would be a denial of human nature to say that he was free from envy or did not have his detractors. George Clark, for example, did not take kindly to Bill beating his records nor failing to seek his assistance, which led to his getting Rowe involved. Once Rowe was on the scene there were undoubtedly some who wished to see him get the better of Bill as was to be the case later with Capes. Hamish Davidson is another who has been critical of Bill. Although the pair were companionable during competition,

Hamish has expressed the opinion that in order to preserve his own domination, Bill failed to encourage newcomers entering the circuit once Rowe left. He also felt Bill had been unduly critical of his prospects when he began on the circuit and attributed that to concern on Bill's part about his continued superiority, claims not accepted by Bill. On the other hand, Willie Robertson remembers beating Bill once in the shot putt at Portree and Bill immediately congratulating him by shaking his hand which impressed Willie very much. In Willie's opinion the integrity of the games was paramount for Bill.

According to Doug Edmunds, Bill had 'all our respects. Not only was he the best on the field but off it he was free from any of the excesses that some of us occasionally fell prey to.' As in any walk of life where competition is central to the activity concerned, factions arose and it would be naive to assert that all were in Bill's camp. But his extraordinary success and the manner in which he achieved it led to his acquiring over the years considerable stature in games' circles where the vast majority of those involved welcomed his success and considered him an iconic figure whose involvement was central to the success of the games.

Throughout most of the 1980s Geoff Capes was to be a major figure on the games' stage. His high profile attracted a lot of publicity and added an extra edge to competition among the heavies. Other heavies who arrived on the scene about this time included Alan Sim, from Fettercairn, and Brian Robin from Isle of Seil, Oban. Jim McBeath from Dunbeath, the excellent all-round athlete, had latterly been placing more emphasis on the heavy events. And within a few years Alistair Gunn from Halkirk, who would go on to be one of the leading heavies of the next twenty plus years, would emerge at national level.

The level of competition was such therefore that it ensured Capes did not have it all his own way. Naturally he dominated the shot putts but it took him some time to master the traditional Scottish events. He became very strong at the 28lb weight for distance and the 56lb weight over the bar and much of the time was excellent at the caber although inconsistent with it. However, he never properly mastered the hammers and for someone of his strength and power never did himself justice. That weakness in his repertoire meant he never dominated in championships as much as he might have as he did not score the requisite points in that event, which allowed the Andersons, Grant and Bill, and others in to acquire points.

In the 28lb weight event Hamish Davidson was capable of some magnificent throws and the same was true for Grant Anderson in the

56lb weight over the bar. Although not the force he had once been, Bill still was performing very well at all events particularly the caber, the hammers and the 28lb weight. From time to time others, apart from Bill, Capes, Grant Anderson and Davidson, would score wins, such as McKenzie, Robin, McBeath, Edmunds, Sim and soon Gunn. As a result honours were spread a little more widely than they had been in Bill and Arthur Rowe's heyday. Then it was a question really of who was going to be third in every event and while there was good competition among the heavies on the level below Arthur and Bill, there was never any realistic likelihood of any being able to dislodge Bill and Arthur from the top spots.

Capes won the Scottish title in his first season on the circuit in 1981 but Bill and Grant Anderson shared the British title at Lochearnhead, while Bill won the European title at Dundee. Grant Anderson had by now really emerged as Capes' biggest rival and having trained assiduously to improve his technique in the traditional events now did not have a weak link in his armoury. He was regularly throwing about 50' in the light putt, over 130' in the light hammer and over 115' in the heavy hammer, about 75' in the 28lb weight for distance, 16' plus in the 56lb weight for height and was first rate with the caber. He won at Aboyne inflicting a rare defeat there on Bill but had to concede to Capes at Braemar. He had been progressively improving, having already notched a win at Aboyne in 1979, and in Bill's absence from Santa Rosa that year, tied for first place with Oldfield in the American heavy events championship. In 1980 in Pomona, Los Angeles, he won a World Heavy Events championship before a very disappointing crowd, edging out Bill and Alec MacKenzie while in 1981 he recorded his first of four consecutive successes in the US championship, with Bill finishing runner up most of these years.

1981 also took Bill to London for a demonstration of caber tossing in Green Park, courtesy of VAT 69 whisky, as a promotional event for the Scotch Whisky Festival being held at the Athenaeum Hotel in Piccadilly. Much to the astonishment of passing commuters a number of publicity photos were taken of Bill in his kilt crossing a busy street with the caber over his shoulder, with the words VAT 69 along its length.

He also made his third trip to Australia to compete, this time in the World Heavy Events Championship held at the Junction Oval, Melbourne. The event was well supported by the Australian government, with the Chieftain of the Games being Sir Billy Snedden, the Speaker in the Australian Parliament, who issued an invitation to Bill's wife Frances to join Sir Ian Hamer, the Prime Minister of Victoria, and his wife for lunch and to join them at the Games. Bill and Frances also attended a reception hosted by the Government of Victoria, as well as a party hosted by the Australian Prime Minister, Sir Malcolm Fraser, and his wife at their private residence. All the dignitaries they met were charming and went out of their way to make Bill and Frances welcome. Fraser, who was of Scots' descent, even suggested Bill and Frances might like to consider staying on in Australia!

To make the trip particularly memorable Bill won the title in the face of stiff competition from Grant Anderson, Jim McBeath, Billy Binks, Colin Mathieson, Keith Tice, Fred Vaughan and Dave Harrington, to collect $2002. He was particularly pleased at the age of forty three to secure this title. It was deeply satisfying at this advanced stage of his career, when he could no longer lay regular claim to being the top man, to defeat such good opposition on such a stage. And his hammer throw of 135'11" was the second best recorded that year, about a foot less than the best which was also his mark.

Over the next few years Capes and Grant Anderson battled for supremacy in the Scottish championship at Crieff. In 1982 they shared the title before Grant went on a winning sequence from 1983 to 1985 and then they shared it again in 1986. All this time Bill succeeded in finishing each year in the top three to preserve his record of always being there since 1958. One ploy adopted by Capes in the early 80s to boost his chances of winning championships was to persuade a former international amateur shot putter team-mate of his, Bob Dale from Manchester, to come north to take part in the heavy events. The thinking was that Dale would place second in the shot putt events and thus deprive the Andersons of points for their aggregate totals.

Such a ploy was not new. It was said in 1979 that Hamish Davidson had offered Willie Robertson £5 for every point he took from Grant Anderson at the Scottish championship, as Grant was then deemed to be his biggest rival. Whether because of that or not, Willie did beat Grant at the 28lb weight thus costing Grant a valuable point and Hamish did go on to win his only Scottish title that year. Bill continued to have success, winning at Aboyne in 1983, 1984 and 1986 and the World Caber Tossing Championship in 1982 and 1985. He also recorded several wins in the Glenfiddich Grampian Heavy Events League, based on total points collected in a number of Games held in the Grampian area.

He also continued his globetrotting and entered pastures new in 1984 when he went with Grant Anderson and Robin to Dubai for the first of three trips, to compete in their Highland Games. It was a fairly novel experience to be tossing cabers and hammers around in baking heat in February amid desert-like terrain. The event was organised by the local Caledonian Club for the benefit of expatriates living there but never succeeded in attracting very big crowds. The displays by the hundreds of Arab pipers and drummers, which included the Sultan of Oman's and the Kuwait Pipe Bands, were quite spectacular.

Another new destination in 1986 was Vancouver, where Games were being held in connection with the Vancouver Trade Fair. Most of the top North American heavies were there including Jim McGoldrick, then the top man there, and the Australian Billy Binks. The venue was very good and a good crowd attended although Bill was a little disappointed with some Canadian officials whom he felt showed some bias in judging the caber towards their own compatriots.

And of course he continued returning each year to Santa Rosa, competing there for the last time in 1986 when he finished a very respectable fourth. Having competed there each year since 1976, with the exception of 1979 when injury ruled him out, Bill had endeared himself to many there and had made a number of good friends. Grant Anderson thought Bill was 'revered' there. Brian Robin has some memories of Bill's last games there. The 56lb weight for height event took place directly in front of the packed stand which, as Bill made to take his first attempt, rose to its feet as one to give him an ovation the like of which Brian never heard anywhere else at any Highland Games. And that night at a Games dinner in Bill's honour most of those present in the room stood up to pay an individual tribute to Bill and present him with gifts. One was a presentation set of Texas steer horns which Bill recalls were handed over at the same time as the benefactor said, 'They're to hang your hat on, Bill, when you retire!'

Since his retirement Bill has twice been invited back to be Honorary Chieftain of the Caledonian Club of San Francisco's Games and has also hosted Games coaching clinics at a number of venues including Sacramento and Colorado.

10. The Final Fling and Last Word

ALTHOUGH he did not know it at the time, 1987 was to be Bill's final season on the games' circuit in Scotland. He was now in his fiftieth year and inexorably his power was slipping away. No man can reverse nature and although Bill had given it a damned good try, the evidence against him was gradually mounting. Although still attaining distances which for the average heavy athlete were extremely good, by his own high standards they were a little disappointing at times. He still thought of himself as 'in the pack' if not leading it. Ironically perhaps what had always been his 'speciality' event, the hammer, had begun to drop as had his putts but his caber, weight for distance and weight for height were still up there with the best. Apart from his performance level lowering, however, he had also begun to detect aches and pains that he had never felt before. Training had started to become a bit of a chore. This was his thirtieth season on the circuit and for the past twenty three years he had been doing heavy weight training.

Throughout his whole career on the circuit he had been engaged in heavy manual work. Initially this had been on the farm and then from about 1964 onwards he had worked as a concrete layer for a number of building companies including Bovis, Doric, Macraes of Inverness, Lilley's, Hall and Tawse, Millers of Edinburgh, and had just begun what was to be a fourteen year stint till retirement with Aberdeen based Stewart Milne Construction. Bill's Games' contacts could be of some help to him in securing employment and thereafter obtaining time off work to compete. He recalls with amusement at his interview for the Milne Construction job one of the managers saying to him, 'I'm the silly young loon that used to carry the hammer back at Aboyne!' The only period when he was not engaged in concreting was in the early 70s when he worked for a spell as a brickworks' manager on the outskirts of

Aberdeen. Concrete laying was physically demanding as steel mesh had to be manoeuvred about before being fitted while floors had to be levelled, which involved a lot of bending and lifting. After a hard day of such activity the prospect of lifting weights in the evening for two hours began to hold less appeal now. For the first time he began feeling stiffness the morning after a training session. He was also experiencing the same reaction once he started his customary throwing training when Spring started.

Bill trained in a very committed fashion. One well known Aboyne heavy, Neil Fyvie, recalled joining Bill for a training session once. Having spent what appeared to Neil an interminably exhausting time throwing the heavy hammer, Bill turned to him and said, 'That's enough of that', much to Neil's relief. But the relief was short lived as Bill went on, 'Now, let's move on to the light hammer.' Given the physical reactions he was experiencing, he started to wonder whether he could continue at a satisfying level. He recalled wryly having given an interview to the local newspaper about twenty years ago stating that, 'he expected to retire by the time he was forty' because 'approaching forty, heavy events were more likely to do a man harm than good and that he would then think about starting to run a pub.' However, once he reached forty, he was still going very strong and the notion for the pub had by then left him.

Now things were different. His old adversary Sandy Gray who himself continued competing well into his forties advised him to keep going as he could still win places even though he was no longer finishing first all the time. That was not really reflective of Bill's approach to competition yet it placed him in a dilemma. Not being consistently the top man was hard for him to accept. On the other hand the Games had been such a huge part of his life for so long that in a sense walking away from them seemed unreal. And that dilemma was not eased by the good results he began to achieve that summer. In early August he recorded his twenty third success in the heavy events championship at Aboyne Games before going on two weeks later to secure his sixteenth outright success (plus two shared with Arthur Rowe) at the Scottish championship at Crieff. Again the importance of Bill's comprehensive ability at all the heavy events was underlined again there as he only won one event, the 28lb weight for distance with 73'. In the course of the season he recorded about a dozen wins in that event while in the 56lb weight over the bar he reached 15'6" at Oldmeldrum to tie with Brian Robin and he also won the caber at about ten Games including Aboyne and Lonach. Taking stock at the end of the season, he decided to continue for another year.

Near the end of December 1987 Bill flew to Australia with Alistair

Gunn to take part in the Combined Societies of New South Wales' 119th Annual Highland Gathering which was to take place at Wentworth Park, Sydney, as part of the year of Australia's Bi Centennial celebrations. Alistair remembers Bill and he doing a training session together throwing the hammers two days before the Games and Bill appearing quite weary. The Games took place on New Year's Day 1988 and the heavies comprised a formidable field including apart from Bill and Alistair, Jim McGoldrick, Dan Marcovic of Canada and top Australians Joe Quigley, Craig Watson and Colin Mathieson. This was to turn out to be Bill's competitive finale although he had not planned it this way. As he threw the hammer he realised it was not happening for him. What had once been there in abundance was no longer there – the power, the snap, the dig. Try as he did, the body was just not responding and he had the impression that was the way it was going to be from now on. He felt tired and was fatigued from the training session with Gunn. Although his intention had been to continue that year that decision had only been reached after some hesitation. In Sydney after a few rounds of the hammer, he felt he 'no longer had it in him' and there and then decided his competitive career was finished, thirty two years after that initially tentative start at Alford.

It was curious that twelve thousand miles should separate the scene of his début from the scene of his finale. He did feel sadness but the end was not wholly unexpected, subconsciously he had been preparing himself for it for some time. Unless he could give of his best, he was not interested and the time was now right to draw a line under it. Hamish Davidson having been occasionally critical of Bill nevertheless thought highly of him for taking the decision then to retire. He knew Bill could have carried on for some time picking up prizes which in one sense would have been the easier option to pursue but applauded him for going when he did.

Shortly after his return from Australia Bill took part in a local radio interview with Robbie Shepherd, the well known Games' commentator and broadcaster, in which he formally announced his retirement. He did participate in a couple of demonstrations of heavy events in Northern Ireland later in the summer but that was the extent of his hands-on involvement. He maintained his connection with the Games after a short break by becoming a heavy events judge, at Aberdeen, Braemar, Crieff and Aboyne, which he still does.

His continuing interest in the Games was also stimulated by the involvement of two of his sons, Mark and Craig. Mark, who was born in 1970, competed in the heavy events in the under-25 category for a period and showed promise. But rugby injuries and his university course in architecture combined to discourage his fledgling career and he did not pursue it. Craig however pursued his interest in the heavy events over a longer period and achieved a good measure of success. Born a year after Mark, his highlights included winning the World Caber Tossing Championship in 1997, the Scottish Caber Tossing Championship for three consecutive years between 1998 and 2000 and the Glenfiddich Heavy Events League Trophy in 1998. He and Bill are the only father and son duo to have won the World Caber Tossing Championship and the Glenfiddich Trophy. Despite showing considerable ability and potential he chose not to continue and retired before he reached thirty. Mark is now an architect in Edinburgh, Craig a civil servant in Perth, while another son Kenneth is a police inspector in Aberdeen where daughter Rosemary is a nursing sister.

Looking back on his career, Bill has much cause for satisfaction. As he says, 'The Games have been good to me.' A quick perusal of the countless trophies and medals he has won in the course of his career confirms that. Many trophies have been donated to Braemar for exhibition at the new Centre being planned. He is, privately, rightly proud of his outstanding achievements and grateful for the opportunity his success gave him to travel the world and the variety of otherwise unimaginable experiences it has yielded him.

Bill Anderson is the last man to beat his own drum but he truly was a giant on the Highland Games' heavy events' stage both at home and abroad. Newspaper headlines regularly dubbed him 'King of the Heavies' and with good reason. Gordon Forbes considers him the last great 'farmyard heavy' and likens his stature in the games and his temperament to that of Jack Nicklaus in golf. Curiously, Nicklaus won eighteen 'majors' – the same number of Scottish titles won by Bill.

Blessed with considerable natural talent, he rigorously applied himself over a long period to developing it and did so essentially single handedly. His performances lifted the heavy events out of the doldrums and breathed new life into the games. His well documented rivalry with Arthur Rowe markedly increased the profile of the games which was maintained through later periods of his career when he faced up to the challenge of former amateurs and strength athletes like Grant Anderson, Geoff Capes and others. He acknowledges with gratitude that the games have been good for him financially and contributed to a decent standard of living which, without the games, might have been difficult to attain. Although the rewards were good, he could never have contemplated becoming a full-time professional. Economically it would not have been viable but Bill also thinks that in being able to combine his sporting career with his work (with generous time off for competing) he had the best of both worlds. He was always careful to ensure a prompt return to work after being abroad on trips, when he was often the recipient of five star hospitality, to avoid any risk of temporarily opulent lifestyles corrupting him!

Even had it been economically viable, he doubts if he would have enjoyed the lifestyle of a full-time athlete. The money only followed on good performances and those were his principal motivation. He rates Rowe as his most difficult opponent. He was very good at all the events and extremely competitive on the field. Later in his career, Hamish Davidson, Grant Anderson and Geoff Capes were very worthy opponents but he was meeting them at a stage of his career when he had passed his peak.

He had respect for a number of other heavies who on their day at their particular event were capable of causing him problems. Sandy Gray at his best was a formidable opponent at the caber and the 56lb weight over the bar. Colin Mathieson and Doug Edmunds were outstanding caber tossers (Edmunds won the World Caber Tossing Championship in 1976 and 1978) and Laurence Bryce a very useful 28lb weight thrower. Hamish Davidson was another excellent all-round heavy although his lack of height hindered him slightly at the hammer events. Sandy Gray's training mainly consisted of his farm work and had he dedicated time to training and doing weight training Bill is in no doubt he would have been even more formidable. Neither Edmunds nor Davidson really fulfilled their potential in Bill's opinion but with more dedication might have done so. Alistair Gunn's great potential was recognised by Bill although his career was taking off just as Bill's was drawing to a close. Gunn was originally from a farming family in Caithness with a longstanding association with Halkirk Games. Despite a relative lack of height it was no surprise to Bill that Gunn developed into a top all-round heavy claiming seven Scottish titles and excelling at the caber. Perhaps Bill saw a bit of himself in Gunn who was also entremely competitive and capable of pulling out a winning final throw. Alistair's younger brother Murray also became an accomplished heavy.

Many of Bill's records have now gone although much to his credit his Scottish Championship record at Crieff for the heavy hammer, of 123'5", set in 1969 still stands. It also remained as a world best till 1983 when Grant Anderson edged past it with 123'8$\frac{1}{2}$" with an extra throw at Santa

Rosa in the US championships. As for the future, one current young heavy who Bill thinks has great potential is Craig Sinclair of Drumoak.

His achievements have been acknowledged with the award of an MBE in 1977 when along with wife Frances and children Kenneth and Rosemary he went to Buckingham Palace to be decorated by the Queen Mother for services to Highland Games. In addition he was honoured by Aberdeen Sports Council in 1990 with a Special Award, their highest honour, for his contribution to sport in the area and in 2007 was admitted as a member of the Scottish Sports' Hall of Fame, alongside such as footballer Ally McCoist and Commonwealth Games gold medallist Lachie Stewart. He is the only 'Hall of Famer' awarded the honour for Highland Games.

There is no doubt that had Bill been an amateur athlete he would have represented his country. While that would have been a matter of considerable pride to him he has no regrets about having been a professional. He never gave much thought to a career as an amateur or what he might have missed out on. From his background the natural arena to enter was the professional one at the games and as he grew up his heroes whom he wished to emulate were heavies.

Geoff Capes was quoted as saying that had Bill dedicated himself exclusively to one of the amateur throwing disciplines such as wire hammer, shot putt or discus, he had the capability to be an Olympic medallist. Tom McNab, one of Britain's most highly respected coaches, shares that opinion and is in no doubt that the heavy events are at least as equally demanding technically and physically as these Olympic events. Jim Brown MBE, well known Games' official and former amateur heavy, reckons he would have been an outstanding wire hammer thrower not only because of his strength and explosive power but because, despite his size, he was very nimble on his feet thanks to a lifelong involvement in dancing.

Bill retired from full-time work about seven years ago but soon took up part-time employment with the Do It Yourself store B&Q, in Bucksburn, Aberdeen, where he works five mornings a week. He and Frances have been enthusiastic dancers since they met many years ago and spend many evenings doing 'Old Time Dancing' in Aberdeen. Hurling large weights around has been swapped for a more genteel and less physically challenging activity but one which both find fulfilling and enjoyable. He is still a much recognised figure in and around the North East of Scotland and an extremely well remembered and popular figure in games' circles everywhere. Not only was he the outstanding exponent

Bill at Buckingham Palace with MBE and son Kenneth, wife Frances and daughter Rosemary

of the art of the heavy events but he conducted himself in a very sportsmanlike and modest manner, with great integrity. He was an exemplary ambassador throughout the world, not only for Scotland's Highland Games but also for Scotland and was rightly proud of always being invited back to compete wherever he went. And Alford always retains a special place in his heart.

On his retiral from competition in the USA in 1986 a fellow competitor there, Walter Carruthers, sent Bill, as a tribute, a photographic album chronicling his career in America with the following dedication:

> 'Your career in Scottish athletics will live in the minds and hearts of all who had the pleasure of competing on the same field. You are truly the Grand Gentleman of the Games.'

Apposite, succinct and warm – and a fitting tribute to Bill Anderson's career. ●

RECORDS AT CRIEFF, ABOYNE & BRAEMAR 1962-73

1962	BILL ANDERSON	ARTHUR ROWE
CRIEFF	49'6" 16lb Shot	NOT PRESENT
	40'7" 22lb Shot	
	79'3$^{1}/_{2}$" 28lb Weight	
ABOYNE	106'7$^{1}/_{2}$" 24lb Hammer	57'6$^{3}/_{4}$" Light stone (16lb)
	131'4$^{1}/_{2}$" 16lb Hammer	42'9$^{1}/_{2}$" Heavy stone (22lb)
BRAEMAR	————	52'10$^{1}/_{2}$" Light stone (16lb)
		33'6$^{1}/_{2}$" Braemar Stone (28lb)
1963		
CRIEFF	134'3" 16lb Hammer	57'0" 16lb Shot
	114'8" 22lb Hammer	47'7" 22lb Shot
	84'3" 28lb Weight	15'0" 56lb Weight/height
ABOYNE	107'1$^{1}/_{2}$" 24lb Hammer	57'7" Light Stone
		43'11" Heavy Stone
		79'8$^{1}/_{2}$" 28lb Weight
		(breaking George Clark's 1934 record of 76'4")
BRAEMAR	111'5$^{1}/_{2}$" 22lb Hammer	53'11$^{1}/_{2}$" Light Stone
		36'8" Braemar Stone
		77'7" 28lb Weight
		14'2" 56lb Weight/height

1964	BILL ANDERSON	ARTHUR ROWE
CRIEFF	———	48'8$^1/_2$" 22lb Shot
ABOYNE	132'0" 16lb Hammer	108'1"24lb Hammer
	(Rowe threw 130'11")	(beat Anderson's 1963 record by 11")
		57'9$^1/_2$" Light Stone
		45'6$^1/_2$" Heavy Stone
BRAEMAR	136'5" 16lb Hammer	56'0" Light Stone
	116'4$^1/_2$" 22lb Hammer	14'8$^1/_2$" 56lb Weight/height
1965		
CRIEFF	121'6" 16lb Hammer	57'10" 16lb Shot
	86'8" 28lb Weight	141'2" 16lb Hammer
		(beat Anderson's 1963 record by 6'11")
		15'1" 56lb Weight/height
ABOYNE	115'5" 24lb Hammer	46'0" Heavy stone
	(beat Rowe's 1964 record by 7'4")	
	137'3$^1/_2$" 16lb Hammer	
	79'9" 28lb Weight	
	(beat Rowe's '63 record by $^1/_2$")	
BRAEMAR	141'4" 16lb Hammer	38'2$^1/_2$" Braemar Stone
	118'9" 22lb Hammer	
1966		
CRIEFF	87'2" 28lb Weight	123'0" 22lb Hammer
		(beat Anderson's 1965 record by 1'6")
ABOYNE	———	———
BRAEMAR		56'3" Light stone
1967		
CRIEFF	141'8" 16lb Hammer	48'9" 22lb Shot
	(beat Rowe's 1965 record by 6")	
ABOYNE	———	———
BRAEMAR	———	56'11" Light stone

1968	BILL ANDERSON	ARTHUR ROWE
CRIEFF	143'5" 16lb Hammer	———
ABOYNE	138'7$^1/_2$" 16lb Hammer	46'10" Heavy stone
	80'6" 28lb Weight	15'7" 56lb Weight/height
	41'11" 56lb Weight/Distance	
BRAEMAR	143'2" 16lb Hammer	57'9" Light stone
	119'7" 22lb Hammer	38'7" Braemar Stone
	14'8$^1/_2$" 56lb Weight/Height	14'8$^1/_2$" 56lb Weight/Height
	77'9" 28lb Weight	
	(beat Rowe's 1963 record by 2")	
1969		
CRIEFF	123'5" 22lb Hammer	
	*(Still the record today and beat Rowe's 1966 record by 5")	
ABOYNE	———	———
BRAEMAR	121'2" 22lb Hammer	14'9" 56lb Weight/Height
	14'9" 56lb Weight/Height	
1970		
CRIEFF	———	———
ABOYNE	15'8" 56lb Weight/Height	
	(beat Rowe's 1968 record by 1")	
BRAEMAR	121'3" 22lb Hammer	39'5" Braemar Stone
	79'7" 28lb Weight	
	14'10" 56lb Weight/Height	14'10" 56lb Weight/Height
1971		
CRIEFF	———	———
ABOYNE	———	———
BRAEMAR	14'11" 56lb Weight/height	
	(beat Rowe's 1970 record by 1")	
1972		
CRIEFF	———	———
ABOYNE	81'2" 28lb Weight	———
BRAEMAR	———	———

1973	BILL ANDERSON	ARTHUR ROWE
CRIEFF	15'3" 56lb Weight/height	
	(beat Rowe's 1965 record by 2")	
ABOYNE	———	———
BRAEMAR	15'0" 56lb Weight/height	

(1973) At ABOYNE BRIAN OLDFIELD set 2 records:

    61'7" Light Stone

    49'0" Heavy Stone

At BRAEMAR BRIAN OLDFIELD set 2 records:

    63'2" Light Stone

    40'7" Braemar Stone

OTHER NOTEWORTHY MARKS

	BILL ANDERSON	ARTHUR ROWE
1964	113'3" 22lb Hammer Aberdeen	54'5" 16lb Stone Aberdeen
		44'3" 22lb Stone Aberdeen
	41'3" 22lb Shot Invergordon	
	(beat Ed Anderson's 1931 record)	
	47'5" 16lb Shot Invergordon	
	111'9" 22lb Hammer Invergordon	
	70'8" 28lb Weight Invergordon	
	14'6" 56lb Weight/height Invergordon	
	140'3" 16lb Hammer Dunbeath	
	81'2" 28lb Weight Dunbeath	
	14'6" 56lb Weight/height Dunbeath	
1965	142'10" 16lb Hammer Strathpeffer	142'0" 16lb Hammer Oban
		142'0" 16lb Hammer Tobermory
		115'2" 22lb Hammer Pitlochry
1966	115'1" 22lb Hammer Oban	143'3" 16lb Hammer Pitlochry
	137'0" 16lb Hammer Luss	118'11" 22lb Hammer Oban
	49'8" 16lb Shot Markinch	83'9" 28lb Weight Auchterarder
		82'0" 28lb Weight Lochearnhead
1967	52'4" 16lb Shot Strathpeffer	15'4" 56lb Weight Luss
	144'6" 16lb Hammer Pitlochry	83'5" 28lb Weight Lochearnhead
	118'0" 22lb Hammer Pitlochry	

	BILL ANDERSON	ARTHUR ROWE
1968	146'8" 16lb Hammer Oban	
	146'6" 16lb Hammer Birnam	
	120'0" 22lb Hammer Pitlochry	
	15'4" 56lbWeight/height Birnam	
1969	144'1" 16lb Hammer Glenisla	58'9" 16lb Shot Invergordon
	15'0" 56lb Weight/height Glenisla	85'6" 28lbWeight Lochearnhead
		85'5" 28lb Weight Pitlochry
1970	122'8" 22lb Hammer Halkirk	54'1" 16lb Shot Halkirk
	82'1" 28lb Weight Halkirk	45'8" 22lb Shot Halkirk
	40'5" 56lb Weight/distance Halkirk	138'8" 16lb Hammer Halkirk
1971	142'1" 16lb Hammer Thornton	
	141'11" 16lb Hammer Balloch	
	119'1" 22lb Hammer Balloch	
	83'9" 28lb Weight Balloch	
	15'6" 56lb Weight/Distance Balloch	
1972	51'1" 16lb Shot Inveraray	80'2" 28lbWeight Thornton
	141'4" 16lbHammer Oban	
1973	50'1" 16lb Shot Blackford	83'0" 28lb Weight Alva
	82'3" 28lbWeight Galashiels	
	144'7" 16lbHammer Thurso	

Acknowledgements

I have been fortunate to receive assistance from a number of sources in the compilation of this book, most notably Bill Anderson himself who gave freely of his time over a course of many interviews. Many others provided information, photographs and reminiscences and my thanks are due to the following:

Aberdeen City Library, Bob Aitken, Charlie Allan, Grant Anderson, Edward Anderson – Ballater Games, Jane Anderson – Blair Castle; Jim Brown MBE, Dr Laurence Bryce, Mrs J Buchanan – Dornoch Games;

Angus Cameron – Lochearnhead Games, Mrs Anne Cameron, Mrs Chalmers – Invercharron Games, Adam Crawford – SGA; Carla Davidson and David McCrear, Hamish Davidson, Jock Davidson – Glenisla Games, Lorna Davidson – Glenisla Games, Craig Dunbar – Alva Games;

Dr Douglas Edmunds, Doug Fales, Dr C Fishburne – Lochearnhead Games, Gordon Forbes, John Freebairn, Patricia Grant – Tomintoul Games, W Grant – Dornoch Games, Sandy Gray, Alastair Gunn;

Prof Grant Jarvie – Stirling University, Jim McBeath, Morag McBeath – Aboyne Games, Jock McColl, Alan McDonald – Arisaig Games, Angus McEwan – Lochinver Games, Gibbie McIntosh – Lonach Games, Mrs I McKay – Durness Games, David McMaster – Strathpeffer Games, Tom McNab, R Millar – Crieff Games, Alistair Moffat;

Anne Paterson – Luss Games, Patsy Paton – Cortachy Games, Tom Pow;

Alastair Roberts – Mallaig Games, Jean Swanston/Robertson, John Robertson, Bill Robertson – photographer, Sauchie, Willie Robertson, Brian Robin, Betty Rowe, Stephen Rowe, W Ruzzak – Inverkeithing Games;

Scottish National Library, Alison Stewart – Invergordon Games, Sandy Sutherland, Ardross and Sandy Sutherland, Edinburgh, Finlay Walker – Tomintoul Games, David Webster, Andrew Wiseman – School of Scottish Studies, Edinburgh University.

My apologies to anyone I have omitted through oversight. I have made every effort to be wholly accurate but the responsibility for any errors is mine.

Jack Davidson
April 2009